The *Guitarist* Book of

GUITAR PLAYERS

Cliff Douse

1994

The *Guitarist* Book of

GUITAR PLAYERS

Cliff Douse

1994

MUSIC MAKER BOOKS

Music Maker Books Ltd,
Alexander House, Forehill, Ely, Cambs, CB7 4AF

First published in Great Britain in 1994 by Music Maker Books

Printed in the UK by The Lavenham Press, Suffolk

ISBN: 1 870951 22 0

Contents

ACKNOWLEDGEMENTS

I would like to thank Goldsmiths' College Library, the National Sound Archive and the
Westminster Public Library (all in London).

Thanks to Phil Alexander (*Kerrang!* magazine, London),
Eddie Allen, BMG Classics (London), Lynne Bond (Atlantic Records, LA),
Rosie Birchall, Charlie Charlton, Cathy Curwood, Dave at Akai UK, Narayani Diorio,
Dave Donnell (Epic Records, London), EG Management, EMI Records (London),
Marcus Ehresmann (Roadrunner), Kim Ewing (Blue Note, New York),
Hardy Fox (Cryptic Corporation, LA), Mitchell Fox Management (Nashville), Hilary Giltrap,
Karen Goodman (MCA, LA), Peter Grant (Music For Nations, London),
Dieter Hann (FMP, Berlin), Margot Harrell (Geffen Records, LA),
Katherine Howard (Sony Classical, London), Jeffrey Hudson, Gibson Keddie,
Yumi Kimura (Warner Brothers, Nashville), Susie and Margit Lithman, Neville Marten,
David Mead, Paul Myers (Decca Records), Mark Palmer (Roadrunner), Suzanne Randall,
Martin Stone, Victoria Strommer (Geneva) and Chrissie Wild (Decca Records).

A very special thanks to the following for their contributions to this book:
Simon Craige for the use of his computer and house;
the magazines *Guitar Player, Guitar World, Guitar Extra* (all US)
and especially *Guitarist* (UK); Lisa Dedman for layout; Sarah Brierley for production;
Non Bohman, Mark Edwards and Garry Millson for their proofreading,
additions, advice and patience.

CONTACT ADDRESS FOR UPDATES AND COMMENTS:
Music Maker Books Ltd
Alexander House
Forehill
Ely
Cambs, CB7 4AF

FOREWORD

One of the biggest problems associated with writing a book of this nature is deciding who to include and who not to include. My aim was simply to feature the most popular and influential guitarists from each genre, along with the most exciting new talents, in an informative but down-to-earth reference book that might appeal to musicians and non-musicians alike.

A selected discography section is included in the appendix for those who would like to investigate a particular type of music further. All selections were chosen from a guitar player's point of view. 'Family' trees are also included to highlight the most influential jazz, rock, blues and classical guitarists. Hope you enjoy it!

C.D. November 1993

A

John ABERCROMBIE

Modern jazz player. Born in Portchester, New York on December 16, 1944. Picked up the guitar while at high school in Connecticut and played in local bands. Early influences included Elvis Presley and Bill Haley. Later became inspired by jazz players such as Tal Farlow, Barney Kessel and Jim Hall. Studied at Berklee College of Music in Boston (1962-66). Worked with organist Johnny 'Hammond' Smith (1968) and drummer Chico Hamilton (1971), before pursuing a solo career. Played guitars and guitar synthesizers on a number of exploratory fusion projects with other musicians such as Ralph Towner, Michael Brecker, Marc Johnson, Jack DeJohnette, Peter Erskine and Jan Hammer. Recordings on ECM include *Timeless* (1974), *Gateway* (1975), *Characters* (1977), *M* (1981), *Night* (1984), *Current Events* (1986), *Getting There* (1988) and *While We're Young* (1993). His style encompasses fusion, bebop, rock and experimental music. A gifted, versatile and unpredictable player.

William ACKERMAN

Folk and new age acoustic guitarist. Born in Germany during November 1949. Moved to California at age 9 and took up the guitar by the time he was 12. Influences included John Fahey and Leo Kottke. Set up his own record label Windham Hill in 1976 and released a number of sparse, atmospheric recordings over the years. Also signed other artists such as Michael Hedges and Alex de Grassi to the label, which became the world's most prominent new-age record company. Recordings include *In Search Of The Turtle's Navel* (1976), *It Takes A year* (1977), *Passage* (1981), *Past Light* (1983), *Conferring With The Moon* (1986) and *Imaginary Roads* (1990).

Bryan ADAMS

Canadian singer/songwriter and rock guitarist. Born in Vancouver, British Columbia, 1959. Influenced by Bruce Springsteen and other singer/songwriters. Worked with Ian Lloyd and Prism during the late '70s, before forming his own five-piece band (guitarist Keith Scott joined in 1980) and signing to A&M. Toured with Foreigner and Tina Turner. Became one of the most successful rock artists of the '80s with a string of down-to-earth hits such as 'Run To You' (1985), 'Heaven' (1985), 'Summer Of 69' (1985) and 'Heat Of The Night' (1987). Longest running number one with 'Everything I do', from *Robin Hood, Prince of Thieves*. Also wrote 'Tears Are Not Enough' for a Canadian Band Aid recording. Big success on MTV video channel. Played a number of charity gigs, including Live Aid and the Nelson Mandela 70th Birthday Concert. Best-selling albums on A&M include *Bryan Adams* (1980), *Cuts Like A Knife* (1983), *Reckless* (1984), *Into The Fire* (1987) and *Waking Up The Neighbours* (1991).

Jan AKKERMAN

Rock guitarist. Born in Amsterdam, Holland on December 24, 1946. Started learning guitar at age 5. Joined his first band at age 10. Played in local nightclubs as a teenager. Early influences included Django Reinhardt, Larry Coryell and Julian Bream. Worked with bands such as Friendship and Brainbox in the '60s. Formed classically-influenced rock band Focus with keyboardist Thijs Van Leer in the early '70s. They recorded a number of critically acclaimed albums on Polydor: *Moving Waves* (1971) boasted 'Hocus Pocus', with idiosyncratic yodelling from Van Leer; double album *Focus III* (1972) featured infectious riffing on 'Sylvia', as well as a number of interesting extended solos. Other albums include *Hamburger Concerto* (1974) and *Mother Focus* (1975). Left the band on the eve of UK sell-out tour in 1976 (replaced by Belgian guitarist Philip Catherine). Later solo albums on Harvest, Atlantic, WEA, Charly and Nospeak include *Profile* (1972), *Tabernakel* (1974), *Jan Akkerman* (1978), *3* (1980), *Pleasure Point* (1981), *It Could Happen To You* (1985), *Can't Stand The Noise* (1986) and *The Noise Of Art* (1990). One of the most influential guitar players of the '70s.

Duane ALLMAN

Rock slide/bottleneck pioneer. Born in Nashville, Tennessee on November 20, 1946.

Early influences included B.B.King, Freddie King and Robert Johnson. Played in various Florida bands with his brother Greg (keyboards, guitar, vocals) from age 16. They moved to Hollywood in 1967 and formed the band Hour Glass, recording two unsuccessful albums. Formed the Allman Brothers Band a year later. Members included 'Dickie' Betts (guitar), Berry Oakley (bass), and Butch Trucks (drums). Recorded critically acclaimed albums on the Capricorn label: *The Allman Brothers Band* (1969), *Idlewild South* (1970) and highly-rated *Live At The Fillmore East* (1971). Also worked with Aretha Franklin, Wilson Pickett and Boz Scaggs. Killed in a motorcycle accident in Macon, Georgia on October 29, 1971. One of the foremost slide guitar players of his time: a big influence on major rock guitar players including Steve Morse, Eric Johnson and Jennifer Batten. Capricorn later released *Duane Allman: An Anthology* (1972) and *Duane Allman: Anthology, Vol II* (1974). On Castle: *The Collection* (1992). Included in *Guitar Player* magazine's 'Gallery Of The Greats' (1991) for his lifetime achievement.

Laurindo **ALMEIDA**

Classical and Bossa Nova guitarist. Born in São Paulo, Brazil on September 2, 1917. Played guitar from an early age and gave his first public recital on the instrument at age 13. Worked for a Brazilian radio station. Travelled to Europe in 1936 and was impressed by Django Reinhardt in Paris. Settled in the United States in 1947. Worked with Stan Kenton, Herbie Mann, Bud Shank and the Modern Jazz Quartet. Helped bring the Bossa Nova to the United States in the '60s. Made a number of solo recordings for Capitol and Concord including *Viva Bossa Nova* (1962), *Guitar From Ipanema* (1964), *Sueños* (1965), *First Concerto For Guitar & Orchestra* (1979), *Brazilian Soul* (1980) with Charlie Byrd and *Artistry In Rhythm* (1983).

Tuck **ANDRESS**

Jazz-influenced player. Born in Tulsa, Oklahoma on October 28, 1952. Developed a formidable fingerstyle technique and extended the boundaries of jazz guitar playing. Often gigged with wife Patti as a duo around San Francisco area. They recorded albums *Tears Of Joy* (1988), *Love Warriors* (1988) and *Dreams* (1991) for the Windham Hill label. Also worked with the Gap Band and a number of

others. Solo albums on Windham Hill include *Reckless Precision* (1991) and *Hymns, Carols & Songs* (1991). Instructional video: *Fingerstyle Mastery* (Hot Licks 1992). A highly respected musician who has influenced many jazz and rock players.

Michael **ANTHONY**

Rock bass player. Born in Chicago on June 20, 1955. Started playing trumpet at age 7, before switching to guitar and bass at junior high school. Moved to Los Angeles at age 14. Studied trumpet and piano at Pasadena City College, while playing bass in a local band. Joined Van Halen in 1974 with Eddie Van Halen (guitar), Alex Van Halen (drums) and David Lee Roth (vocals, later replaced by Sammy Hagar). They proved to be one of the most successful and influential heavy metal bands of the late '70s and early '80s, with Michael's solid bass playing holding the bottom end down. (See Eddie VAN HALEN for more information on the band).

Joan **ARMATRADING**

Singer/songwriter. Born in St. Kitts, West Indies on December 9, 1950. Moved to UK and grew up in Birmingham. Relocated to London in the early '70s. Developed a highly individual acoustic folk style. Met singer/songwriter Pam Nestor while touring for the musical Hair. They recorded *Whatever's For Us* (1972) for David Platz's Cube label, before Armatrading signed to A&M. *Back To The Night* (1975) generated some interest. Big break came with *Joan Armatrading* (1976), featuring some excellent lyrics and tunes. Made the UK Top 20 and featured the hit single 'Love And Affection'. *Show Some Emotion* (1977) and *To The Limit* (1978) continued in the same direction. *Walk Under Ladders* (1981) and *The Key* (1983) were produced by Steve Lillywhite. *Sleight Of Hand* (1986), *The Shouting Stage* (1988) and *Hearts & Flowers* (1990) were more mainstream and produced by Armatrading. Later recordings include *The Very Best Of Joan Armatrading* (1991) and *Square The Circle* (1992).

Chet **ATKINS**

Legendary country guitarist and fingerstyle pioneer. Born Chester Burton Atkins in Luttrell, Tennessee on June 20, 1924. Took an early interest in country music and joined Bill Carlisle

Chet Atkins

and his Dixieland Swingers (playing fiddle) on Knoxville radio while still at school. Later switched to guitar. Developed an advanced

thumb-and-three-fingers technique which inspired many others. Toured with Archie Campbell, Bill Carlisle and Maybelle Carter during the '40s. Appeared on the Grand Ole Opry (legendary country show) in 1948 and worked extensively as a session musician and producer. Became an A&R director with RCA: helped supervise the careers of Elvis Presley, the Everly Brothers, Jim Reeves, Don Gibson, Charlie Pride and many others. Thought to be the most powerful man in Nashville at one time. Elected to the Country Music Hall of Fame in 1973. Recordings on RCA include *Chet Atkins' Gallopin' Guitar* (1953), *In Three Dimensions* (1956), *Fingerstyle Guitar* (1958), *Chet Atkins' Workshop* (1960), *Down Home* (1961), *The Best Of Chet Atkins* (1963), *The Early Years Of Chet Atkins And His Guitar* (1964), *Picks On The Beatles* (1965) and *Pickin' My Way* (1971). On Columbia: *Work It Out* (1983), *Stay Tuned* (1985), *Sweet Dreams* (1986), *Sails* (1987), and *CGP* (1988). With Mark Knopfler: *Neck & Neck* (1990). Compilation: *The RCA Years* (1992). Instructional video/book: *Get Started On Guitar* (Atkins Video Society 1985). One of the most influential guitarists of the 20th century. Included in *Guitar Player* magazine's 'Gallery Of The Greats' after being voted Best Country Guitarist (1970-1974) and Best Overall Guitarist (1972).

B

Derek **BAILEY**

UK experimental guitarist and free-improvisation pioneer. Born in Sheffield, Yorkshire on January 29, 1930. Initially worked as a commercial player in theatres and studios. Started improvising during the '60s and developed an extended technique incorporating flutter-picking, string scrubbing, volume-pedal swells, string bending from behind the bridge, cluster chords, unusual harmonics and other effects. Joined Spontaneous Music Ensemble (S.M.E) with John Stevens, Evan Parker, Trevor Watts and others. Formed Incus records in 1970 with Tony Oxley and Evan Parker. Worked with Steve Lacy, Dave Holland, Tristan Honsinger, Anthony Braxton, Steve Beresford, Lol Coxhill, the Company and others. Recordings on Incus include *Solo Guitar* (1971), *Improvisation* (1975), *New Sights, Old Sounds* (1978), *Aida* (1980), *Notes* (1985), with bassist Barre Phillips *Figuring* (1989), *Solo Guitar Vol.2* (1991) and *Playing* (1992) with John Stevens. Book: *Improvisation - Its Nature & Practice In Music* (British Library 1992). One of the greatest improvising guitar players.

Antonio Carlos **BARBOSA-LIMA**

Classical and latin guitarist. Born in São Paulo, Brazil on December 17, 1944. Child prodigy who made concert debuts in São Paulo and Rio de Janeiro at age 12. Later studied with Segovia. Toured North America, South America and Europe extensively in the '70s. Transcribed many works by Bach, Handel, Mozart, Vivaldi and Scarlatti. Also commissioned works by composers such as Francisco Mignone, Guido Santorsola and John Duarte. Later performed and recorded pieces by Gershwin, Cole Porter, Antonio Carlos Jobim, Scott Joplin and Leonard Bernstein. Recordings on Concord include *Plays Music Of Antonio Jobim And George Gershwin* (1983) and *Music Of The Americas* (1990).

George **BARNES**

Jazz player. Born in Chicago, Illinois on July 17, 1921. Started playing the guitar at age 9. Taught by his father. Early influences included Benny Goodman, Louis Armstrong, Lonnie Johnson and Django Reinhardt. Formed his own quartet at age 14 and played in clarinetist Jimmy Noonan's band two years later. Became a guitarist, conductor and arranger for NBC (Chicago) at age 17. Recorded with Big Bill Broonzy and Blind John Davis in the late-'30s. Drafted into the army in 1942. Signed a contract with Decca (as a guitarist, composer and arranger) in the '50s and found himself working with Frank Sinatra and Bing Crosby. Became well-known for his impressive and highly original guitar duos with Carl Kress. Died after a heart attack in Concord, California on September 5, 1977. Recordings include *Two Guitars And A Horn* (1962), *Something Tender* (1963), *Swing Guitar* (1972), *The Best I've Heard: Braff-Barnes Quartet* (1976) and with Joe Venuti: *Live At The Concord Summer Jazz Festival* (1976).

Martin **BARRE**

UK rock guitarist. Born in Birmingham, England on November 17, 1946. Started playing the guitar at age 15. Also took up the flute and saxophone. Joined legendary rock band Jethro Tull in 1968 with frontman Ian Anderson (vocals, flute, guitar) and others. The band's hard-hitting/innovative brand of folk-rock and Anderson's charismatic one-legged flute playing earned them considerable respect and success from the '70s onwards. The line-up changed a number of times, but Barre and Anderson always remained at the nucleus. Recordings include *Stand Up* (1969), *Benefit* (1970), *Aqualung* (1971), *Thick As A Brick* (1972), *A Passion Play* (1973), *War Child* (1974), *Minstrel In The Gallery* (1975), *Too Old To Rock'N'Roll, Too Young To Die* (1976), *Songs From The Wood* (1977), *Heavy Horses* (1978), *Stormwatch* (1979), *A* (1980), *The Broadsword And The Beast* (1982), *Under Wraps* (1984), *Crest Of A Knave* (1987), *Rock Island* (1989), *Live At Hammersmith* (1991)

and *Catfish Rising* (1991). Barre also set up his own band and recorded solo album *Another View* (1994).

Syd **BARRETT**

Singer/songwriter and guitarist. Born Roger Barrett in Cambridge, England on January 6, 1946. Formed Pink Floyd in 1965 with Roger Waters (bass, vocals), Richard Wright (keyboards) and Nick Mason (drums). Named after bluesmen Pink Anderson and Floyd Council. Had hits with 'Arnold Layne' and 'See Emily Play' in 1967. Recorded critically acclaimed album *Piper At The Gates Of Dawn* (1967), but became unstable due to heavy use of LSD and left the band in 1968. Recorded two highly original solo albums on Harvest: *The Madcap Laughs* and *Barrett* (both 1970, later released together as double album *Syd Barrett* in 1974). Retired from the music scene. A cult-figure who inspired many other rock musicians.

Agustin **BARRIOS**

Classical virtuoso and composer. Born in San Bautista De Las Misiones, Paraguay on May 5, 1885. Started playing guitar at an early age. Recognised as a prodigy by the time he was 13. Moved to Argentina in 1910 and gave concerts all over South America in the '20s. Toured Europe in the mid-'30s but suffered from a bad heart condition and spent his remaining years composing and teaching in El Salvador. Composed more than 300 works for the guitar, some of which are regarded as among the finest solos ever written. Recordings of his compositions include *John Williams Plays Barrios* (CBS) and *Jesus Benites Plays Barrios* (Globo). Included in *Guitar Player* magazine's 'Gallery Of The Greats' (1988) for his lifetime achievement.

Manuel **BARRUECO**

Classical virtuoso. Born in Santiago, Cuba in 1952. Started playing guitar at age 8. Studied with Manuel Puig and at the Esteban Salas Conservatory in Cuba. Moved to the United States in 1967 and continued his studies with Juan Mercadal (Miami), Ray De La Torre (New York) and at the Peabody Conservatory in Baltimore. Soloist with the Peabody Orchestra and winner of the Peabody competition. Has since given highly acclaimed performances throughout the world and made several outstanding recordings on Turnabout including *Works For Guitar* and *Manuel Barrueco Plays Scarlatti/Paganini*. On EMI: *Albeniz And Turina* (1992).

Jennifer **BATTEN**

Rock virtuoso. Born in Montour Falls, New York on November 29, 1962. Moved to California and started learning guitar at around age 9. Early influences included Django Reinhardt, Duane Allman, B.B.King, Jeff Beck and Joe Diorio. Studied with Pat Metheny, Tommy Tedesco and Don Mock at the Guitar Institute of Technology in Hollywood (later taught there). Developed an impressive two-handed lead technique and appeared in *Guitar Player's* 'Spotlight' column (Feb 1984). Author of several guitar instruction books including *The Transcribed Guitar Solos Of Peter Sprague* (1981) and *Two-Handed Rock* (1984). Joined Michael Jackson's band in 1987 and toured the world several times with the megastar. Also worked with Jeff Beck, Jane Child and Sara Hickman. Debut solo album on Voss: *Above, Below & Beyond* (1991). Formed her own band the Immigrants. Columnist with *Guitar Player* magazine. Featured on *Hot Guitarist* video magazine premier issue (1992) and Guitar Recordings CD: *Guitar's Practicing Musicians* (1993). Highly respected player and teacher.

Shaun **BAXTER**

UK rock/fusion virtuoso. Born in Llanyravon, Wales on April 6, 1962. Grew up around Cardiff and played bass in a punk band, before taking up the guitar at age 18. Influences included Michael Schenker, Eddie Van Halen, Yngwie Malmsteen, Michael Brecker and Allan Holdsworth. Developed his own unique style, effortlessly blending bebop licks into a heavy metal format. Worked with a number of artists including John Sloman and Princess during the '80s. Also respected teacher at the Guitar Institute in London and columnist with *Guitar* magazine during the early-'90s. Impressive debut solo album *Jazz Metal* (1993) showcases his dynamic playing and formidable technique. One of the UK's foremost rock and fusion players.

Jeff 'Skunk' **BAXTER**

Session ace. Born in Washington DC on December 13, 1948. Grew up in Washington and Mexico City. Started playing at an early age. Influences included the Ventures, Bill Haley, Howard Roberts and Charlie Parker. Moved to New York in 1965 and met many other musicians including guitarist Sam Brown. Joined Steely Dan for their first three albums: *Can't Buy A Thrill* (1972), *Countdown To Ecstasy* (1973) and *Pretzel Logic* (1974). Also a member of bands fronted by the Doobie Brothers, Elton John and Linda Ronstadt. Sessioned with Donna Summer, Cher, Little Feat, Joni Mitchell, Ritchie Havens, Rod Stewart, Dolly Parton, Stanley Clarke and many others. Respected steel guitar player. Session guitarist and composer for films such as *Beverly Hills Cop*, *Roxanne* and *Bull Durham* during the '80s. Involved with recording console and guitar synthesizer design for Allen & Heath and Roland. Collaborated with the Epiphone guitar company on a special 'Jeff Baxter' model. Also produced many artists including Stray Cats, Nils Lofgren and Nazareth. A talented all-rounder.

Jeff **BECK**

Legendary rock player. Born in Surrey, England on June 24, 1944. Sung in a church choir and played some violin, cello and piano before building his first electric guitar out of wood,

Jeff Beck

George Bodnar/Idols

home-made frets, wire and a pickup. Played with the Del-Tones and the Tridents before replacing Eric Clapton in the Yardbirds in 1965. Left during a gruelling tour of America in 1966 and went solo with producer Mickey Most. They made the successful hit single 'Hi Ho Silver Lining' (1967). Formed the Jeff Beck Group and signed to CBS/Epic for debut album *Truth* (1968), featuring a raw version of Yardbirds' 'Shapes Of Things'. *Beck-Ola* (1969) included a cover of the Presley hit 'All Shook Up', with some impressive leadwork. The group went through several personnel transformations. One of the line-ups included Aynsley Dunbar (drums), Rod Stewart (vocals) and Ron Wood (bass). Another included Tim Bogert (bass) and Carmine Appice (drums). Involved in a serious car crash in 1969 and was unable to play for more than a year. However two more albums *Rough And Ready* (1971) and *Jeff Beck Group* (1972) were released before the band Beck, Bogert and Appice formed in 1972. Following an unsuccessful eponymous debut album in 1973, Beck decided to concentrate on purely instrumental albums: *Blow By Blow* (1975) and *Wired* (1976) had a jazz-rock feel, featuring some amazing lead work (tasteful bends and brilliant control of harmonics/distortion) from the guitarist, as well as a number of top musicians, including keyboardist Jan Hammer. Beck then joined Hammer's band for a tour, resulting in the album *Jeff Beck With The Jan Hammer Group Live* (1977). Later recordings include *There And Back* (1980), *Flash* (1985), *Jeff Beck's Guitar Shop* (1989) and tribute to Cliff Gallup *Crazy Legs* (1993). With Jed Leiber: *Frankie's House* (1992). His unique and highly expressive playing inspired countless guitar players worldwide. One of the most influential guitarists of all time.

Jason BECKER

US rock guitarist. Born in Richmond, California on July 22, 1969. Started playing at age 5. Studied classical guitar. Met Marty Friedman (another guitarist) at high school. They formed a classically-orientated heavy metal band called Cacophony, signed to Mike Varney's Shrapnel label, and recorded *Speed Metal Symphony* (1987) and *Go Off* (1989). Becker had also recorded a highly-rated solo album *Perpetual Burn* (1988). Joined David Lee Roth's band in 1990 as Steve Vai's replacement. The Roth album *A Little Ain't Enough* (1991) on Warner Brothers features some impressive lead work by

the guitarist. Also recorded a raunchy version of Bob Dylan's 'Meet Me In The Morning', which is featured on the compilation CD *Guitar's Practicing Musicians* (1993).

Adrian BELEW

Experimental rock guitarist. Born in Covington, Kentucky in 1949. Developed an unorthadox style, using unique feedback/tremolo effects and guitar synthesizers. Impressed Frank Zappa, who asked him to join his band. Played on Zappa's CBS album *Sheik Yerbouti* (1979). With Talking Heads on Sire: *Remain In Light* (1980) and *The Name Of This Band Is Talking Heads* (1982). With King Crimson on EG: *Discipline* (1981), *Beat* (1982) and *Three Of A Perfect Pair* (1983). With Laurie Anderson on Warner Brothers: *Mr Heartbreak* (1983) and *Home Of The Brave* (1986). Also worked with David Bowie, Paul Simon, Jean-Michel Jarre, Herbie Hancock and others. Solo albums on Island highlighting his eccentric style include *Lone Rhino* (1982), *Twang Bar King* (1983) and *Desire Caught By The Tail* (1986). On Atlantic: *Mr Music Head* (1989) and *Young Lions* (1990). Instructional video: *Electronic Guitar* (DCI).

George Benson

George BENSON

Jazz guitarist and singer. Born in Pittsburg, Pennsylvania on March 22, 1943. Sang in local Pittsburg R&B bands at age 8 and was playing guitar professionally by the time he was 15. Moved to New York in 1963 and joined the Jack McDuff Quartet. Also worked with Herbie Hancock and Wes Montgomery. Recorded jazz albums on Columbia, Verve and CTI such as *It's Uptown* (1965), *Benson Burner* (1966), *Giblet Gravy* (1967), *Beyond The Blue Horizon* (1971) and *Bad Benson* (1974). Later had considerable commercial success with more mainstream recordings on Warner Brothers, including *Breezin'* (1976), *In Flight* (1977), *In Your Eyes* (1983), *20/20* (1985), *When The City Sleeps* (1986), *Twice The Love* (1988) and *Tenderly* (1989). On Telstar: *Midnight Moods* (1991). Well-known for his exciting single-note improvisations and singing in unison with the guitar. Included in *Guitar Player* magazine's 'Gallery Of The Greats' after being voted Best Jazz Guitarist (1976) and Best Pop Guitarist (1980-1983).

Jeff BERLIN

Fusion bass virtuoso. Born in Queens, New York on January 17, 1953. Started playing the violin at age 5. Later picked up the bass guitar during early teens. Influences included Stanley Clarke, Alphonso Johnson and Jaco Pastorius. Soon developed his own unique and formidable technique and became one of the most highly respected jazz and fusion bass players. Worked with Al Di Meola, Lenny White, George Benson, Patrick Moraz, Herbie Mann, Bill Evans, Joe Farrell, David Sancious and many others. Recorded with Bill Bruford on Polydor/EG: *Feels Good To Me* (1978), *One Of A Kind* (1979) and *Gradually Going Tornado* (1980). With Allan Holdsworth on Warner Brothers: *Road Games* (1983). Occasional instructor at the Bass Institute of Technology (B.I.T.) in Hollywood and regular columnist with *Guitar Player* during the '80s. Solo albums on Passport Jazz include *Champion* (1985) and *Pump It* (1986). Author of *A Comprehensive Chord Tone System For Mastering The Bass* (REH 1987).

Chuck BERRY

Rock and roll legend. Born in San Jose, California on October 18, 1926. Moved to St Louis. Sang in a local church choir. Also listened to boogie-woogie, blues and swing at an early age. Started learning guitar while at high school. Influences included Muddy Waters, T-Bone Walker, Charlie Christian, Tampa Red and Carl Hogan (with Louis Jordan). Worked as a trainee hairdresser and formed a trio that played during the weekends in the early '50s. Made a demo tape in 1955 and took it to Chess Records in Chicago (on Muddy Waters'

recommendation). The result was his debut single 'Maybellene'. It became America's No.1 rhythm and blues song by the end of the year. Also recorded other hits such as 'Roll Over

Chuck Berry

Beethoven' (1956), 'Brown Eyed Handsome Man' (1956), 'School Days' (1957), 'Reelin' And Rockin''(1958), 'Johnny B Goode' (1958), 'Little Queenie' (1959) and 'No Particular Place To Go' (1964). Introduced a variety of new double-stops and catchy 4-bar intros; changed the way the instrument was played thereafter. Incarcerated in 1944 for armed robbery, also in 1962 for "transporting a fourteen-year-old across state lines for immoral purposes", and in 1979 for income tax irregularities. Wrote *Chuck Berry: The Autobiography*, which was well received by critics and fans in 1987. The documentary *Hail, Hail, Rock'N'Roll* (1987) features a 60th birthday tribute concert with other musicians including Eric Clapton, Keith Richards and Robert Cray. Compilation albums on Greenline and Chess include *Chuck Berry's Greatest Hits* (1986) and *Chuck Berry Story 1955-1958* (1990). Well-known for his famous "duck walk", wielding a Gibson ES-350T (or 355). An early singer-player-songwriter who was a major influence on '60s performers such as the Beatles and the Rolling Stones. Considered to be the first true rock guitar stylist. Included in *Guitar Player* magazine's 'Gallery Of The Greats' (1984) for his lifetime achievement.

Nuno **BETTENCOURT**

Heavy metal virtuoso. Born in Azores, Portugal on September 20, 1966. Family settled in Massachusetts. Started playing drums before switching to guitar. Influences included Al Di Meola, Eddie Van Halen and Yngwie Malmsteen. Formed his own band in Boston but left to join Extreme (formerly Dream) with Gary Cherone (vocals), Pat Badger (bass) and Paul Greary (drums). Signed to A&M. Bettencourt's formidable technique, innovative

Nuno Bettencourt

soloing and powerful riffs soon become an essential component of the band's sound and stage act. His impressive lead style broke out of the usual HM cliches. The band's ballad 'More Than Words' reached No.1 in the US charts (No.2 in UK) in 1990. Albums include *Extreme* (1989), *Pornograffitti* (1990) and *Three Sides To Every Story* (1992). Bettencourt was also featured on the CD *Guitar's Practicing Musicians* (1993).

Ed **BICKERT**

Jazz player. Born in Manitoba, Canada on November 29, 1932. Picked up the guitar at age 8. Played in his parents country dance band as a teenager. Moved to Toronto in the early '50s and worked as a sideman for Chet Baker, Red Norvo, Milt Jackson and Paul Desmond. Also did extensive studio and television work. His tasteful chordal embellishments earned him considerable respect within the jazz community.

Recordings on Sackville and Concord Jazz include *In Concert At The Garden Party* (1981), *Border Crossing* (1983), *Ed Bickert 5 At Toronto's Bourbon Street* (1983), *I Wished On The Moon* (1985) and *Third Floor Richard* (1989).

Ritchie **BLACKMORE**

Rock guitarist. Born in Weston-Super-Mare, England on April 14, 1945. Started playing skiffle. Worked with Screaming Lord Sutch, Joe Meek's Outlaws and Jerry Lee Lewis in the '60s. Formed Deep Purple in 1968 with Jon Lord (keyboards), Ian Paice (drums), Rod Evans (vocals) and Nick Simper (bass). This line-up had success in the US charts with *Shades Of Deep Purple* (1968), *Book Of Taliesyn* (1969) and *Deep Purple* (1969). Evans and Simper left the band and were replaced by Ian Gillan (vocals) and Roger Glover (bass) for *Concerto For Group And Orchestra* (1970) with the Royal Philharmonic Orchestra. Also recorded *Deep Purple In Rock* (1970); one of the most influential British heavy rock albums ever. Had

Ritchie Blackmore

a hit (UK No.2) with single 'Black Night' the same year. Continued success with *Fireball* (1971), *Machine Head* (1972) and the live *Made In Japan* (1972). Tracks such as 'Child In Time' and 'Smoke On The Water' soon became rock classics. The band was dogged by personality clashes, with Gillan and Glover leaving after the recording of *Who Do We Think We Are?* (1973). Bass player Glenn Hughes and vocalist David Coverdale were brought in for *Burn* (1974) and *Stormbringer* (1974), which showed a change in musical direction. Blackmore was dissatisfied with the band's new 'funky' sound and left to form his own band Rainbow. The line-up varied and members included vocalist Ronnie James Dio, drummer Cozy Powell and keyboardist Don Airey. Recordings include *Ritchie Blackmore's Rainbow* (1975), *Rainbow Rising* (1976), *On Stage* (1977), *Long Live Rock'n'Roll* (1978), *Down To Earth* (1979), *Difficult To Cure* (1981), *Straight Between The Eyes* (1982) and *Bent Out Of Shape* (1983). Re-formed Deep Purple with Lord, Paice, Glover and Gillan for further albums: *Perfect Strangers* (1984), and *The House Of Blue Light* (1987), *Slaves And Masters* (1990) and *The Battle Rages On* (1993). A highly influential rock guitarist, who inspired heavy metal players such as Yngwie Malmsteen, Vinnie Moore and Jeff Watson.

'Scrapper' BLACKWELL

Blues guitarist and singer. Born Francis Hillman Blackwell in Syracuse, South Carolina on February 21, 1903. One of sixteen children. His nickname came from fighting with one of his brothers. Built a guitar out of a cigar box at age 6 and taught himself to play. Developed a unique style falling somewhere between blues and jazz. Became a moonshiner during the Prohibition period. Met singer/pianist Leroy Carr and they collaborated on several recordings from 1928 up until Carr's death in 1935. Left full-time music and worked on an asphalt plant until 1958. Later resumed recording and gave a few club performances. Shot to death in Indianapolis, Indiana on October 7, 1962. Albums include compilations such as *The Virtuoso Guitar Of Scrapper Blackwell* (Yazoo), *Singing The Blues* (Yazoo) and *Blues That Make Me Cry* (Agram).

Blind BLAKE

Blues guitarist and singer. Born Arthur Blake (or Phelps) in Jacksonville, Florida c.1890. Early years spent as itinerant performer. Ragtime-influenced fingerstyle player. Moved to Chicago and recorded for Paramount during the late '20s. Inspired players as diverse as Big Bill Broonzy, Rev. Gary Davis, Blind Boy Fuller and

Leon Redbone. Impressive ragtime solos include 'Southern Rag' and 'Blind Arthur's Breakdown'. Mystery surrounds his death: some say he was murdered in Joliet, Illinois in 1932, while others claim he was killed in an Atlanta road accident in 1941. Albums include Biograph compilations such as *Bootleg Rum Dum Blues*, *Search Warrant Blues* and *Rope Stretching Blues*.

Mike BLOOMFIELD

Blues guitarist. Born in Chicago on July 28, 1944. Frequented Chicago blues clubs as a teenager. Became influenced by Muddy Waters and Albert King. His own style was sparse and highly expressive. Played in clubs with harmonica player Charlie Musselwhite before working with Paul Butterfield, Bob Dylan, Stephen Stills and Dr. John on various projects. Released a number of solo albums including *Super Session* (1968), *Fathers & Sons* (1969), *Triumvirate* (1973), *Try It Before You Buy It* (1975), *There's Always Another Record* (1976), *If You Love These Blues...* (1977), *Analine* (1977) and *Cruisin' For A Bruisin'* (1980). Died of a drug overdose in San Francisco on February 15, 1981. Included in *Guitar Player* magazine's 'Gallery Of The Greats' after being voted Best Electric Blues Player (1976) and Best Acoustic Blues Player (1978-1982). Columbia later released compilation *Mike Bloomfield* (1983). One of the most popular and influential white blues players. Biography: *The Rise & Fall Of An American Guitar Hero* by Ed Ward.

Marc BOLAN

Pop singer/songwriter and guitarist. Born Mark Feld in Hackney, London on July 30, 1947. Became a male model at age 15 and pursued a career under the names Toby Tyler and Marc Bowland. Formed a duo called Tyrannosaurus Rex with percussionist Steve Peregrine-Took in the late '60s. Took was replaced by Mickey Finn in 1969 and the band eventually became T-Rex. Had numerous glam-rock hits in the '70s, including 'Hot Love' (1971), 'Get It On' (1971) and 'Telegram Sam' (1972). Influenced later pop groups such as Bauhaus and Siouxsie & the Banshees. Albums on Regal Zonophone, Fly, T-Rex and K-Tel include *Unicorn* (1969), *T-Rex* (1970), *Electric Warrior* (1971), *Tanx* (1973), *Zip Gun Boogie* (1974), *Futuristic Dragon* (1976) and compilation *Best Of The 20th Century Boy* (1985). Also recorded a number of solo albums. Perished in a car crash on September 16, 1977.

Tommy **BOLIN**

Rock/jazz-rock player born in Sioux City, Iowa on August 1, 1951. Started playing drums at age 13 before switching to guitar. Early influences included Jimi Hendrix, Django Reinhardt and Carl Perkins. Left high school at age 16, moved to Denver and formed a band called Zephyr. Later worked for Albert King, Billy Cobham, the James Gang and Alphonse Mouzon, before joining Deep Purple in 1975 to replace Ritchie Blackmore. Appeared on their R&B/funk influenced EMI album *Come Taste The Band* (1975). Also recorded solo albums on Nemperor and Columbia: *Teaser* (1975) and *Private Eyes* (1976). Compilation: *The Ultimate: Tommy Bolin* (1989). Died of a drug overdose in Miami, Florida on December 4, 1976.

Luiz **BONFA**

Latin, jazz and classical guitarist. Also composer. Born in Rio de Janeiro, Brazil on October 17, 1922. Started playing the guitar at age 12. Had lessons with his father and later studied with Uruguayan classical virtuoso Isaias Savio. Played and sang in several groups in Brazil and became one of the most celebrated performers in the country. Moved to the United States in 1958 and worked with singer Mary Martin and saxophonist Stan Getz. Achieved considerable success as a composer and performer of film and TV music. Albums include *Braziliana* (Philips), *The New Face Of Bonfa* (RCA), *Bonfa* (Dot), *The Brazilian Guitar Of Luiz Bonfa* (Capitol), *Jacaranda* (Ranwood), *Le Roi de la Bossa Nova* (Fontana), *Amor* (Atlantic) and *The Bonfa Magic* (Caju). One of the first to apply classical technique to jazz and bossa nova.

Mick **BOX**

Rock guitarist. Born in London, England on June 8, 1947. Played in Stalkers and Spice in the late-'60s, before forming Uriah Heep with David Byron (vocals), Ken Hensley (keyboards, guitar), Paul Newton (bass) and Lee Kerslake (drums). The band, named after a Dickens character, highlighted Box's extrovert guitar work and Byron's shrill vocals. Several personnel changes over the years (later members included bassist John Wetton and guitarist Clem Clempson), although Box always remained at the nucleus. Recordings on Bronze, Legacy and Castle include *Very 'Eavy, Very 'Umble* (1970), *Look At Yourself* (1971),

Demons And Wizards (1972), *Uriah Heep Live* (1973), *Wonderworld* (1974), *Return To Fantasy* (1975), *High And Mighty* (1976), *Firefly* (1977), *Innocent Victim* (1978), *Conquest* (1980), *Head First* (1983), *Equator* (1985), *Anthology* (1985), *Live In Moscow* (1988), *Raging Silence* (1989), *Still 'Eavy, Still Proud* (1990) and *Different World* (1991).

Liona **BOYD**

Classical virtuoso. Born in London, England in 1952. Family moved to Canada in 1962. Played classical guitar from age 14. Studied at the University of Toronto. Also with Eli Kassner in Toronto, Julian Bream in Ontario and Alexandre Lagoya in France. Won the Juno Award (Canada) for Instrumental Artist Of The Year in 1982. Signed a major deal with CBS and made several successful recordings including *Liona Boyd*, *Spanish Fantasy*, *Liona Live In Tokyo*, *A Guitar For Christmas*, *Persona* and *Miniatures For Guitar*. Joined the advisory board for *Guitar Player* magazine during the '80s. Also performed with Gordon Lightfoot, Chet Atkins and many others.

Doug **BOYLE**

UK heavy metal player. Born in Buckhurst Hill, Essex on September 6, 1962. Got his first guitar at age 11. Became influenced by Jimi Hendrix and heavy-rock bands such as Led Zeppelin, Deep Purple and Black Sabbath. Formed a fusion band in the late '70s before joining Robert Plant's group. His impressive playing can be heard on the Robert Plant albums on Atlantic: *Now And Zen* (1988) and *Manic Nirvana* (1990). Also on Polydor/Castle compilation *Knebworth - The Album* (1990 charity concert) with Plant. Later worked with LA singer/songwriter Ryan Douglas and numerous others, as well as concentrating on a solo project (due for release in 1994).

Julian **BREAM**

English classical virtuoso and lutanist. Born in Battersea, London on July 15, 1933. Started playing guitar at age 11. Became fascinated by the jazz guitar playing of Django Reinhardt. Studied piano and cello at the Royal Academy of Music in London. Also studied classical guitar with Segovia. Made his professional debut on the instrument in 1947. Joined the British Army in 1952 and spent three years there, during which time he played some jazz.

Later performed extensively in Europe, America and Asia. Became widely acknowledged as a master of Renaissance, Baroque and Romantic music. Also broadened the guitar repertoire by commissioning works from new composers such as Leo Brouwer, Benjamin Britten, William Walton, Lennox Berkley, Hans Werner Henze and Peter Fricker. Made many recordings since 1955 and won several prizes, including two

BMG Records Ltd

Julian Bream (left)

Grammy awards (1963 and 1966) and two Edison awards (1964 and 1974). Albums on RCA Red Seal include *20th-Century Guitar* (1966), *Classic Guitar* (1968), *The Winds So Wild* (1972), *Lute Music Of John Dowland* (1976), *Plays Villa-Lobos* (1977) and *Dedication* (1981). Famous collaborations with John Williams include *Together* (1971) and *Together Again* (1974). RCA presented him with a Platinum Disc in 1979 to mark UK record sales of half a million. Awarded a C.B.E. in 1984. Considered by many to be the finest lutanist of his generation.

Lenny BREAU

Fingerstyle jazz virtuoso. Born in Auburn, Maine on August 5, 1941. Son of country performers Hal Breau and Betty Cody. Started playing guitar at age 8. Played with his parents' band in country circuits by the time he was 12. Early influences included Chet Atkins and jazz

players such as Tal Farlow and Barney Kessel. Moved to Winnipeg, Manitoba in Canada. Spent years practicing jazz and country before working as a studio musician for the local Canadian Broadcasting Company. Chet Atkins was so impressed with Lenny's playing he offered him a recording contract. The result was a critically acclaimed album *Guitar Sounds From Lenny Breau* (RCA) and also *The Velvet Guitar Of Lenny Breau Live* (RCA). There were no more recordings for nearly ten years (mainly because of alcohol and drug problems), until 1978, when he joined forces with pedal steel player Buddy Emmons for the project *Minors Allowed* (Flying Fish). Also worked with Chet Atkins. Later recordings include *Lenny Breau* (Direct Disc), *Five O'Clock Bells* (Adelphi) and *Mo' Breau* (Adelphi). Died mysteriously (apparently strangled) in a swimming-related incident on August 12, 1984. He was well known for his unique melodic sense and impressive control of harmonics.

Big Bill BROONZY

Early blues performer. Born in Scott, Mississippi on June 26, 1893. Worked in corn and cotton fields at age 7. Made a home-made guitar out of a goods box at age 10. Took guitar lessons in the early '20s and played at house rent parties. By the mid '20s he met (and became influenced by) major exponents of the blues such as Blind Lemon Jefferson and Blind Blake and had recorded several 78 rpm records, including 'Rent House Stomp'. Continued to make recordings up until 1957 with musicians such as Memphis Slim and Big Maceo. Died of throat cancer on August 15, 1958. Major country-blues player who inspired later guitarists ranging from B.B.King to Eric Clapton. Albums include compilations such as *Big Bill's Blues* (1968), *The Young Big Bill Broonzy* (1969), *Bluebird No.6* (1976), *Midnight Steppers* (1986), *Sings Folk Songs* (1989), *Remembering Big Bill Broonzy* (1990), *Big Bill Broonzy & Washboard Sam* (1991) and *Do That Guitar Rag 1928-35* (1992).

Leo BROUWER

Classical virtuoso/composer. Born in Havana, Cuba in 1939. Started learning guitar at age 13. Had lessons with Cuban classical guitarist Isaac Nicola. Built up a considerable repertoire by the time he was 16. Studied at Cuba's National Conservatory and then at the Juilliard School in New York, until he had to return to his homeland when Cuba and the United States broke relations in 1962. Since then he has composed many pieces and has taught, performed and conducted at various international festivals. Works published by Schott & Co (London) include *Danza Characteristica*, *Elogio de la Danza*, *Canticum*, *Tres Apuntes* and *La Espiral Eterna*. Recordings on Deutsche Grammophon, Musical Heritage Society and Select include *El Cimarron*, *The Classics Of Cuba*, *Rara*, *Domenico Scarlatti* and *Music For Guitar*.

Clarence 'Gatemouth' BROWN

Blues/bluegrass guitarist and singer. Born in Vinton, Louisiana on April 18, 1924. Grew up in Orange, Texas. Started learning the guitar from age 5. Also played drums, harmonica and fiddle. Worked as a drummer in various bands before flying to LA to record for the Aladdin label in 1947. Moved to Houston in 1949 and signed to Peacock Records with Don Robey. Recorded several hits during the '50s, including 'Dirty Work At The Crossroads' and 'Ain't That Dandy'. Later incorporated elements of jazz, country and cajun music into his style and led various big bands during the '60s and '70s. Worked with Roy Clarke, the Oak Ridge Boys and Hank Wangford. Studio work included commercials for Lone Star Beer. Also did a spell as Deputy Sheriff of San Juan County, New Mexico. His guitar solos inspired many others, including Jimi Hendrix, Frank Zappa and Albert Collins. Albums on Rounder and Alligator include *One More Mile* (1983), *Atomic Energy* (1984), *Pressure Cooker* (1986), *Real Life* (1987) and *No Looking Back* (1991).

Jackson BROWNE

Singer/songwriter and guitarist. Born in Heidelberg, Germany on October 9, 1948. Grew up in Orange County, California. Early influences included Bob Dylan, Buffy Sainte-Marie and John Hurt. Worked with the Nitty Gritty Dirt Band and Nico (ex-Velvet Underground) in the '60s, before going solo. Recordings on Asylum, Elektra and WEA include *Jackson Browne* (1972), *For Everyman* (1973), *Late For The Sky* (1974), *Hold Out* (1980), *Lawyers In Love* (1983), *Lives In The Balance* (1986), *World In Motion* (1989) and *I'm Alive* (1993). Also worked as a producer and had his songs recorded and performed by many singers, including Tom Rush, the Jackson Five, Bonnie Raitt and Linda Ronstadt. A highly-respected songsmith.

Bob BROZMAN

Blues, ragtime and jazz guitarist. A bottleneck specialist. Raised in Brooklyn, New York. Started playing guitar at age 6. Played rock and roll as a teenager. Became interested in blues players such as Robert Johnson and Charley Patton. Later inspired by Hawaiian music and jazz. Studied at Washington University in St. Louis. Played with the Cheap Suit Serenaders (a wacky string band). Also became known for his solo performances, which are laced with humour and showmanship. Solo albums on Kicking Mule include *Blue Hula Stomp* (1982) and *Snappin' The Strings* (1983). On Rounder: *Hello Central...Give Me Dr. Jazz* (1985) and *Devil's Slide* (1988). Author of *The History & Artistry Of National Resonator Instruments* (Hal Leonard). Specialises in Prohibition-period guitar styles and is a leading authority on Hawaiian music.

Jack BRUCE

Legendary rock bass player. Born in Scotland, 1945. Studied the cello at the Royal Scottish Academy of Music at age 17. Played upright bass in various Glasgow jazz clubs. Worked with Graham Bond Organisation and John Mayall in the mid '60s. Formed Cream in 1965 with Eric Clapton and Ginger Baker. One of the first rock bands to use extended improvisations in their repertoire (see Eric CLAPTON). Bruce's solid, inventive and dextrous bass playing set a new standard for the instrument. Cream split up in 1969 and Bruce later worked with many other musicians including Leslie West, Robin Trower, Tony Williams, John McLaughlin and Allan Holdsworth. Solo albums on Polydor, RSO, Epic, Castle and CMP include *Songs For A Tailor* (1969), *Out Of The Storm* (1974), *How's Tricks?* (1977), *A Question Of Time* (1989), *Willpower* (1989), *Jack Bruce - The Collection* (1992) and *Something Else* (1993). One of the most influential bass players of all time.

Jimmy BRYANT

Country guitar player born in Moultrie, Georgia on March 5, 1925. Started learning fiddle from his father (he was beaten if he didn't practice). Joined the US army in 1943 and served in Europe, where he was wounded.

Picked up guitar while convalescing in hospital. Became influenced by Django Reinhardt and Tony Mottola. Moved to California, where he met vocalist Eddie Dean and played in his band. Also worked with Bing Crosby, Speedy West, Tex Williams, Sheb Wooley, Stan Kenton, Kay Starr and many others. Died of lung cancer on September 22, 1980. Solo albums on Imperial include *Laughing Guitar/Crying Guitar*, *The Fastest Guitar In The Country*, *Bryant's Back In Town* and *We Are Young*. On Stetson: *Country Cabin Jazz*.

Roy **BUCHANAN**

Blues-rock player born in Ozark, Tennessee on September 23, 1939. Grew up in Pixley, California. Picked up guitar at age 5. Early influences included Barney Kessel, B.B.King and Jimmy Nolan. Began playing for Dale Hawkins at age 17 and later spent a lot of time as a studio sideman in Nashville and the East Coast. Asked to play guitar with the Rolling Stones after Brian Jones died but turned it down. Voted Best New Guitarist by *Guitar Player* magazine readers in 1972. Played a Fender Telecaster, which gave his distinctive treble sound. Suffered from booze and drug dependancy. Died in Fairfax, Virginia (found hanged in a jail cell) on August 14, 1988. Recordings on Polydor, Atlantic and Sonet include *Roy Buchanan* (1972), *Second Album* (1973), *That's What I'm Here For* (1973), *In The Beginning* (1974), *Rescue Me* (1975), *A Street Called Straight* (1976), *Loading Zone* (1977), *You're Not Alone* (1978), *When A Guitar Plays The Blues* (1985), critically acclaimed *Dancing On The Edge* (1986), *Hot Wire* (1987) and compilation *Sweet Dreams: The Anthology* (1992).

Lindsey **BUCKINGHAM**

Rock player. Born in Palo Alto, California on October 3, 1947. Started learning guitar at age 8. Self-taught. Influenced by folk music and later rock guitarists such as Eric Clapton and Peter Green. Recorded an album titled *Buckingham/Nicks* (1974) with his girlfriend singer Stevie Nicks while still at college. The pair joined Fleetwood Mac in the mid '70s. The resulting band was highly successful, having massive hits with Warner Brothers albums such as *Fleetwood Mac* (1975), *Rumours* (1976), *Tusk* (1979) and *Mirage* (1982). Relationship with Nicks turned sour and he eventually left the band in 1987. Solo albums include *Law*

And Order (1981), *Go Insane* (1984) and *Out Of The Cradle* (1992).

Hiram **BULLOCK**

Rock/fusion player and session ace. Born in Osaka, Japan in 1955. Family moved over to Boston. Started learning the piano at age 3. Took up bass when he was 13 and switched to guitar several years later. Early influences include Eric Clapton, Allman Brothers, John McLaughlin and Steve Miller. Studied at the University of Miami. Started playing professionally in New York during the mid '70s and his reputation soon grew. Since then has worked with Billy Joel, Carla Bley, Chaka Khan, Barbra Streisand, Michael Brecker, Al Jarreau, David Sanborn (tasteful soloing by the guitarist on the Sanborn's Warner Brothers album *Straight To The Heart*), Kenny Loggins and others. Solo albums on Atlantic include *From All Sides* (1986), *Give It What U Got* (1987) and *Way Kool* (1992).

Teddy **BUNN**

Jazz guitarist. Born in Freeport, Long Island in 1909. Picked up the guitar at an early age. Initially played calypso, before switching over to jazz. Developed a subtle, laid-back style which won him considerable respect among fellow musicians and jazz fans. Recorded with the Duke Ellington Orchestra during the late '20s. Later with the Washboard Serenaders, Ben Bernie, Spirits of Rhythm, Jack McVie, Louis Jordan, Hot Lips Page, Lionel Hampton and many others. Suffered from ill health during the '60s and '70s. Died of a heart attack on July 20, 1978. Recordings include *Washboard Rhythm Kings* (RCA), *Swing Street Vol 1* (Epic) with Spirits of Rhythm and *Feelin' High And Happy* (RCA) with Hot Lips Page. Compilations include *Teddy Bunn* (1930-39 sessions).

Jean-Jacques **BURNEL**

New wave bassist. Born in London on February 21, 1952. Joined the Stranglers during the mid-'70s with Hugh Cornwell (guitar, vocals), Dave Greenfield (keyboards) and Jet Black (drums). Their gloomy rock style was compared to the Doors, but was more powerful. Received critical and commercial acclaim with provocative songs such as 'Grip', 'Peaches', 'No More Heroes' and 'Nice 'N Sleazy' during the late '70s. Surprise cover version of Dionne Warwick hit 'Walk On By' in 1978. All songs featured Burnel's solid and aggressive bass style. Became notorious for provoking disturbances at their concerts (and their treatment of journalists). Biggest hit was more laid back 'Golden Brown' (UK No.2 in 1982). Later material covered a broader range. Cornwell left in 1990. Albums include *IV/Rattus Norvegicus* (1977), *No More Heroes* (1977), *Black And White* (1978), *Live: X-Cert* (1979), *The Raven* (1979), *Themeninblack* (1981), *La Folie* (1981), *Feline* (1983), *Aural Sculpture* (1984), *Dreamtime* (1986), *All Live And All Of The Night* (1988), *The Singles* (1989), *Greatest Hits* (1990) and *10* (1990). Burnel solo albums were generally less commercial: *Euroman Cometh* (1979), *Fire And Water* (1983) with Dave Greenfield and *Un Jour Parfait* (1989). Also formed the Purple Helmets for cover versions of '60s classics.

Kenny **BURRELL**

Popular jazz guitarist. Born in Detroit, Michigan on July 31, 1931. Started playing the guitar at age 12. Went to the same school as saxophonist Yusef Lateef and vibraphonist Milt Jackson. Early influences included Charlie Christian and Oscar Moore. Later studied music at Wayne University. Worked with Dizzy Gillespie in 1951, Oscar Peterson in 1955 and Benny Goodman in 1957. Recorded with Astrud Gilberto, Stan Getz, John Coltrane, Tommy Flanagan, Gil Evans and many others. Became one of the most sought after guitarists for studio work, concerts and seminars. Albums on Blue Note, Fantasy, Verve and Muse include *At The Five Spot Cafe Vol.1* (1959), *Guitar Forms* (1965), *Ellington Is Forever* (1975), *Kenny Burrell In New York* (1981), *Handcrafted* (1978), *Generations* (1987) and *Blue Lights Vols 1&2* (1989).

James **BURTON**

Country-rock pioneer. Born in Shreveport, Louisiana on August 21, 1939. Started learning guitar at age 13. Influenced by blues players such as Muddy Waters and Lightnin' Hopkins and country guitarists including Chet Atkins and Hank Williams. Started playing professionally at age 14. Recorded with rockabilly Dale Hawkins a year later. Also took up steel guitar. Appeared in a local radio program, the Louisiana Hayride (KWKH Radio). Later became famous through his work with Ricky Nelson, Jerry Lee Lewis, Elvis Presley and Gram Parsons. His sound, a strong

James Burton

rockabilly-influenced style (innovative string bending and slurring), inspired many younger players. Can be heard on the Ricky Nelson compilation albums including *The Rick Nelson Singles Album* (Liberty) and *The Decca Years* (MCA). Also on Elvis RCA recordings such as *In Person At The International Hotel* (1969), *From Elvis In Memphis* (1969) and *Aloha From Hawaii* (1973). Solo recordings include *The Guitar Sound Of James Burton* (1971). Hot Licks instruction video: *The Legendary Guitar Of James Burton* (1991). Included in *Guitar Player* magazine's 'Gallery Of The Greats' (1987) for his lifetime achievement.

Bernard **BUTLER**

UK guitarist. Born on May 1, 1970. Started playing the instrument at age 14. Influences included Neil Young, Jimmy Page and Johnny Marr. Formed indie band Suede with singer Brett Anderson and bassist Mat Osman in October 1989. Simon Gilbert was added on drums. Gained critical and commercial acclaim with singles such as 'The Drowners' (1992), 'Metal Mickey' (1992), 'Animal Nitrate' (1993), 'So Young' (1993) and 'Stay Together' (1994). Butler's versatile guitar playing is heavily featured on all and ranges from atmospheric acoustic to indie-metal, reminiscent of Jimmy Page. Also plays keyboards. Suede debut album on Nude/Columbia: *Suede* (1993). One of the most striking bands of the genre.

Charlie **BYRD**

Jazz and classical player. Born in Suffolk, Virginia on September 16, 1925. Started playing the guitar at age 9. Early influences included local blues guitarists, as well as guitar giants such as Les Paul, Charlie Christian and Django Reinhardt. Studied theory with his father. Later studied classical guitar with

Sophocles Papas and Andrés Segovia. Worked with Woody Herman, Stan Getz, Herb Ellis, Barney Kessel, Nat Adderley and Laurindo Almeida. Bossa nova pioneer during the early '60s. Formed a very popular jazz trio with Keeter Betts (bass) and Berstell Knox (drums). Recorded many latin-tinged easy-listening albums on the Concord label, including *Brazilian Byrd* (1965), *Great Guitars* (1974), *Byrd By The Sea* (1974), *Blue Byrd* (1978), *Sugarloaf Suite* (1979), *Latin Odyssey* (1983), *Isn't It Romantic* (1984), *It's A Wonderful World* (1988) and *Bossa Nova Years* (1991). Owner of Charlie's Georgetown nightclub in Washington D.C.

David **BYRNE**

Singer/songwriter/guitarist. Born in Dumbarton, Scotland on May 14, 1952. Family emigrated to America and he grew up in Baltimore, Maryland. Self-taught. Early influences included Bob Dylan, the Beatles, Jimmy Nolan (with James Brown) and Neil Young. Formed Talking Heads in 1974 with drummer Chris Frantz and bass player Tina Weymouth. Keyboard player Jerry Harrison joined in 1976. They had a number of original hits featuring Byrne's quirky songs and vocal delivery. Albums on Sire include *Talking Heads '77* (1977), *Fear Of Music* (1979), *Remain In Light* (1980), *The Name Of The Band Is Talking Heads* (1982) and *Popular Favorites/Sand In The Vaseline* (1992). On EMI: *Little Creatures* (1985), *True Stories* (1986) and *Naked* (1988). Also impressive experimental project *My Life In the Bush Of Ghosts* (1981) with Brian Eno. Solo albums on Sire and Warner Brothers include *Catherine Wheel* (1982), *Brazil Classics* (1989) and *Forro* (1991).

J.J. **CALE**

Singer/songwriter/guitarist. Born Jean-Jacques Cale in Oklahoma on December 5, 1938. Grew up in Tulsa. Played in high school bands with Leon Russell. Influences included country and blues musicians. Formed a rock'n'roll group Johnny Cale & The Valentines. Moved to Los Angeles to work with other ex-Tulsa musicians Leon Russell and Carl Radle. Developed an effortless 'minimalist' blues style. Gained a cult following through several laid-back albums on A&M, Mercury, Phonogram, RCA, Hannibal and Silvertone including *Naturally* (1972), *Really* (1973), *Okie* (1974), *Troubadour* (1976), *Five* (1979), *Shades* (1981), *Grasshopper* (1982), *No.8* (1983), compilation *Nightriding* (1988), *Travel-Log* (1989) and *Fragments Of A Rainy Season* (1992). Also with Delaney & Bonnie and others. His laconic style inspired many others including Eric Clapton and Mark Knopfler.

Vivian **CAMPBELL**

UK heavy metal player. Born c.1963. Grew up in Belfast, Northern Ireland. First became interested in the guitar at age 8. Early influences include Marc Bolan, Rory Gallagher and Gary Moore. Formed the band Sweet Savage after being expelled from school in 1979. They toured with Motörhead and Thin Lizzy. Big break came when he was invited over to England to work with Ronnie James Dio. They recorded a number of albums on Warner Brothers/Vertigo, including *Holy Diver* (1983), *The Last In Line* (1984), *Sacred Heart* (1985) and *Intermission* (1986). Later worked with Whitesnake, River Dogs and Def Leppard. His soloing is fiery and rich in harmonics. Hot Licks instructional video *Lead Master Class* (1986) was received warmly.

Larry **CARLTON**

Jazz/fusion guitarist and studio ace. Born in Torrance, California on March 2, 1948. Early influences included blues and jazz musicians. Started working professionally as a session musician in the late-'60s. Joined jazz-funk band the Crusaders in 1971, appearing on MCA recordings including *Chain Reaction* (1975) and *Free As The Wind* (1976). Also worked with top artists such as Joni Mitchell and Steely Dan and became the most sought-after session player

Larry Carlton

in the West Coast. Left the Crusaders in 1978 to pursue a solo career. Debut album *Larry Carlton* (1978) on Warner Brothers featured impressive 'Room 335' and some beautiful fluid guitar tones. A sophisticated mixture of blues, jazz and rock. Later recordings on Warners, MCA and GRP include *Strikes Twice* (1979), *Friends* (1983), *Discovery* (1987), *Collection* (1991) and *Kid Gloves* (1992). Instructional video: *Larry Carlton* (Star Licks). An exceptional guitarist with a unique, concise and highly expressive style.

Maybelle **CARTER**

Folk guitarist/singer. Born Maybelle Addington in Copper Creek, Virginia on May 10, 1909. Also played banjo and autoharp. Formed a country trio the Carter Family with cousin Sara (vocals, guitar) and Sara's husband Alvin Pleasant Carter (vocals, fiddle). Started singing at local church functions before making their first recordings during the late '20s. Became very influential in the folk music scene (revolutionised the genre by bringing vocals to the foreground) and later had songs performed by Joan Baez, Emmylou Harris, the Weavers and many others. Maybelle joined the Grand Ole Opry in 1950. Appeared at the Newport Folk Festival in 1967. Close friends with Johnny Cash (he married Maybelle's daughter June in 1967). Elected to the Country Music Hall of Fame in 1970. Albums include *The*

Famous Carter Family (1961), *The Carter Family* (1963), *Home Among The Hills* (1965), *The Country Album* (1967), *The Carter Family On Border Radio* (1972), *Country's First Family* (1976) and *Legendary Performers* (1978). Maybelle died in Nashville on October 23, 1978.

Al **CASEY**

Jazz guitarist. Born in Louisville, Kentucky on September 15, 1915. Started playing violin at age 8 and switched to acoustic guitar by the time he was 15. Moved to New York in 1930. Studied at the Martin Smith Music School and graduated in 1933. Joined Fats Waller and His Rhythm in 1934 and played on most of their subsequent records until Waller's death in 1943. Also worked for pianist Teddy Wilson during 1939-40. Switched to amplified guitar and formed his own band in 1943. Later recordings on Prestige, JSP and Storyville include *Buck Jumpin'* (1960), *Six Swinging Strings* (1981) and *Al Casey With Fessor's Session Boys* (1983).

Philip **CATHERINE**

Jazz and fusion player. Born in London, England on October 27, 1942. Grew up in Brussels, Belgium. Played in local bands as a teenager. Early influences included Django Reinhardt and Rene Thomas. Started playing professionally at age 17. Worked with French violinist Jean-Luc Ponty in the early '70s, before studying at the Berklee College of Music in Boston in 1972. Later performed and recorded with Larry Coryell, Chet Baker, Palle Mikkelborg, Toots Thielemans and Niels-Henning Ørsted Pedersen. Albums on Atlantic, CMP, Elektra, Pablo, Inak, Criss Cross and Enja include *September Man* (1974), *Sleep, My Love* (1978), *Babel* (1980), *The Viking* (1983), critically-acclaimed *Transparence* (1988), *Moods Vol 1* (1992) and *Spanish Nights* (1992).

Carlos **CAVAZO**

Heavy metal player born in Atlanta, Georgia on July 8, 1958. Grew up in Los Angeles and South America. Started learning guitar at age 8. Took lessons at age 10 and also learned from other friends. Early influences include Jimi Hendrix, Jeff Beck and Michael Schenker. Formed the bands Speed Of Light and Snow before joining Quiet Riot (as Randy Rhoads' replacement) with Kevin DuBrow (vocals),

Rudy Sarzo (bass) and Frankie Banali (drums). Cavazo and DuBrow made the band a potent live act. They had considerable success with the Epic album *Metal Health* (1983). It sold more than 3,000,000 copies in its first year and became the best-selling heavy metal debut album ever. Further success continued with further recordings including *Critical Condition* (1984), *Quiet Riot III* (1986) and *Wild, Young And Crazee* (1987). Instructional video/cassette: *Carlos Cavazo* (Star Licks).

Eugene CHADBOURNE

Experimental guitarist. Born c.1954. Grew up in Boulder, Colorado. Started playing guitar in the fourth grade. Influences as diverse as Jimi Hendrix, Frank Zappa, Captain Beefheart, Tommy Bolin, Derek Bailey, Conlon Nancarrow (composer of highly unusual music for player-pianos), Spike Jones and Iannis Xenakis (Greek composer). Impressive fingerpicking and slide guitar techniques. Also uses garden tools, household utensils (including a toilet plunger!) and toy instruments. Recorded some highly original and unconventional albums on Fundamental, Delta and Intakt: *Country Protest* (1985), *Corpses Of Foreign Wars* (1986), *Vermin Of The Blues* (1987), *Blotter* (1992) and *Strings* (1992).

Craig CHAQUICO

Rock player. Born in Sacramento Valley, California on September 26, 1954. Picked up his first guitar at age 10. Broke both of his arms and a leg in a car crash when he was 14. Recovered and formed a high school band called Steelwind. Recorded on the Paul Kantner/Grace Slick album *Sunfighter* (Grunt, 1971) while still in his teens. Later replaced Jorma Kaukonen in Jefferson Airplane (renamed Jefferson Starship). His soaring and melodic rock solos can be heard on several band albums on Grunt, including *Dragon Fly* (1974), *Red Octopus* (1975), *Spitfire* (1976), *Earth* (1978), *Winds Of Change* (1982) and *Nuclear Future* (1984). Later shortened name to Starship. *Knee Deep In The Hoopla* (1985) featured US No.1 hits 'We Built This City' and 'Sara'. Other recordings include *No Protection* (1987) and *Love Among The Cannibals* (1989).

Charlie CHRISTIAN

Jazz and electric guitar pioneer. Born in Dallas, Texas on July 29, 1916. His father was a blind guitar player. Family moved to Oklahoma City in 1921. Started playing trumpet at age 12 and was soon also playing piano, double bass and acoustic guitar. Later switched to electric guitar, after hearing Eddie Durham and Floyd Smith experiment with the instrument. Developed a unique single-note electric lead style and a percussive rhythm technique, utilizing a lot of augmented and diminished chords in a way that would later be known as bebop. Joined Al Trent's band in the late '30s and astonished other musicians and audiences alike with his playing. Later with Benny Goodman, Charlie Parker, Dizzie Gillespie, Thelonius Monk and many others. Died of tuberculosis in New York on March 2, 1942. A legendary figure who is generally considered to be the father of bebop guitar. Influenced many major jazz players such

Charlie Christian

as Tal Farlow, Barney Kessel, Herb Ellis and Jim Hall. One of the most influential guitar players of all time. Recordings include compilations on Columbia and Charly: *The Genius Of Electric Guitar* (1987) *and Guitar Wizard* (1993). Included in *Guitar Player* magazine's 'Gallery Of The Greats' (1984) for his lifetime achievement.

Eric CLAPTON

English blues/rock legend. Born in Ripley, Surrey on March 30, 1945. Grew up with his grandparents. Influenced by early blues players such as Big Bill Broonzy, Muddy Waters and Robert Johnson. Joined pop band the Yardbirds in 1963. They recorded the EMI album *Five Live Yardbirds* (1964). Clapton left the band to

Eric
Clapton

concentrate more on playing the blues and joined John Mayall's band the Blues Breakers in 1965. They released the landmark album *Bluesbreakers* (1965) on Decca. The guitarist's contribution to the album was outstanding. He pioneered the feedback-assisted sustain and overdrive sounds, playing solos of a previously unheard of intensity. Also used light gauge strings to get a crisper sound and enhance note bending. By then he had achieved cult-figure status in the UK; graffitti proclaiming "Clapton is God" started to appear on walls, signposts and even rocks. Left Mayall in 1966 to form Cream with Jack Bruce (bass) and Ginger Baker (drums). Cream were one of the first rock bands to gain mass appeal through their instrumental abilities. They recorded several successful albums on RSO including *Fresh Cream* (1966), *Wheels Of Fire* (1968) and *Goodbye* (1969). Some of their songs, such as 'Badge' and 'Sunshine Of Your Love', have since become rock classics. The band split up in 1969 and Clapton spent brief periods with Blind Faith (with Stevie Winwood and Ginger Baker) and Delaney & Bonnie & Friends. Formed Derek & The Dominoes in 1970 with guitarist Duane Allman for the Polydor album *Layla And Other Assorted Love Songs* (1970). The recording was a critical and commercial flop (although the song 'Layla' was later a smash hit in 1972) and the band soon split up. This marked the beginning of a traumatic period for the

guitarist. His friends Jimi Hendrix and Duane Allman died in 1970 and 1971 respectively. He also lost his grandfather, who had brought him up. Became temporarily addicted to heroin and alcohol; gave some below-par performances during the early '70s before picking up again. Albums on RSO, Duck and Reprise include *Eric Clapton* (1970), *461 Ocean Boulevard* (1974), *E.C. Was Here* (1975), *Slowhand* (1977), *Backless* (1978), *Just One Night* (1980), *Money And Cigarettes* (1983), *Backtracking* (1984), *Behind The Sun* (1985), *August* (1986), *Journeyman* (1989), *24 Nights* (1991) and *Unplugged* (1992). Inspired players as diverse as Robert Cray, Paul Kossoff, Alex Lifeson, Brian May, Michael Schenker, Angus Young, Eddie Van Halen, Bill Connors, Steve Lukather and many others. One of the most influential guitarists of all time. Included in *Guitar Player* magazine's 'Gallery Of The Greats' after being voted Best Rock Guitarist (1971-1974) and Best Electric Blues Guitarist (1980-1982). Videos include *The Cream Of Eric Clapton* (1990). Various books: *Slowhand - The Story Of Eric Clapton* by Harry Sharpiro (Proteus), *Eric Clapton* by John Pidgeon (Panther) and *Survivor*, an authorised biography by Ray Coleman (Warner Books).

Roy **CLARK**

Country guitarist and singer. Born in Meherrin,

Virginia on April 15, 1933. Played in his father's band as a child. Won the USA country banjo championship twice by the time he was 17. Worked with Jimmy Dean, Marvin Rainwater and George Hamilton IV in the '50s. Solo albums on various labels include *The Lightning Fingers Of Roy Clark* (1962), *The Tip Of My Fingers* (1963), *Guitar Spectacular* (1965), *Roy Clark* (1966), *Live* (1967), *Happy To Be Unhappy* (1967), *Urban, Suburban* (1968), *I Never Picked Cotton* (1970), *The Incredible Roy Clark* (1971), *Classic Clark* (1974), *Hookin' It* (1977), *Labour Of Love* (1978), *Live From Austin City Limits* (1982) and compilation *20 Golden Pieces* (1984).

Stanley CLARKE

Bass virtuoso born in Philadelphia, Pennsylvania on June 30, 1951. Started learning violin at age 12. Later switched to cello, double-bass and bass guitar by the time he was 16. Early influences included James Brown, Jimi Hendrix, the Beatles and Bach. Studied

Stanley Clarke

symphonic double-bass playing at the Philadelphia Musical Academy. Also played popular music with local groups. Worked with jazzers Horace Silver, Joe Henderson and Stan

Getz in 1970. Joined Chick Corea's fusion band Return To Forever in 1972. They were one of the most impressive and adventurous jazz-rock bands of the '70s. The most popular line-up included guitarist Al Di Meola and drummer Lenny White. They recorded several albums on Polydor and Columbia including *Where Have I Known You Before* (1974) and the amazing *Romantic Warrior* (1976). Clarke later worked with Jeff Beck, George Duke, Paul McCartney and the acoustic guitar virtuosos Strunz & Farah. His unique slapping, popping and rapid solo passages set a new standard for the electric bass. A major influence on Mark King, Stu Hamm, Marcus Miller and many others. Solo albums on Atlantic include *Stanley Clarke* (1974), *Journey To Love* (1975), *School Days* (1976). On Epic: *Rocks, Pebbles And Sand* (1980), *Time Exposure* (1983), *Find Out* (1985), *Hideaway* (1986), *If This Bass Could Talk* (1988) and *East River Drive* (1993).

Zal CLEMINSON

Scottish rock guitarist. Born on May 4, 1949. Early influences included rock players such as Jimi Hendrix, Eric Clapton and Jeff Beck. Joined the Sensational Alex Harvey Band in the early '70s. Had considerable success as a live act in the UK with Harvey's crazed charisma and Cleminson dressed as a clown. Singles included manic cover of Tom Jones hit 'Delilah' (1975) and 'Boston Tea Party' (1976). Recorded a number of albums on Vertigo, including *Framed* (1972), *Next* (1973), *The Impossible Dream* (1974), *Sensational Alex Harvey Band Live* (1975), *Tomorrow Belongs To Me* (1975), *The Penthouse Tapes* (1976) and *Rock Drill* (1978). Cleminson left to join Nazareth in 1978 and Harvey died of a heart attack on February 4, 1981.

Kurt COBAIN

Rock guitarist and singer. Born on February 20, 1967. Influenced by rock bands of the '70s and '80s. Formed grunge-rock band Nirvana with Krist Novoselic (bass) and Aaron Burckhard (drums, later replaced by several others) in 1987. Debut album *Bleach* (1989) on Sub Pop featured second guitarist Jason Everman, who left after US tour. Music was angry, aggressive and distinctive. Geffen recording *Nevermind* (1991) featured new drummer Dave Grohl. The album went gold within 3 weeks of its release. Toured with the Red Hot Chilli Peppers and Pearl Jam that year. Played a concert at San

Francisco's Cow Palace in aid of rape survivors in Bosnia. Cobain married Courtney Love of

Kurt Cobain

Hole on February 24, 1992. Later Nirvana recordings include compilation of B-sides *Incesticide* (1992) and *In Utero* (1993).

Eddie COCHRAN

Rock and roll singer/songwriter/guitarist. Born on October 3, 1938 in Oklahoma City, Oklahoma. Started learning trombone and then guitar. Family moved to Bell Gardens, California in 1952. Formed bands with friends at high school and became heavily influenced by Chet Atkins. Performed with Hank Cochran (no relation) as the Cochran Brothers during 1954/55. Later worked as a session guitarist in LA and wrote many songs with Jerry Capeheart. Had a stream of classic hits including 'Sitting In The Balcony' (1957), 'Summertime Blues' (1958), 'C'Mon Everybody' (1959) and 'Three Steps To Heaven' (1960). Killed in a car crash in London after a successful tour. Albums include *Eddie Cochran* (Liberty), *Best Of Eddie Cochran* (EMI/Liberty), *Singing To My Baby* (Liberty), *The Early Years* (Ace) and *The Eddie Cochran Singles Album* (United Artists).

Albert COLLINS

Blues singer/songwriter/guitarist. Born in a log cabin in Leona, Texas on October 1, 1932. Family moved to Houston. Took lessons from his cousin Lightnin' Hopkins, who taught him to tune the guitar to an F minor chord.

Developed a powerful blues style, using his thumb and first two fingers for picking. Influenced mainly by horn and organ players. Played with Clarence 'Gatemouth' Brown by the time he was 15. Later recorded instrumental singles such as 'The Freeze' (1952) and 'Frosty' (1962). Albums include *The Cool Sound Of Albert Collins* (1965), *Love Can Be Found Anywhere, Even In A Guitar* (1968), *Alive And Cool* (1971), *Ice Pickin'* (1979), *Frostbite* (1980), *Don't Lose Your Cool* (1982), *Live In Japan* (1984), *Cold Snap* (1986), *The Ice Man* (1991) and *Molten Ice* (1992). Also collaborated with Robert Cray and Johnny

Albert Collins

Copeland on *Showdown!* (1985). His graunchy double-stop bends, treble sound and aggressive string snaps inspired players as diverse as Larry Carlton, Stevie Ray Vaughan, Robben Ford and Robert Cray. Died of lung cancer on November 24, 1993.

Allen COLLINS

Rock guitarist born in Jacksonville, Florida in 1952. Picked up the guitar from an early age and taught himself to play. Formed a band with school classmates Ronnie Van Zant (vocals) and Gary Rossington (guitarist), which eventually became the nucleus of southern rock band Lynyrd Skynyrd. Co-wrote the famous song 'Freebird' in 1974. They recorded a number of albums on MCA: *Pronounced Leh-Nerd Skin-*

Nerd (1973), *Second Helping* (1974), *Nuthin'
Fancy* (1975) and *One More For The Road*
(1976). The band split in 1977, after Van Zant
and two others perished in a plane crash.
Collins formed the Rossington-Collins Band
with Gary Rossington. Became paralysed from
the waist down after a serious road accident.
Died of pneumonia in January 1990.

Eddie CONDON

Jazz guitarist. Born in Goodland, Indiana on
November 16, 1905. Taught himself to play
banjo and four-string guitar as a youngster.
Recorded with the Chicagoans during the '20s.
Moved to New York City in 1928. Worked
with Louis Armstrong, Artie Shaw, Bobby
Hackett, Red McKenzie, Bix Beiderbecke and
many others. Became well-known as an
organiser of gigs and recording sessions.
Actively involved in the jazz scene until his
death in New York on August 4, 1973. Albums
include *Jam Session Coast To Coast* (1953),
Bixieland (1955) and *Live In Tokyo* (1964).
Compilations include *The Spirit Of London*
(1979), *Chicago Style* (1985) and *The
Liederkrantz Sessions* (1987). Also wrote an
autobiography *We Called It Music* (Holt 1947).

Bill CONNORS

Jazz-rock and classical player. Born in Los
Angeles on September 24, 1949. Early
influences included Eric Clapton and Joe Pass.
Played with numerous musicians before joining
Chick Corea's fusion band Return To Forever
in the early '70s for the Polydor recording
Hymn Of The Seventh Galaxy (1973). Left the
band to do session work in New York. Took up
classical guitar after hearing Julian Bream and
recorded acoustic albums including *Theme To
The Guardian* and *Of Mist And Melting* (both
on ECM). Started playing electric guitar again
in the early '80s and formed an impressive
fusion trio with virtuosos Tom Kennedy (bass)
and Dave Weckl (drums). They signed to
Pathfinder Records and recorded *Step It* (1984).
Weckl left to join the Chick Corea Elektric
Band and was replaced by Kim Plainfield on
drums for two more albums: *Double Up* (1986)
and *Assembler* (1987).

Ry COODER

Blues and folk guitarist. Also highly respected
slide player. Born Ryland Peter Cooder in Los
Angeles on March 15, 1947. Started learning

the guitar at age 4. Took lessons from the Rev.
Gary Davis. Formed a duo with Jackie
DeShannon as a teenager. Worked with Taj
Mahal, Captain Beefheart, Randy Newman,
Phil Ochs and the Rolling Stones in the late
'60s. Recorded an eponymous debut solo album
in 1970 and has since recorded many others on
Reprise and Warner Brothers, including *Into
The Purple Valley* (1971), *Boomer's Story*
(1973), *Paradise & Lunch* (1974), *Chicken Skin
Music* (1976), *Jazz* (1978), *Bop Till You Drop*
(1979), *Borderline* (1980), *Why Don't You Try
Me Tonight?* (1986) and *Get Rhythm* (1987).
Also worked on several film soundtracks,
including *Southern Comfort* (1981), *Alamo Bay*
(1985), *Paris, Texas* (1985), *Crossroads* (1986)
and *Trespass* (1992). Also joined forces with
Nick Lowe, John Hiatt and Jim Keltner for
Little Village (1992). Included in *Guitar Player*
magazine's 'Gallery Of The Greats' after
winning several blues and acoustic guitar
categories during the '80s.

Larry CORYELL

Jazz and fusion guitarist. Born in Galveston,
Texas on April 2, 1943. Grew up in
Washington and taught himself guitar. Early
influences included Chet Atkins and Chuck
Berry. Later inspired by Wes Montgomery, Tal
Farlow and Barney Kessel. Moved to New York
in 1965. Worked with Chico Hamilton, Gary
Burton and Herbie Mann in the late '60s.
Recorded solo albums such as *Basics* (1968),
Spaces (1970) and *At The Village Gate* (1971),
before forming pioneering fusion group the
Eleventh House in 1972. They recorded
Introducing The Eleventh House (1972) and
Larry Coryell And The Eleventh House (1974).
Other albums include *Return* (1979), *Coming
Home* (1985), *Together* (1986) with Emily
Remler, *A Quiet Day In Spring* (1988) and *Just
Like Being Born* (1989). A regular columnist
with *Guitar Player* magazine during the '80s.
Also worked with Charles Mingus, Al Di
Meola, John McLaughlin, Steve Khan, John
Scofield and many others. Author of instruction
video *Advanced Jazz Guitar* (Hot Licks 1990).

Pete COSEY

Jazz-influenced guitar player. Born in Chicago,
Illinois on October 9, 1943. Initially took up
accordion and later started playing guitar at age
14. Early influences include Freddie King,
B.B.King, and jazzmen such as Ornette
Coleman and John Coltrane. Formed his own

band in the '60s and also worked with Ike & Tina Turner and Bobby Bland. Started experimenting and developed radical distortion and wah-wah techniques, which he later used with Miles Davis on the Columbia album *Agharta* (1976). A unique guitarist who influenced players as diverse as Henry Kaiser, Vernon Reid, Elliott Sharp and Robert Quine.

Libba COTTEN

Born Elizabeth Cotten in 1893. Daughter of a cook and a miner. Grew up near Chapel Hill in North Carolina. Married at age 15. Later divorced and moved to Washington DC. Taught herself to play the guitar and composed songs ranging from hymns to ragtime and blues. Played a Martin acoustic upside down and left-handed. Developed a two-fingered picking style which became a folk standard. Her songs have been performed by Maria Muldaur, the Grateful Dead and many others. Chas McDevitt had a hit with 'Freight Train' (she composed it at age 11) in 1957. Won the Burl Ives award in 1972 for her contribution to folk music and a Grammy award for Best Traditional Folk Music in 1985 for *Elizabeth Cotten Live* (Arhoolie). Other recordings on Folkways include *Folksongs And Instrumentals With Guitar* (1958 sessions), *Shake Sugaree* (1967) and *When I'm Gone* (1979). Died in Syracuse, New York on July 29, 1987.

Robert CRAY

Singer/blues guitarist. Born in Columbus, Georgia on August 1, 1953. Began playing guitar at age 12. Early influences included Jimi Hendrix, Eric Clapton, Steve Cropper and other exponents of blues, R&B and jazz. Formed the Robert Cray Band in 1974. Their blend of soul and traditional blues developed and became very popular in the '80s. Cray's fluid and exciting blues guitar playing won him critical acclaim. Admired by major bluesmen such as Muddy Waters, John Lee Hooker and Jimmy Vaughan. Debut album *Who's Been Talking* (1979) was re-released on the Charly label. Albums on High Tone include *Bad Influence* (1983) and *False Accusations* (1985). With Albert Collins and Johnny Copeland: *Showtime* (1985). On Mercury: *Strong Persuader* (1986), *Don't Be Afraid Of The Dark* (1988), *Midnight Stroll* (1990) and *I Was Warned* (1991). On Tomato: *Too Many Cooks* (1991). Cover versions of his songs have also been recorded by Eric Clapton, Albert King and others.

Robert Cray

Ian Astle

Jim CROCE

Folk singer/songwriter and guitarist. Born in Philadelphia, Pennsylvania on January 10, 1943. Started playing accordion at age 6 and later switched to guitar. Spent some time as a university disc jockey and performed as a duo with his wife Ingrid in bars and coffee-houses. Also worked as a truck driver and telephone engineer. Secured a record deal with ABC and later released best-selling (US) folk albums such as *You Don't Mess Around With Jim* (1972), *Life And Times* (1973) and *I Got A Name* (1973). Died in a plane crash at Natchitoches, Louisiana on September 20, 1973. ABC released the compilation *Photographs and Memories - His Greatest Hits* (1974). Later releases on Castle include *The Final Tour* (1990) and *The 50th Anniversary Collection* (1992).

Steve CROPPER

Rock guitarist. Born in Willow Springs, Missouri on October 21, 1941. Formed a band called the Mar-Keys at school. They had a hit with 'Last Night' (1961). Joined Booker T & The MG's (Memphis Group) with Booker T Jones (organ), Lewis Steinberg (bass) and Al Jackson (drums). Debut single 'Green Onions' (1962) featured a blues-organ groove slashed through by Cropper's gritty blues licks. It was a huge success and was followed up by a number of smaller hits. Albums on London and Stax include *Green Onions* (1962), *Soul Limbo* (1968) and *Greatest Hits* (1973). Considered to be one of the greatest R&B groups of all time. Solo Cropper album: *With A Little Help From My Friends* (1971). Also worked with Otis Redding, Wilson Pickett, Pop Staples, Albert King and the Blues Brothers band.

Warren **CUCURULLO**

US rock guitarist. Born c.1957. Grew up in Brooklyn, New York. Picked up the guitar at age 10 and soon played in various local bands. Early influences included the Beatles, Cream and Johnny Winter. Sent solo demo tapes to Frank Zappa, who was impressed and asked him to join his band in 1979. Appeared on several Zappa albums including *Joe's Garage, Act I* (1979), *Tinseltown Rebellion* (1981) and *Shut Up And Play Your Guitar* (1981). Formed the band Missing Persons with Terry Bozzio (drums), Dale Bozzio (vocals), Patrick O' Hearn (bass) and Chuck Wild (keyboards). Albums on Capitol include *Missing Persons, Spring Session*

M and *Rhyme & Reason*. Later joined Duran Duran. Cuccurullo's textural rock style incorporates a number of distortion, flange and delay effects.

Jan **CYRKA**

UK rock player/composer. Born in Halifax, West Yorkshire on October 31, 1963. Started playing the guitar seriously from age 16. Early influences included Steve Howe, Dave Gilmour and Jeff Beck. Joined Zodiac Mindwarp And The Love Reaction as guitarist 'Flash Bastard' on *Tattoed Beat Messiah* (1987). Also worked on TV commercials including Adidas, McDonalds and Irn Bru (humorous heavy metal parody). Later pursued solo career with instrumental music: debut album *Beyond The Common Ground* (1992) on Food For Thought featured 'Western Eyes' (used by Tommy Vance for BBC Radio One's 'Friday Rock Show'). *Spirit* (1993) was more atmospheric and covered a broader range. An original and melodic guitarist who has drawn praise from the likes of Joe Satriani and Brian May.

D

Reverend Gary **DAVIS**

Early bluesman. Born in Laurens, South Carolina on April 30, 1896. Taught himself guitar, piano and harmonica from age 6. Performed on street corners and in church. Lost his sight during his late twenties. Became a Baptist minister in 1933. Earliest recordings were spiritual and blues songs during the mid-'30s. Moved to New York in 1940 and played the folk circuit. Appeared at the Newport Festival in 1968. Influenced musicians as diverse as Bob Dylan, Ry Cooder (one of his students), Donovan and Stefan Grossman. Died in Hammonton, New Jersey on May 5, 1972. Recordings include compilations such as *1935-1949* (Yazoo), *Ragtime Guitar* (Kicking Mule) and *When I Die* (Fantasy).

Jimmy 'Fast Fingers' **DAWKINS**

Blues guitarist and singer. Born James Henry Dawkins in Tchula, Mississippi on October 24,

1936. Taught himself to play guitar as a teenager. Formed his own band and played in clubs. Later worked with Wild Child Butler, Koko Taylor, Sleepy John Estes, Luther Allison, Jimmy Rogers, Johnny Young and a number of others. Recordings on Delmark include *Fast Fingers*, *All For Business* and *Blisterstring* (all '70s). Also wrote for *Blues Unlimited* magazine. Played at the Ann Arbor Blues Festival in 1972 with Otis Rush. JSP later released a Chicago '85 recording session as *Feel The Blues* (1988). Little known, but highly respected guitarist.

Paco **DE LUCÍA**

Flamenco virtuoso. Born Francisco Sánchez Gómez in Algeciras, Spain on December 21, 1947. Son of flamenco guitarist Antonio Sánchez Pecino. Brothers Ramón de Algeciras and Pepe de Lucía also flamenco players. Moved to Barcelona at age 5 and began learning the guitar two years later. Early influences included Niño Ricardo, Sabicas and Mario Escudero. Practised for up to twelve hours a day and developed a unique and formidable technique. First recording *Los Chiquitos de Algeciras* (1961), made with Pepe, caused a sensation in the flamenco world. Toured Europe with the Festival Flamenco Gitano in 1967. Later made a number of outstanding recordings on Philips including *The Fabulous Guitar Of Paco de Lucía* (1967), *Fantasiá Flamenca de Paco de Lucía* (1969), *Fuente y Caudal* (1973), *Paco de Lucía en Vivo Desde el Teatro Real* (1975), *Almoraima* (1976), *Paco de Lucía Interpreta a Manuel de Falla* (1978), *Solo Quiero Caminar* (1981), *Sirocco* (1987), *Zyryab* (1990) and *Concierto de Aranjuez* (1991). Also recorded impressive *Friday Night In San Francisco* (1981) and *Passion, Grace & Fire* (1983) with fusion virtuosos Al Di Meola and John McLaughlin. A supremely gifted player who has helped reshape the course of flamenco, as well as introduce it to a wider audience. Included in *Guitar Player* magazine's 'Gallery Of The Greats' after being voted Best Flamenco Guitarist (1977-1981).

Warren **DE MARTINI**

Heavy metal player. Born c.1964. Picked up a guitar at age 7, but soon smashed it up after seeing Pete Townshend play with The Who. His parents refused to get him another guitar and so he had to buy the next one himself when he was 15. Early influences included Jimi Hendrix, Eddie Van Halen and Michael Schenker. Joined the heavy metal band Ratt on the recommendation of guitarist Jake E. Lee. The initial line-up included Robbin Crosby (guitar), Stephen Pearcy (vocals), Juan Croucier (bass) and Bobby Blotzer (drums). De Martini's impressive and dextrous guitar work played a large role in the band's subsequent success. Ratt albums on Atlantic include *Out Of The Cellar* (1984), *Invasion Of Your Privacy* (1985), *Dancing Undercover* (1986), *Reach For The Sky* (1988) and *Detonator* (1990).

Rick **DERRINGER**

Rock guitarist/producer. Born Richard Zehringer in Fort Recovery, Ohio on August 5, 1947. Picked up the guitar at age 9. Played rhythm guitar in a high school swing band at age 15. Also formed the McCoys while still in his teens. They had hits with 'Hang On, Sloopy' and 'Fever' in 1965. Later worked with Johnny and Edgar Winter, Todd Rundgren, the

Osmonds, Steely Dan (allegedly inspired the title of the song 'Rikki Don't Lose That Number'), Bette Midler, Alice Cooper and 'Wierd Al' Yankovic. Recorded a number of solo albums including *All American Boy* (1973), *Spring Fever* (1975), *Derringer* (1976), *Sweet Evil* (1977), *Live* (1977), *If You Weren't So Romantic* (1978), *Guitars And Women* (1979), *Face To Face* (1980), *Rick Derringer* (1981), *Good Dirty Fun* (1983) and *Back To The Blues* (1993). Instructional video: *Secrets* (Warner Brothers).

Neil **DIAMOND**

Singer/songwriter. Born in Brooklyn, New York on January 24, 1941. Picked up the guitar as a teenager after seeing Pete Seeger perform. Hired as staff writer by Sunbeam Music. Wrote the hits 'I'm A Believer' and 'A Little Bit Me, A Little Bit You' for the Monkees during 1966-67. Later had a number of hits himself with 'Sweet Caroline' (1969), 'Cracklin' Rosie' (1970) and 'Song Sung Blue' (1972). Popularity increased into the '70s with ambitious albums on Uni and MCA such as *Tap Root Manuscript* (1972), *Moods* (1972) and *Rainbow* (1973). Later recordings on CBS/Columbia include film soundtrack *Jonathan Livingston Seagull* (1973), *Serenade* (1974) and *Beautiful Noise* (1976), soundtrack for his own film *The Jazz Singer* (1980), *Primitive* (1984), *Headed For The Future* (1986), *The Best Years Of Our Lives* (1989) and *The Greatest hits 1966-1992* (1992).

Bo **DIDDLEY**

R&B singer, songwriter and guitarist. Born Ellas Bates in McComb, Mississippi on December 30, 1928. Started learning violin but "couldn't see nothin' happening for a black violin player" and switched to guitar. Influences included Muddy Waters, John Lee Hooker and Jimmy Rogers. Developed the unique 'hambone' style (unconventional rhythmic chopping technique) that influenced later songwriters such as Buddy Holly and the Rolling Stones. Had a big hit with the Chess single 'Bo Diddley' (1955), although he apparently had to change its original title 'Dirty Motherfucker' so it could be released for radio airplay. Other songs include 'Little Girl' (1955), 'Hey Bo Diddley' (1957), 'Hush Your Mouth' (1958) and 'Bo Meets The Monster' (1958). Became very popular in the UK during the early and mid-'60s (along with other Chess bluesmen Muddy Waters and Howlin' Wolf). Recorded albums such as *Bo Diddley Is A Lover* (1961),

Bo Diddley

Bo Diddley (1962), *Bo Diddley & Company* (1963), *Hey Good Looking* (1964), *Let Me Pass* (1965), *Super Blues Band* (1968), *London Sessions* (1973) and *The Black Gladiator* (1975). Appeared in a sports footwear TV advert during the late '80s. Elected to the Rock'N'Roll Hall Of Fame (1987) and received a star in the Hollywood Walk Of Fame (1989). Also well-known for playing unusual rectangular-shaped guitars. Ace compilation: *Bo's Blues* (1993). Included in *Guitar Player* magazine's 'Gallery Of The Greats' (1989) for his lifetime achievement.

Al **Di MEOLA**

Fusion guitarist and composer. Born in Jersey City, New Jersey on July 22, 1954. Started learning guitar at age 9. Early influences included Larry Coryell, Tal Farlow, Kenny Burrell, Doc Watson and George Benson. Studied at the Berklee College of Music in Boston. Joined Chick Corea's Return To Forever in 1974 with Corea (keyboards), Stanley Clarke (bass) and Lenny White (drums). They recorded pioneering fusion albums such as *Where Have I Known You Before?* (1974), *No Mystery* (1975) and *Romantic Warrior* (1976), before Di Meola left to pursue a solo career with CBS. His first album *Land Of The Midnight Sun* (1976) also featured Corea and bass player Jaco Pastorius. The next two recordings *Elegant Gypsy* (1977) and *Casino* (1978) justly received critical acclaim. Both albums highlighted Di Meola's

flair for composition as well as his formidable picking technique. Often muted the strings with his right hand while picking, to produce what he

Al Di Meola

called the 'Mutola' effect. This sound became a trademark and also featured heavily on the next studio album *Splendido Hotel* (1980). Formed an acoustic guitar trio with John McLaughlin and Paco de Lucía. They released the well-received *Friday Night In San Francisco* (1981). More solo albums followed: *Electric Rendezvous* (1982), *Tour De Force - Live* (1982) and *Scenario* (1983). Switched to Manhattan label. Marked change in style for the eclectic acoustic album *Cielo e Terra* (1985). Guitar synthesizers and vocals prominent in later Manhattan and Tomato recordings: *Soaring Through A Dream* (1985), *Tirami Su* (1987) and *Kiss My Axe* (1991). With acoustic group World Sinfonia: *World Sinfonia* (1990) and *Heart Of The Immigrants* (1993). His rapid picking and use of latin rhythms inspired many jazz and rock players. Books include *Al Di Meola's Picking Technique*, *A Guide To Chords, Scales & Arpeggios* and *Cielo e Terra* (all 21st Century). Instructional video: *Al Di Meola* (REH). Included in *Guitar Player* magazine's 'Gallery Of The Greats' after being voted Best Jazz Player (1977-1981) and Best Acoustic Steel-string Player (1983-1987).

Joe DIORIO

Jazz guitarist. Born in Waterbury, Connecticut on August 6, 1936. Started taking guitar lessons at age 13. Moved to Chicago and then Miami. Influences included Django Reinhardt and Tony Mottola. Worked with Stan Getz, Eddie Harris, Stanley Turrentine, Ira Sullivan, Sonny Stitt, Wally Cirillo and Horace Silver. Also on television shows. Became a highly respected teacher at the Guitar Institute of Technology in Hollywood (pupils included Scott Henderson and Jennifer Batten). Various recordings on Spitball, Zdenek, RAM and other labels include *Solo Guitar* (1975), *Peaceful Journey* (1977), *Bonita* (1982), *Earth-Moon-Earth* (1988), *Minor Elegance* (1989), *Italy* (1989), *We Will Meet Again* (1993), *Double Take* (1993) with Ricardo del Fra and *Rare Birds* (1993) with Mick Goodrick. Books include *Joe Diorio Guitar Solos* (Zdenek), *21st Century Intervallic Designs* (REH) and *The Ten Book* (Musicians Institute). Instructional video: *Creative Jazz Guitar* (REH).

Sacha DISTEL

Jazz guitarist and singer. Born in Paris, France on January 29, 1933. Started learning the piano at age 5. Took up the guitar at 15. Became inspired by Dizzy Gillespie. Won an amateur music contest in 1950. Later worked with Stan Getz, Lionel Hampton, Dizzy Gillespie, Kenny Clarke and the Modern Jazz Quartet. Won the International Jazz Club prize in 1957. Developed his own individual singing style in the late '50s and had hits with 'The Good Life' and 'Raindrops Keep Falling On My Head'. Albums include *Love Is All* (1976), *From Sacha With Love* (1979) and *Move Closer* (1985).

Jerry DONAHUE

Country-rock player. Born in New York City on September 24, 1946. Started playing guitar at age 12. Early influences included James Burton, the Ventures, Duane Eddy, Amos Garrett and Richard Thompson. Formed folk-rock group Fotheringay in 1970 with singer Sandy Denny and others. Joined Fairport Convention a couple of years later, playing on Island recordings *Rosie* (1973) and *Nine* (1973). Worked with Gerry Rafferty on London recording *North & South* (1988). Also with Ralph McTell, Sandy Denny and Joan Armatrading. Released a highly acclaimed solo album *Telecasting* (1987), followed by *Meetings* (1988) and *Neck Of The Wood* (1992). Also made an instruction video *Country Tech* (REH). His impressive style incorporates fluid runs and lilting multiple-string bends.

K.K.DOWNING

British heavy rock guitarist. Noted for his playing in conjunction with other guitarist Glen Tipton in heavy metal band Judas Priest. They formed during the early '70s in Birmingham, England. The line-up for their first album *Rocka Rolla* (1974) was Rob Halford (vocals), Glen Tipton (guitar), K.K.Downing (guitar), Ian Hill (bass) and John Hinch (drums). The drummer left in 1975 and was replaced by several others in the following years. The combination of Halford's shrill vocals and the unique guitar duo made Judas Priest one of the most popular HM bands on both sides of the Atlantic. Other albums include *Sad Wings Of Destiny* (1976), *Sin After Sin* (1977), *Stained Glass* (1978), *Killing Machine* (1978), *Unleashed In The East* (1979), *British Steel* (1980), *Point Of Entry* (1981), *Screaming For Vengeance* (1982), *Defenders Of The Faith* (1984), *Turbo* (1986), *Priest Live* (1987), *Ram It Down* (1988), *Painkiller* (1990) and *Judas Priest - The Collection* (Castle 1989).

John DUARTE

Classical guitarist/composer. Born in Sheffield, England on October 2, 1919. Started playing ukulele at age 14 and took up the guitar a year later. Decided to devote his time to composing and writing instruction books for the guitar, as well as studying it in a broader sense. Won an international competition organised by the Classical Guitar Society of New York with his composition 'The Colorado Trail' in 1958. Composed many other works, many of which have been performed by major classical guitarists such as Andrés Segovia, John Williams and Alexandre Lagoya. Published a technical reference book endorsed by Segovia. Author of a number of articles for *Guitar Player* magazine and sleeve notes for many guitar records.

Billy DUFFY

Rock guitarist. Born in Manchester, England on May 12, 1961. Played with Theatre Of Hate before joining new wave band The Death Cult in 1983. Within a year they had shortened their name to the Cult. First stable line-up included Ian Astbury (vocals), Jamie Stewart (bass) and Les Warner (drums). Influences included Jimi Hendrix and Led Zeppelin. Adopted a gothic image with Duffy's raunchy guitar up front. Their punk/heavy metal amalgam proved to be a success, with hit singles such as 'She Sells Sanctuary' (1985) and 'L'il Devil' (1987). Albums on Beggars Banquet include *Dreamtime* (1984), *Love* (1985), *Electric* (1987), *Sonic Temple* (1989) and *Ceremony* (1991).

Eddie DURAN

Bebop player. Born in San Francisco on September 6, 1925. Started learning piano and picked up the guitar at age 8. Studied harmony and theory while at school. Early influences include Eddie Lang, Charlie Christian, Django Reinhardt and Carl Kress. Gigged in local clubs at age 15. Drafted into the US Navy during World War II and discharged in 1946. Played regularly in the San Francisco Bay area and gained a considerable reputation both as an accompanist and for his melodic bebop improvisations. He was soon working with Charlie Parker, George Shearing, Stan Getz, Red Norvo and Benny Goodman. Recorded solo albums including *Eddie Duran-Jazz Guitarist* (Fantasy) and *Ginza* (Concord Jazz).

Eddie DURHAM

Jazz guitarist, trombonist, composer and arranger. Born in San Marcos, Texas on August 19, 1906. Studied theory and composition at US School of Music. First professional experiences were as a trombonist. Toured with Bennie Moten, Count Basie, Cab Calloway, Andy Kirk and many others during the '30s. First jazzman to play electric guitar: introduced Charlie Christian and Floyd Smith to the instrument in 1937. Recorded electric guitar solos with John Hammond and Lester Young as early as 1938. Best known for his compositions and arrangements for Glenn Miller, Count Basie, Artie Shaw and many others. Concentrated on the trombone during his final years. Died on March 6, 1987. Recordings on RCA and JSP include *Eddie Durham* (1973) and *Blue Bone* (1981).

Bob DYLAN

Legendary singer/songwriter. Born Robert Allen Zimmerman in Duluth, Minnesota on May 24, 1941. Moved to Hibbing, Minnesota (mining town) at age 6. Started playing the guitar at age 12 and formed various groups at high school. Became influenced by Woody Guthrie and determined to become a famous folk singer. Went to New York to perform in Greenwich Village and adopted the name Bob Dylan (after the writer Dylan Thomas). His earthy acoustic renditions of traditional songs and idiosyncratic harmonica playing caused a stir. Signed to CBS in 1962. Debut album *Bob Dylan* (1962) featured covers of standard folk tunes and established Dylan as an outstanding performer. *The Freewheelin' Bob Dylan* (1963) and *The Times They Are A-Changin'* (1964) consisted mainly of original protest songs. *Another Side Of Bob Dylan* (1964) was more personal. Became influenced by the Beatles and the Animals and used electric guitar on *Bringing It All Back Home* (1965), *Highway 61 Revisited* (1965) and *Blonde On Blonde* (1966). Outraged folk purists booed at many performances, including the Newport Festival in 1965. Hostility from the public soon died down, although opinions have been divided on later albums such as *Self-Portrait* (1970), *Planet Waves* (1974), *Blood On The Tracks* (1975), *Street Legal* (1978), *Empire Burlesque* (1985), *Knocked Out Loaded* (1986) and *Good As I Been To You* (1992). Dylan has been one of the most influential figures in the development of folk and rock music. His songs have been covered by countless others and his lyrics have inspired generations of aspiring singer/songwriters. Books include *Bob Dylan* by Anthony Scaduto and *Performing Artist* by Paul Williams.

Snooks **EAGLIN**

Blues guitarist/singer. Born Fird (Ford) Eaglin in
New Orleans on January 21, 1936. Took up
acoustic guitar at age 5 and electric when he
was 15. Influenced by local bluesmen, as well as
blues giants such as Robert Johnson and T-
Bone Walker. Blinded after an operation to
remove a brain tumour when he was 19.
Recorded with Sugarboy and the Cane Cutters
on Chess album *Jockamo* (1954). By then
Snooks had a considerable reputation. Solo
albums on Folkways, Prestige, Storyville, GNP
and Arhoolie include *Street Singer* (1958),
Rural Blues (1961), *Portraits In Blues Volume
1* (1962), *Snooks Eaglin* (1971), *Possum Up A
Simmon Tree* (1971). On Black Top: *Baby, You
Can Get Your Gun* (1987) and *Teasin' You*
(1992).

Nathan **EAST**

Bass player. Born in Philadelphia c.1956. Grew
up in San Diego. Started learning the cello
before picking up bass instruments at age 14.
Played in the jazz band and orchestra at high
school. Influences included Verdine White,
James Jamerson, Ron Carter and Larry
Graham. Studied classical technique (double
bass) at University of California in San Diego
before moving to Los Angeles to pursue a
studio career. Worked with artists as diverse as
Barry White, George Benson, Phil Collins, Al
Jarreau, Kenny Rogers, Eric Clapton, Diana
Ross, Barbra Streisand, Julio Iglesias, Jeff
Lorber and many others. Film and TV work
includes *Brewsters Millions*, *Private Benjamin*
and *Fame*.

Duane **EDDY**

Rock and roll guitarist. Born in Corning, New
York on April 26, 1938. Grew up in Arizona.
Started playing guitar at age 5 on a Martin
acoustic. Later played a Gibson Les Paul and a
Gretsch Chet Atkins guitar. Influenced by Chet
Atkins, Les Paul, B.B.King, Barney Kessel,
Howard Roberts and others. Well known for
his simple-melody instrumental tunes played on
the bass strings of the guitar, although producer
Lee Hazlewood also contributed to that 'big'

Duane Eddy

sound by using a grain silo as a reverberator.
Eddy was also distinguished by the sliding and
vibrato effects he achieved with the tremolo
arm. Recordings include the classic Outline
album *Have Twangy Guitar, Will Travel*
(1958). One of the most influential guitar
players of the late '50s and early '60s.
Compilations include *Compact Command
Performances* (1988) and *$1,000,000 Dollars
Worth Of Twang* (1990).

The **EDGE**

Rock guitar player. Born David Evans in Dublin
on August 8, 1961. Started playing guitar at age
13. Formed the band U2 with other
schoolmates Paul 'Bono' Hewson (vocals),
Adam Clayton (bass) and Larry Mullen
(drums). Early influences included the Patti
Smith Group, Tom Verlaine and Neil Young.
His sparse and highly distinctive lead and
rhythm styles became an essential component of

28

The Edge

the band's sound. Signed to Island Records. Their debut album *Boy* (1980) was produced by Steve Lillywhite and included the classic track 'I Will Follow'. The next two albums *October* (1981) and *War* (1983) established U2 as a major band in the UK. Achieved global success with *The Unforgettable Fire* (1984), which boasted the hit single 'In The Name Of Love'. Later recordings, including *The Joshua Tree* (1987), the blues orientated *Rattle and Hum* (1988), *Achtung, Baby!* (1991) and *Zooropa* (1993) were all commercial successes. U2 have a reputation for being an outstanding live band and The Edge has achieved guitar-hero status. Also recorded film soundtrack *Captive* (1986) with Sinead O'Connor.

Dave **EDMUNDS**

UK rock guitarist. Also singer and producer. Born in Cardiff, Wales on April 15, 1944. Played in local bands in the '60s, before having a hit with an instrumental rock version of Khachaturian's 'Sabre Dance' in 1968. Other hits with numerous cover versions. Albums including *Rockpile* (1972), *Subtle As A Flying Mallet* (1975), *Get It* (1977), *Tracks On Wax* (1978), *Repeat When Necessary* (1979), *Seconds Of Pleasure* (1980), *Twangin'* (1982), *Information* (1983), *Riff-Raff* (1984), the live *I*

Hear You Rockin' (1987), *Closer To The Flame* (1990) and *The Complete Early Dave Edmunds* (1991). Also worked (as a producer and performer) with Jeff Beck, Fabulous Thunderbirds, Shakin' Stevens, Stray Cats, the Everly Brothers, Paul McCartney, Eric Clapton, George Harrison, k.d. lang, Status Quo and Ringo Starr. An important figure in the world of popular music.

Mark **EGAN**

Bass player. Born in Brockton, Massachusetts on January 14, 1951. Started playing guitar at age 10 but soon switched to trumpet after uninspiring lessons. Took up bass as second instrument when he was 13. Played trumpet in jazz bands and orchestras. Became influenced by bass players such as Jack Bruce, Harvey Brooks and James Jamerson. Studied at University of Miami, where he first met Pat Metheny. Worked with Ira Sullivan, Eumir Deodato and David Sanborn, before joining the Pat Metheny Group for the ECM albums *Pat Metheny Group* (1978) and *American Garage* (1980). Also with Carly Simon, Flora Purim, Stan Getz and Bill Connors. Formed the band Elements with drummer Danny Gottlieb (also ex-Pat Metheny Group) for Antilles albums *Elements* (1982) and *Forward Motion* (1984). Solo albums on Hip Pocket and GRP include *Mosaic* (1985) and *A Touch Of Light* (1988).

Herb **ELLIS**

Jazz player. Born Mitchell Herbert Ellis in Farmersville, Texas on August 4, 1921. Started playing banjo and guitar from an early age. Self-taught. Met other jazz players such as Jimmy Giuffre and Gene Roland at North Texas State College. Joined Jimmy Dorsey's band in 1945. Formed trio Soft Winds with Lou Carter (piano, vocals) and John Frigo (bass, vocals). Joined the Oscar Peterson Trio in 1953. Later accompanied Ella Fitzgerald and Julie London. Formed guitar duos with Joe Pass and Barney Kessel. Also worked extensively in TV. Formed Great Guitars with Barney Kessel and Charlie Byrd. Very popular swinging guitarist, whose style also incorporates elements of blues and hillbilly music. His many recordings on Verve, CBS, Dot, MPS, Concord, Atlas and other labels include *Ellis In Wonderland* (1956), *Thank You Charlie Christian* (1960), *The Midnight Roll* (1962), *Man With A Guitar* (1965), *Hello Herbie* (1969), *Wildflower* (1977), *Herb Ellis At Montreux* (1979), *Herb*

Mix (1981) and *When You're Smiling* (1983). Author of instructional video *Swing Jazz - Soloing And Comping* (REH).

Rik **EMMETT**

Canadian rock guitarist and singer. Born in Toronto, Ontario on July 10, 1953. Took up guitar at age 12 at a local music school. Early influences included the Beatles, Jimi Hendrix, Led Zeppelin, Cream and Charlie Byrd. Studied jazz for a while at Humber College. Played in various bands including Zon and Act III. Formed the rock trio Triumph in 1975 with Mike Levine (bass) and Gil Moore (drums). They had considerable success as a live act and with albums such as *Triumph* (1976), *Rock & Roll Machine* (1977), *Just A Game* (1979), *Allied Forces* (1981), *Never Surrender* (1982), *Thunder Seven* (1984), *Stages* (1985), *The Sport Of Kings* (1985) and *Surveillance* (1987). Emmett solo album: *Absolutely* (1991). Regular columnist with *Guitar Player* magazine during the '80s. Instruction video: *Rik Emmett* (Star Licks).

Buddy **EMMONS**

Steel guitarist. Born in Mishawaka, Indiana on January 27, 1937. Started playing the fiddle at age 10 and soon switched to lap-top steel guitar. Played with Little Johnny Dickens by the time he was 18. Worked with Ernest Tubb's Troubadors and Ray Price's Cherokee Cowboys in the '50s and '60s. Later did sessions for Roger Miller, Judy Collins, Ricky Skaggs, Henry Mancini, Linda Ronstadt, Danny Gatton and many others. Recordings include *Steel Guitar* (1975), *Sings Bob Wills* (1976), *Buddies* (1977) with Buddy Spicher, *Minors Aloud* (1979) with Lenny Breau, *First Flight* (1984) and *Christmas Sounds Of The Steel Guitar* (1987). Also steel guitar designer and co-founder of the Sho-Bud Guitar Company with Shot Jackson. Included in *Guitar Player* magazine's 'Gallery Of The Greats' after being voted Best Steel Guitarist (1978-1992).

John **ENTWISTLE**

UK rock bass player. Born in Chiswick, London on October 9, 1944. Went to the same school as singer Roger Daltrey. They formed the Detours with guitarist Pete Townshend in the early '60s. Changed name to the Who and Keith Moon was added later on drums (see Pete TOWNSHEND for more information on the

Who). Entwistle's solid bass playing influenced many younger players including Geddy Lee (Rush) and Jerry Peek (Steve Morse Band). Nicknamed 'The Ox'. Compiled the Who album *Odds And Sods* (1974) out of previously unreleased tracks. Recorded several solo albums on Track, Decca and WEA including *Smash Your Head Against The Wall* (1971), *Whistle Rhymes* (1972), *Rigor Mortis* (1973), *Mad Dog* (1975) and *Too Late The Hero* (1981). A highly influential musician.

John **ETHERIDGE**

Jazz, fusion guitarist. Born in London on January 12, 1948. Started learning piano at age 6 and took up guitar at age 13. Self-taught. Early influences included Hank Marvin, the Ventures, Django Reinhardt, Wes Montgomery, Joe Pass, Jimi Hendrix, Jeff Beck, Eric Clapton and John McLaughlin. Joined Darryl Way's band Wolf in 1972. They recorded three albums before Etheridge left in 1974 to join Global Village Trucking Company for a brief spell. A year later Allan Holdsworth left Soft Machine to work with Tony Williams and recommended Etheridge as his replacement. The band agreed and recorded two impressive albums on Harvest: *Softs* (1976) and *Alive And Well In Paris* (1978), with substantial contributions from the guitarist. Also worked with Second Vision and played acoustic guitar with violinist Stephane Grappelli. Gigged with various jazz and fusion bands in the UK. Regular teacher at London's Guitar Institute.

Kevin **EUBANKS**

Jazz-influenced guitarist. Born in Philadelphia, Pennsylvania on November 15, 1957. Started learning classical violin and switched to guitar. Played in local bands at age 13. Early influences included Wes Montgomery and George Benson. Studied composition at Berklee College of Music in Boston. Worked with Art Blakey in 1980 (the only guitar player ever featured in the drummer's band). His style ranges from sensitive/atmospheric acoustic work to high-energy jazz, fusion, rock, blues and funk. Recorded several solo albums on Elektra, GRP and Blue Note including *Kevin Eubanks: Guitarist* (1982), *Opening Night* (1985), *Face To Face* (1986), *The Searcher* (1989), *Promise Of Tomorrow* (1990) and *Turning Point* (1992).

Don **EVERLY**

Singer/songwriter/guitarist. Born on February 1, 1937. Grew up in Brownie, Kentucky. His father was a well-respected country guitarist and brother Phil was also a gifted player. Don and Phil formed the Everly Brothers. They had a stream of hits including 'Bye Bye Love', 'Wake Up, Little Susie' and 'When Will I Be Loved?' during the '50s. Albums on Rhino, Cadence, Warner Brothers and RCA include

Songs Our Daddy Taught Us (1959), *Fabulous Style Of The Everly Brothers* (1960), *A Date With The Everly Brothers* (1960), *Golden Hits* (1962) and *Roots* (1968) and *Pass The Chicken And Listen* (1973). Don had a few minor hits during the '70s, before the brothers made a successful comeback in 1984 with a concert at London's Albert Hall. It was recorded and released as *The Everly Brothers* (1984).

John **FAHEY**

Acoustic guitar player. Born in Takoma Park, Maryland on February 28, 1939. Self-taught. Became influenced by folk legend Sam McGee and blues players such as Blind Willie Johnson. Studied at UCLA and wrote his PhD thesis on the life of bluesman Charley Patton. Developed his own original blues-folk style. Gained considerable respect as a composer and guitar player, despite rare public performances. Formed his own Takoma label, recording himself, Leo Kottke, Bukka White and others. Albums on Takoma, Vanguard, Varrick and Rounder include *The Transfiguration Of Blind Joe Death* (c.1959), *John Fahey I* (1966), *Days Are Gone By* (1967), *Requia* (1967), *John Fahey II* (1968), *The Yellow Princess* (1969), *Of Rivers And Religions* (1972), *After The Ball* (1973), *The New Possibility* (1974), *Old Fashioned Love* (1975), *Live In Tasmania* (1981), *Let Go* (1984), *Rain Forests, Oceans & Other Themes* (1985) and *Old Girlfriends And Other Horrible Memories* (1992).

Ardeshir **FARAH**

Acoustic flatpicker. Born in Iran on December 12, 1954. Took up guitar at age 12. Became very interested in flamenco, rock and fusion. Influences include John McLaughlin and Paco de Lucía. Developed a formidable technique and impressed acoustic virtuoso Jorge Strunz, who invited him to form an acoustic duo Strunz & Farah. Debut album on Ganesh *Mosaico* (1982) also featured Indian violinist L.Subramaniam and a number of other players. Switched to Milestone label. *Frontera* (1984)

included Farah's composition 'Reng', which has a Persian feel and features instruments such as the santur (like a dulcimer) and dombak (drum). Other recordings on Milestone and Mesa include *Guitarras* (1985), *Primal Magic* (1990) and *Americas* (1992).

Tal **FARLOW**

Jazz guitar legend. Born Talmadge Holt Farlow in Greensboro, North Carolina on June 7, 1921. Started learning mandolin at age 9 and picked up guitar later as a teenager. Early influences included Charlie Christian, trumpeter Dizzy Gillespie and saxophonists Lester Young and Charlie Parker. Worked as a commercial artist while playing in local groups. Joined vibraphonist Red Norvo's band in 1949 with Charles Mingus on bass. Also worked with clarinetist Artie Shaw and formed his own trio in the '50s. A pioneer of thumb-style guitar. Also noted for his long melodic lines and impressive control of harmonics. Won the *Downbeat* New Star Award in 1954. Since 1958 Tal has recorded several albums and given many performances, interspersed between a number of periods of semi-retirement. Recordings on Verve, Xanadu, Inner City, Prestige and Concord include *The Tal Farlow Album* (1954), *Autumn In New York* (1954), *Fuerst Set* (1956), *Tal* (1956), *Guitar Player* (1969), *Trilogy* (1976), *A Sign Of The Times* (1976), *Chromatic Palette* (1981) and *The Legendary Tal Farlow* (1983). Also wrote an instruction book *Tal Farlow Method* (Guitar Player Productions). Included in *Guitar Player's* 'Gallery Of The Greats' (1992) for his lifetime

Tal Farlow

achievement. One of the most influential jazz guitarists of all time.

Jose **FELICIANO**

Singer/songwriter/guitarist. Born blind in Lares, Puerto Rico on September 10, 1945. Grew up in Spanish Harlem, New York. Left high school to play at various clubs in Greenwich Village. Considerable success with debut RCA album *The Voice And Guitar Of Jose Feliciano* (1967). Other recordings on RCA, Private Stock, Motown, Optimism, Woodford and Capitol include *Feliciano!* (1968), *Sweet Soul Music* (1976), *Jose Feliciano* (1980), compilation *Portrait* (1985), *Steppin' Out* (1990), *The Very Best Of Jose Feliciano* (1991) and *Latin Street '92* (1992). His style incorporates elements of latin, folk, rock and soul music. Very popular during the late '60s and early '70s.

Leo **FENDER**

Guitar player and luthier. Born in Orange County, California in 1909. Built his first acoustic guitar at age 16 and was working with pick ups by the 1930s. First guitar maker to use separate magnets (one for each string) on the pickups to get a clearer sound. Designed a series of guitars that played an essential role in the evolution of rock and pop music. The two famous models were the Telecaster (popularised by Steve Cropper and Jeff Beck) and the Stratocaster (immortalised by Hank Marvin and Jimi Hendrix). They had solid bodies, which practically eliminated feedback.

Eduardo **FERNÁNDEZ**

Uruguayan classical virtuoso. Born in Montevideo in 1952. Began studying guitar at age 7 and gave concerts with his brother (as a guitar duo) by the time he was 11. Studied economics at university before continuing his guitar lessons with classical player Guido Santorsola. Won first prize in the Uruguayan Guitar Society Competition in 1971 and took honours in the Segovia Competition in Spain four years later. Gave a highly acclaimed performance at his United States debut in New York (1977). Later acknowledged globally as one of the major post-Segovia guitar players. Recordings on London include *Concierto De Aranjuez* and *Etudes And Preludes*. Later on Decca: *The World Of The Spanish Guitar* (1987) and *Avant-Garde Guitar* (1993).

Boulou **FERRE**

French jazz player. Born in Paris on April 24, 1951. Started playing the guitar at age 8. Taught by his father, who had played with Django Reinhardt in the Quintet du Hot Club de France. Gave his first public performance at age 9 and was regarded as a child prodigy. Later studied classical and jazz. Influences included Django Reinhardt, Wes Montgomery and Tal Farlow. Recorded his first album at age 12 and later worked with Stephane Grappelli, T-Bone Walker and Dexter Gordon. Also formed an acoustic duo with his brother Elios. Solo albums include *Boulou* (Barclay) and *Trinity* (Steeplechase).

Eliot **FISK**

Classical virtuoso. Born in Philadelphia, Pennsylvania on August 10, 1954. Picked up guitar at age 7, taught himself, and built up a considerable repertoire by the time he was 12. Studied with Oscar Ghiglia in Aspen, Colorado. Joined the Aspen Music Festival's teaching staff while still in his teens. Graduated from Yale with the school's first master degree in classical guitar, winning several prizes including a Phi Beta Kappa key. Went on to teach classical guitar at Yale and Mannes College of Music (New York). Also transcribed many pieces by Mozart, Haydn, Scarlatti and Beethoven for the instrument. Recordings on Musicmasters and EMI include *Performs His Own Transcriptions Of Works By Baroque Composers* (1985) *and Latin American Guitar Music* (1988).

Ray FLACKE

Country-rock player. Born in Milford-On-Sea, England in 1949. Grew up in Bognor Regis. Started playing acoustic guitar at age 11. Early influences include Hank Marvin, Chet Atkins, Ritchie Blackmore and Roy Nichols. Played with many bands in the UK and Europe. Moved to Nashville and got into session work during the late '70s. Well-known for his exciting Telecaster playing with Ricky Skaggs on recordings such as *Waiting For The Sun To Shine* (1981) and *Highways & Heartaches* (1982). Also worked with Lacy J.Dalton, Emmylou Harris and others. Recorded solo album on RJM: *Untitled Island* (1990). Instructional video: *Ray Flacke* (Star Licks).

Lita FORD

Heavy metal player and songwriter. Born in London, England on September 23, 1959. Grew up in Los Angeles. Picked up first guitar at age 11. Self-taught. Early influences included Jimi Hendrix, Led Zeppelin, Black Sabbath, UFO and AC/DC. Joined all-girl teenage heavy rock group the Runaways in the mid-'70s with Joan Jett (guitar/vocals), Jackie Fox (drums) and others. They recorded a number of albums on Mercury including *The Runaways* (1976), *Queens Of Noise* (1977), *Live In Japan* (1977) and *And Now...The Runaways* (1979). The band split up in 1980 with both Joan and Lita following successful solo careers. The Lita Ford Band became a powerful live act. Albums released on Mercury and RCA include *Out For Blood* (1983), *Lita* (1988) and *Stiletto* (1990).

Robben FORD

Blues guitarist. Born in Woodlake, California on December 16, 1951. Started learning saxophone before switching over to guitar. Early influences includeed Eric Clapton and Mike Bloomfield. Played in harmonica player Charlie Musselwhite's band at age 18. Later worked with saxophonist Tom Scott, the Yellowjackets, Miles Davis, Joni Mitchell, George Harrison, Kiss, Barry Manilow and others. Developed an impressive high-energy jazz-influenced blues style. Taught at the Guitar Institute of Technology in Hollywood and also released instructional courses. Albums on WEA, Stretch and GRP include *Robben Ford* (1985), *Talk To Your Daughter* (1988), Grammy-nominated *Robben Ford & The Blue Line* (1992) and *Mystic Mile* (1993). Author of book

Rhythm Blues (Hal Leonard) and instructional videos include *Playin' The Blues* and *The Blues & Beyond* (both REH).

Bruce FORMAN

Bebop player. Born in Springfield, Massachusetts on May 14, 1956. Started learning piano at age 6 before picking up guitar at age 13. Moved to San Francisco and learned a lot through friend Ratso Harris (bassist) and local teacher Jackie King. Played gigs in the San Francisco Bay area. Later travelled over to New York to sit in with Roland Hanna (piano) and Sam Jones (drums). His performance impressed a Choice Records representative so much the company offered him a recording deal. Has since worked with Elvin Jones, Oscar Peterson, Grover Washington and many others. Highly respected player who is capable of playing exciting and intricate solos at very fast tempos. Albums on Concord include *Full Circle* (1985), *There Are Times* (1988) and *Pardon Me* (1989). Switched to Kamei for *Still Of The Night* (1991). Author of *The Jazz Guitarist's Handbook* (Music Sales 1992).

Mo FOSTER

UK bass guitarist. Born in Byfleet, Surrey on December 22, 1944. Picked up the bass at around age 15. Also played drums and guitar while studying physics at Sussex University. Moved to London and started session work. Impressive playing and sight-reading earned him a reputation as one of the UK's top session men. Toured extensively and played on albums ranging from Jeff Beck's *There And Back* (1980) to Phil Collins' *Hello, I Must Be Going* (1982). Appeared at the *Secret Policeman's Other Ball* in 1982 with Beck, Clapton and Sting. With Gary Moore: *Corridors Of Power* (1982) and *Victims Of The Future* (1984). With jazz composer Gil Evans: *The British Orchestra* (1983) and live *Take Me To The Sun* (released 1990). With Gerry Rafferty: *Night Owl* (1979), *Snakes & Ladders* (1980) and *On A Wing And A Prayer* (1993). Also worked with Judy Tzuke, Hank Marvin, Andrew Lloyd Webber, Jan Cyrka, the LSO and many others. Solo recordings: *Bel Assis* (1988) and *Southern Reunion* (1990).

Roddy FRAME

Scottish singer/songwriter and guitarist. Born in 1964. Influenced largely by '60s music and '70s new-wave. Formed Neutral Blue in 1979 with Malcolm Ross (guitar), Campbell Owens (bass) and David Ruffy (drums). Performed cover versions of songs by the Velvet Underground and the Clash, before changing the group name to Aztec Camera. Frame's catchy acoustic-based tunes won the band considerable critical acclaim during the '80s and '90s. Hits include 'Oblivious' (1983), 'All I Need Is Everything' (1984) and 'Working In A Goldmine' (1988). Albums on Rough Trade and WEA include *Highland, Hard Rain* (1983), *Knife* (1984), *Love* (1987), *Stray* (1990) and *Dreamland* (1993).

Peter **FRAMPTON**

UK rock guitarist and singer/songwriter. Born in Beckenham, Kent on April 22, 1950. Started playing guitar at age 7. Formed a band called The Herd when he was 16. They had hits with 'From The Underworld', 'Paradise Lost' and 'I Don't Want Our Loving To Die' (all Fontana) in the late '60s. Formed rock band Humble Pie in 1969 with Steve Marriott (guitar), Greg Ridley (bass) and Jerry Shirley (drums). Their albums on A&M included *Humble Pie* (1970), *Rock On* (1971) and *Performance: Rockin' The Fillmore* (1971). The band became increasingly dominated by Marriott and Frampton left to pursue a solo career. Formed Frampton's Camel in the early '70s and released a few albums, before the big break came with the double LP *Frampton Comes Alive* (1976). It went platinum and also included the hit single 'Show Me The Way', which featured a trademark voice-box guitar effect. Other albums include *I'm In You* (1977), *Where I Should Be* (1979), *Breaking All The Rules* (1981), *The Art Of Control* (1982), *Premonition* (1986) and *Shine On - A Collection* (1992).

Paul **FRANKLIN**

Pedal-steel player. Born in Detroit on May 31, 1954. Started playing guitar at age 8. Early influences included Buddy Emmons, Jimmy Day, Hal Rugg and Charlie Chalker. Played sessions at local clubs by the time he was 16 and moved to Nashville a year later. Became one of the most sought-after steel session players of the '70s and '80s. Played with Jerry Reed on RCA: *Half And Half* (1974). With Linda Hargrove on Capitol/Elektra: *Love, You're The Teacher* (1975), *Just For You* (1976) and *Impressions* (1977). With Mel Tillis on MCA/Elektra: *Mr.Entertainer* (1979), *The*

Great Mell Tillis (1979) and *Your Body Is An Outlaw* (1980). Also worked with Barbara Mandrell, Lynn Anderson and many other country artists. Solo albums include *Just Pickin'* and *Play By Play* (both on Scotty's Music). Joined Dire Straits for *On Every Street* album and tour.

Robert **FRIPP**

Experimental rock player, composer and teacher. Born in Wimborne, Dorset on May 16, 1946. Joined a group of backing musicians the League Of Gentlemen (a name later used for one of his own bands) in London during the late-'60s. Formed the innovative progressive rock band King Crimson in 1969 with Michael Giles (drums), Ian McDonald (keyboards, sax, flute) and Greg Lake (bass and vocals). They recorded the highly-acclaimed album *In The Court Of The Crimson King* (1969). The group line-up changed many times since then and featured many notable musicians including John Wetton (bass, vocals), Eddie Jobson (keyboards,

Robert Fripp

violin), Tony Levin (bass), Adrian Belew (guitar) and Bill Bruford (drums). Other albums include *Lizard* (1971), *Island* (1972), *Earthbound* (1972), *Larks' Tongues In Aspic*

(1973), *Starless And Bible Black* (1974), *Red* (1974), *USA* (1975), *Discipline* (1981), *Beat* (1982) and *Three Of A Perfect Pair* (1983). Fripp is also a unique and influential player, best known for his forceful (often abrasive) electric style. Developed Frippertronics, a system that recycles his improvised guitar lines by using tape loops and various other effects. Solo albums on Polydor and EG include *Exposure* (1979), *God Save The Queen* (1980), *Let The Power Fall* (1981) *God Save The King* (1985). Also worked with Andy Summers, Brian Eno, Peter Gabriel, Talking Heads, Daryl Hall, David Bowie, Blondie and many more. Highly respected as a teacher through his Guitar Craft seminars. Recordings with the League Of Crafty Guitarists: *Robert Fripp And The League Of Crafty Guitarists Live* (1986), *Live II* (1990) and *Show Of Hands* (1991). Book: *Robert Fripp - From King Crimson To Guitar Craft* by Eric Tamm.

Bill FRISELL

Unique and innovative electric guitar player. Born in Baltimore, Maryland on March 18, 1951. Early influences included Jimi Hendrix, Wes Montgomery, Jim Hall and saxophonist John Coltrane. Studied at North Colorado University and at the Berklee College of Music in Boston. Also took lessons with Jim Hall. Worked with John Zorn, Bass Desires, Lyle Mays, Paul Bley, Eberhard Weber, Paul Motian, John Scofield and many others. Highly individual style incorporates extensive use of delay, distortion and other effects, controlled with volume pedals. Solo albums on ECM and Elektra include *In Line* (1983), *Rambler* (1984), *Lookout For Hope* (1988), *Before We Were Born* (1988), *Is That You?* (1990), *Where In The World* (1991) and *Have A Little Faith* (1993, material ranging from Charles Ives to Madonna!). With Bass Desires on ECM: *Bass Desires* (1986) and *Second Sight* (1987).

Fred FRITH

UK experimental guitarist. Born in Yorkshire c.1949. Formed avant-garde rock band Henry Cow while at Cambridge University in 1968. Original line-up included Chris Cutler (drums), Tim Hodgkinson (keyboards, reeds) and John Greaves (bass). Made several highly unusual recordings on Virgin and Broadcast such as *Legend* (1973), *Unrest* (1974), *In Praise Of Learning* (1975) with the band Slapp Happy and *Western Culture* (1979) with vocalist

Dagmar Krause (ex-Slapp Happy). They later became Art Bears. Frith had also developed a unique, brutal and impressive prepared guitar technique, and recorded highly acclaimed *Guitar Solos* (1974) for Caroline. *Guitar Solos II* (1976) featured contributions from Derek Bailey, Hans Reichel and G.F.Fitzgerald. *Guitar Solos III* (1981) on Rift featured a number of players, including Keith Rowe. Other recordings on Ralph and RecRec include *Cheap At Half The Price* (1983) and *Step Across The Border* (1989). Joined forces with guitarists John French, Henry Kaiser and Richard Thompson for Rhino and Demon releases: *Live, Love, Larf & Loaf* (1987) and *Invisible Means* (1990). With Hans Reichel on Free Music Production: *Stop Complaining* (1991). Also worked with Violent Femmes, the Residents, Robert Wyatt, Skeleton Crew and Brian Eno.

Blind Boy FULLER

Blues guitarist and singer. Born Fulton Allen in Wadesboro, North Carolina in 1908. Played the guitar from an early age. Influenced by Blind Blake and the Reverend Gary Davis. Started losing his sight during his teens and was totally blind by the time he was 20. Played on streets and at parties. Also performed with Sonny Terry and Rev. Gary Davis. 'Discovered' by the American Recording Company in 1935 and recorded many swinging blues tunes. His vigorous blues style influenced many later players, including Eric Clapton. Popular tunes included 'What's That Smells Like Fish?' and 'Get Your Yas Yas Out'. Died of blood poisoning following a kidney operation in Durham, North Carolina on February 13, 1941. Compilation albums include *Truckin' My Blues Away* (1991) on Yazoo.

Lowell FULSON

R&B guitarist/singer. Born in Tulsa, Oklahoma on March 31, 1921. Son of a Cherokee Indian. Influences included his family (many were musical) and early blues performers. Entertained in the US Navy during the mid-'40s. Performed as a guitar duo with his brother Martin. Later worked with Hot Lips Page, Clifton Chenier and Ivory Joe Hunter. Had a number of hits in the '50s, including 'Blue Shadows' (1950) and 'Reconsider Baby' (1954). Numerous TV appearances during the '50s and '60s. Recordings on various labels include *Lowell Fulson* (1965), *Soul* (1966), *Tramp*

(1967), *In A Heavy Bag* (1970), *Let's Go Get Stoned* (1971), *I've Got The Blues* (1973), *Love Maker* (1978), *Think Twice Before You Speak*

(1984), *I Don't Know My Mind* (1987) and *Back Home Blues* (1992). Also appeared on B.B.King's *Blues Summit* (1993).

Eric GALE

Jazz guitarist. Born in New York on September 20, 1938. Taught himself to play the guitar. Toured with a number of blues musicians during the '60s and developed a solid R&B/jazz style. Became a popular session player: worked with Jimmy Smith, Aretha Franklin, Grover Washington, Stanley Turrentine and many others. Later recorded a number of solo albums on Kuda, Columbia, Elektra and Emarcy Including *Forecast* (1973), *Ginseng Woman* (1976), *A Touch Of Silk* (1980), *Blue Horizon* (1981), *Island Breeze* (1982) and *In A Jazz Tradition* (1988).

Rory GALLAGHER

Irish blues guitarist. Born in Ballyshannon, Co. Donegal on March 2, 1949. Grew up in Cork. Became influenced by blues players such as Freddie and Albert King. Left school to join the Fontana Showband at age 15. They played in Ireland and the UK before splitting up in 1965. Formed Taste with Richard McCracken (bass) and John Wilson (drums) in the late '60s. They signed to Polydor and recorded *Taste* (1969), *On The Boards*, (1970) and *Live* (1971), before splitting up in 1971. Gallagher started performing under his own name with Gerry McAvoy (bass) and Wilgar Campbell (drums), although the band line-up changed many times since then. Well known for his high-octane playing (especially bottleneck) and raw, unpretentious vocals. Albums on Chrysalis and Demon include *Rory Gallagher* (1971), *Live In Europe* (1972), *Blueprint* (1973), *Against The Grain* (1975), *Calling Card* (1976), *Stage Struck* (1980), *Jinx* (1982), *Defender* (1987), *Fresh Evidence* (1990) and *Edged In Blue* (1992). Also worked with Muddy Waters, Jerry Lee Lewis, Lonnie Donegan and Mike Batt.

Frank GAMBALE

Australian rock/fusion player. Born c.1958. Began playing guitar at age 7 and started his first band when he was 13. Early influences included John McLaughlin and Steely Dan. Worked with Jeff Berlin and Jean-Luc Ponty before joining Chick Corea's Elektric Band. Refined a technique known as 'sweep-picking', which involves minimal movement of the picking hand and facilitates very fast arpeggio playing. Recordings with Chick Corea on GRP: *Light Years* (1987), *Eye Of The Beholder* (1988), *Inside-Out* (1990) and *Beneath The Mask* (1991). With Allan Holdsworth on Legato: *Truth In Shredding* (1991). Solo albums on Legato include *Brave New Guitar* (1986), *A Present For The Future* (1987) and *Live* (1989). On JVC: *Thunder From Down Under* (1990), *Note Worker* (1993) and *The Great Explorers* (1993). One of the foremost rock and fusion players. Instruction books include *The Frank Gambale Technique, Books I & II* (DCI). Videos: *Monster Licks & Speed Picking* and *Modes: No More Mystery* (both DCI).

Jerry GARCIA

Blues-rock player, singer and songwriter. Born Jerome John Garcia on August 1, 1942. Grew up in San Francisco. Picked up the guitar at age 15. Played in folk groups during the early '60s. Formed the Grateful Dead (originally the Warlocks) in 1965 with Ron 'Pigpen' McKernan (keyboards, harmonica, vocals), Bob Weir (guitar, vocals), Phil Lesh (bass, vocals) and Bill Kreutzmann (drums). They were one of the most improvisatory rock bands to emerge from the psychedelic era and became notorious for taking part in public LSD parties (before the drug was made illegal). Attracted a loyal following (called 'Deadheads'). The band went through several personnel changes over the years but Garcia always remained at the helm (although he nearly died after collapsing into a temporary diabetic coma in 1986). Also formed spin-off band New Riders Of The Purple Sage. Garcia's style involves subtle modal/pentatonic improvisation, combined with a charismatic thin vocal delivery. Grateful Dead albums on Warner Brothers, Grateful Dead Records and Arista: *Grateful Dead* (1967), *Anthem Of The Sun* (1968), *Aoxomoxoa* (1969), *Workingman's Dead* (1970), *Vintage Dead* (1970), *Historic Dead* (1971), *Europe '72* (1972), *Wake Of The*

Richie AAron/Redferns

Jerry Garcia

Flood (1973), *From The Mars Hotel* (1974), *Blues For Allah* (1975), *Steal Your Face* (1976), *Terrapin Station* (1977), *Shakedown Street* (1978), *Go To Heaven* (1980), *Reckoning* (1981), *Dead Set* (1981), *In The Dark* (1987), *Built To Last* (1989), *Without A Net* (1990), *Infrared Roses* (1991) and *Still Truckin' - Interview* (1992). Books include *Grateful Dead: The Music Never Stopped* by Blair Jackson. Jerry Garcia solo albums include *Compliments Of Garcia* (1974), *Reflections* (1976) and *Run For The Roses* (1982).

Sonny GARRISH

Steel session ace. Born in Fairplay, Maryland on May 14, 1943. Started playing steel guitar at age 13. Early influences included Jimmy Day, Jerry Byrd and Jimmy Bryant. Joined Bill Anderson's band the Po' Boys in the late '60s and toured extensively. Word of his superb steel licks soon spread and he quickly became Nashville's most sought-after steel guitarist. Sessioned with Hank Williams Jr., Barbara Mandrell, B.B.King, the Judds, Ed Bruce, Eddie Rabbitt and Micky Gilley. Recordings with Hank Williams on Elektra and Warner Brothers: *The Pressure Is On* (1981), *High Notes* (1982) and *Man Of Steel* (1983). Also on Bill Anderson compilations on MCA such as *Greatest Hits Vol 1* (MCA) and *The Bill Anderson Story* (MCA).

Danny GATTON

Rock/country/jazz guitarist. Born in Washington DC on September 4, 1945. Started learning the guitar at age 6. Played in his first rock band the Lancers by the time he was 12. Early influences included Scotty Moore, Les Paul and Lenny Breau. Developed his own unique and virtuosic style, fusing rock, rockabilly, country and jazz. Worked with Robert Gordon, Bobby Charles, Link Wray, Big Al Downing, Chris Isaac and many others. Recordings on NRG, Blue Note and Elektra include *Redneck Jazz* (1978), *Unfinished Business* (1987), critically-acclaimed *88 Elmira Street* (1991), jazzier *New York Stories* (1992) and *Cruisin' Deuces* (1993). Instruction videos: *Hot Licks And Tricks For Guitar* (Pro Video 1987) and *Telemaster* (Hot Licks 1990). Voted Best Country Player in various *Guitar Player* readers polls. A world-class player who deserves greater recognition.

Lowell GEORGE

Rock guitarist and songwriter. Born on April 13, 1945. Played guitar with Frank Zappa's Mothers of Invention in the '60s before forming Little Feat with Roy Estrada (bass), Bill Payne (keyboards) and Ritchie Hayward (drums) in 1969. Zappa provided the band name (from the guitarist's shoe size). George's unique compositions were a rich fusion of blues, country and jazz. His expressive vocals and slide guitar were an essential part of the band's sound. Signed to Warner Brothers and released a number of albums: *Little Feat* (1971), *Sailin' Shoes* (1972), *Dixie Chicken* (1973), *Feats*

Don't Fail Me Now (1974), *The Last Record Album* (1976), *Time Loves A Hero* (1977) and *Waiting For Columbus* (1978). Died of a heart attack (brought on by drug abuse) in Arlington, Virginia on June 29, 1979. He had also played sessions for John Cale, Etta James and many others, as well as recording a solo album for Warner Brothers: *Thanks, I'll Eat It Here* (1979).

Oscar **GHIGLIA**

Classical guitarist. Born in Livorno, Italy on August 13, 1938. Studied at the Santa Cecilia Conservatory in Rome and graduated with honours in 1961. Won first prize at the International Guitar Competition in Paris in 1963. Became Segovia's assistant at the University of California at Berkeley. Gained a considerable reputation as a teacher and gave master classes worldwide. Also taught at various universities in the United States and at the Juilliard School and Mannes College in New York. Pupils included Sharon Isbin and Eliot Fisk. Made several recordings for EMI/HMV including *Paganini For Guitar And Violin* and *The Guitar In Spain*.

Billy **GIBBONS**

Rock guitarist, singer and songwriter. Born in Houston, Texas on December 12, 1949. Played

Tony Wooliscroft/Idols

Billy Gibbons

in Texas bands The Saints, The Coachmen, Ten Blue Flames and Moving Sidewalks in the '60s. Formed ZZ Top with Dusty Hill (bass, vocals) and Frank Beard (drums) in 1969. Their raunchy brand of southern blues-rock and outlandish 'beard and boiler suit' image soon earned them a reputation in the US as the support band headlining acts were reluctant to follow. Hit the big time in the mid-'70s and staged a year-long Worldwide Texas Tour in 1976 with $140,000 worth of Texas livestock on stage. Later went on to have more commercial success with mainstream singles such as 'Give Me All Your Lovin'' and 'Legs' in 1984. Albums on London Records include *First Album* (1970), *Rio Grande Mud* (1972), *Tres Hombres* (1973), *Fandango* (1975), *Tejas* (1976), *Deguello* (1979), *El Loco* (1981). On Warner Brothers: *Eliminator* (1983), *Afterburner* (1985), *Recycler* (1990) and *ZZ Top Greatest Hits* (1992).

Paul **GILBERT**

Heavy metal virtuoso. Prize pupil at the Guitar Institute of Technology in LA (later taught there at age 18!). Formed Racer X with Jeff Martin (vocals), John Alderete (bass) and Harry Gschoesser (drums). Signed to Mike Varney's Shrapnel label and recorded *Street Lethal* (1986). The band was then augmented with guitarist Bruce Bouillet and replacement drummer Scott Travis. Later recorded *Second Heat* (1987) and *Extreme Volume* (1988). Gilbert left to form Mr Big with Billy Sheehan (bass), Eric Martin (vocals) and Pat Torpey (drums). Recordings on Atlantic include *Mr Big* (1989), *Lean Into It* (1991) and *Bump Ahead* (1993). Author of instruction videos *Intense Rock I & II* (REH). An exciting player with a formidable technique.

Brad **GILLIS**

US heavy metal player. Born c.1958. Grew up in San Francisco. Started learning guitar at age 8. Played in a number of bands in the Bay area before forming the heavy rock band Night Ranger with Jeff Watson (guitar), Jack Blades (bass,vocals), Alan Fitzgerald (keyboards) and Kelly Keagy (drums). Night Ranger albums on MCA include *Dawn Patrol* (1982), *Midnight Madness* (1983), *Big Life* (1987), *Greatest Hits* (1989) and *Live In Japan* (1990). Also recorded with Ozzy Osbourne on *Speak Of The Devil* (1982) on Jet. Later solo album on Guitar Recordings: *Gilrock Ranch* (1993). Brad's expressive lead style incorporates heavy use of the tremolo arm.

Dave **GILMOUR**

Rock guitarist, singer and songwriter. Born in Cambridge, England on March 6, 1944. Went to the same school as Syd Barrett, who formed Pink Floyd in 1965 with Roger Waters (bass, vocals), Richard Wright (keyboards) and Nick Mason (drums). Their first album on Columbia *Piper At The Gates Of Dawn* (1967) was well

Wish You Were Here (1975), *Animals* (1977) and *The Wall* (1979). The band staged massive concerts with extravagant props, including a giant inflatable pig, which hovered over the audience during the performance. Split up in the early '80s but Gilmour reformed the group (without Waters) for Capitol recording *Momentary Lapse Of Reason* (1987). Also recorded solo albums for the Fame label: *David Gilmour* (1978) and *About Face* (1984). His guitar solos are melodic, spacey and punctuated by tasteful use of the tremolo arm.

Dave Gilmour

received, but Barrett became unstable due to heavy use of LSD. Gilmour joined the band in early 1968 and Barrett left two months later. They recorded the unusual and spacey *A Saucerful Of Secrets* (1968) the same year. Signed to Harvest and released further progressive rock albums such as *Ummagumma* (1969), *Atom Heart Mother* (1970), *Meddle* (1971) and *Obscured By Clouds* (1972). Their big break came with *Dark Side Of The Moon* (1973). It was superbly recorded and produced and sold over 10 million copies worldwide, staying high in the album charts for more than two years. Two of the album tracks 'Time' and 'Money' boasted excellent/beefy rock solos by Gilmour. Later albums on Harvest included

Transcriptions of his solos are included in the book *Original David Gilmour* (1987) by Steve Tarshis.

Gordon **GILTRAP**

UK guitarist/composer. Born near Paddock Wood, Kent on April 6, 1948. Grew up in Deptford, London. Picked up the guitar at age 12 and formed his first band by time he was 14. Early influences included Bert Jansch and John Renbourn. Developed an unorthadox right hand technique, using a plectrum and his little finger. Had a hit in 1977 with acoustic instrumental 'Heartsong' (later used for *The Holiday Programme* on British TV). Worked with Jansch, Renbourn, Midge Ure and many others. Albums now on Prestige include *Visionary* (1976), *Perilous Journey* (1977), *Fear Of The Dark* (1978), *Elegy* (1987), *A Midnight Clear* (1988) and *The Solo Album* (1991). With jazz guitarist Martin Taylor: *A Matter Of Time* (1991). On Music Maker: *Gordon Giltrap - Guitarist* (1988) and live *On A Summer's Night* (1993). Instructional video: *Giltrap On Guitar* (IMP). His unique classically orientated rock style influenced many other players. Author of a number of books including *The Hofner Guitar - A History* (IMP 1993) with Neville Marten.

Vincente **GOMEZ**

Classical guitarist/composer. Born in Madrid, Spain on July 8, 1911. Started playing flamenco guitar at age 7. Entertained customers in his father's tavern by the time he was 8. Studied classical guitar with Don Quintin Esquembre and later at the Madrid Conservatory. Toured France in 1932 and Russia in 1936. Gave numerous public recitals in the United States and recorded soundtrack music for several Hollywood films during the '40s. Established the Academy of Spanish Arts in Los Angeles in 1953 and has since devoted most of his time to teaching and writing music. Recordings include *Guitar Recital* and *Artistry Of Vincente Gomez* (both Decca).

Mick **GOODRICK**

Jazz guitarist. Born on June 9, 1945. Grew up in Sharon, Pennsylvania. Started playing guitar at age 12. Studied at Berklee College of Music in Boston (later taught there). Developed an impressive fingerstyle technique. Worked with Gary Burton, Charlie Haden, Jack DeJohnette and Michael Brecker. Appeared on a number of Gary Burton ECM albums including *Dreams So Real* (1975) and *The New Quartet* (1988). Solo albums on ECM and CMP include *In Passing* (1978) and *Biorhythms* (1990). With Joe Diorio on RAM: *Rare Birds* (1993). Author of *The Advancing Guitarist* (Hal Leonard). Influenced many other guitarists including Mike Stern and John Scofield. Highly respected as a player and teacher.

John **GOODSALL**

UK fusion guitarist. Born in London, England on February 15, 1953. Started playing the guitar at age 7. Worked with Alan Bown and Atomic Rooster, before going into session work. Formed Brand X with fellow session musicians Percy Jones (bass), Robin Lumley (keyboards) and Phil Collins (drums, also with Genesis). Highly original debut: *Unorthadox Behaviour* (1975) on Charisma. There were a number of personnel changes over the following years and other members included keyboardist Peter Robinson, bassist John Giblin, percussionist Morris Pert and drummers Chuck Burgi, Mike Clarke and Frank Katz. Later albums on Charisma and Ozone include *Masques* (1978), *Product* (1979), *Do They Hurt?* (1980) and, after a very long break, *XCommunication* (1992). All of the above feature Goodsall's unique rock-influenced compositions and solos.

Guthrie **GOVAN**

UK rock player. Born in Chelmsford, Essex on December 27, 1971. Started playing the guitar at age 5. Earliest influences included Chuck Berry, Jimi Hendrix and Zal Cleminson. Appeared on national TV playing 'Purple Haze' (Hendrix) at age 9. Later inspired by Steve Vai, Eric Johnson, Mike Stern and John Scofield. Featured in the Spotlight column in *Guitar Player* magazine (Sept '92). Worked with fusion band What It Is. Won *Guitarist* magazine's Guitarist Of The Year competition (UK) in 1993. Featured on Mark Varney's compilation discs *Guitar On The Edge Vols 4-6* (1993) on Legato. His impressive technique incorporates advanced sweep-picking and eight-fingered tapping.

Larry **GRAHAM**

Funk-bass pioneer. Born in Beaumont, Texas on August 14, 1946. Moved to Oakland, California at age 2. Played guitar, bass, harmonica and drums by the time he was 15. Worked with Jackie Wilson, the Drifters and Jimmy Reed while still at college. Joined Sly and the Family Stone in 1967 with Sylvester 'Sly Stone' Stewart (vocals, keys, guitar), Freddie Stone (guitar), Jerry Martini (saxophone), Cynthia Robinson (trumpet), Rose Stone (piano, vocals) and Greg Errico (drums). Their blend of funk, soul and psychedelic rock became popular on both sides of the Atlantic. Hits included 'Dance To The Music' (1968) and 'Family Affair' (1971). Albums include *Dance To The Music* (1968), *Stand!* (1969) and *There's A Riot Goin' On* (1971). Later formed the funk group Graham Central Station. One of the most influential bass players in the history of rock. Included in *Guitar Player* magazine's 'Gallery Of The Greats' (1988) for his lifetime achievement.

Gary GRAINGER

US funk/fusion bass player. Born in 1954. Grew up in Baltimore, Maryland. Initially played drums and then switched to bass at age 15. Early influences included Stanley Clarke and Larry Graham. Studied art but quit school to play in Arthur Ingram's band. Played fusion with a group called Inner Visions before joining John Scofield's band in 1986. Made a name for himself through his sharp/funky bass playing on several highly acclaimed Scofield albums during the '80s: *Blue Matter* (1986), *Loud Jazz* (1987) and the live *Pick Hits* (1987). All on Gramavision.

Freddie GREEN

Jazz rhythm legend. Born in Charleston, South Carolina on March 31, 1911. Moved to New York City at age 12. Self-taught. John Hammond heard him playing at the Black Cat in Greenwich Village and recommended him to Count Basie. Auditioned in Basie's dressing room at the Roseland Ballroom and joined the band in 1937. The line-up also included Walter Page (bass) and Jo Jones (drums), and was considered to be one of the greatest rhythm sections in history. Green rarely played solo notes and never played amplified guitar, although he could clearly be heard on most of the band's recordings. Basie albums on Roulette and GRP featuring Green include *The Atomic Mr Basie* (1957), *Kansas City Suite* (1960), *The Count Basie Story* (1961) and *Diane Schuur & The Count Basie Orchestra* (1987). Also sessioned with Benny Goodman, Lionel Hampton, Teddy Wilson and many others. Died in Las Vegas on March 1, 1987.

Peter GREEN

UK blues-rock guitarist. Born Peter Greenbaum in Bethnal Green, London on October 29, 1946. Played in several semi-pro bands after leaving school. Early influences included Freddie and B.B.King. Joined John Mayall's Bluesbreakers as Eric Clapton's replacement in 1966 and was heavily featured on Decca recording *A Hard Road* (1966). His sensitive and expressive style soon earned him a reputation as an outstanding guitarist. Left a

year later to form Fleetwood Mac with Mick Fleetwood (drums) and John McVie (bass, ex-Mayall). They had a number of hits with Green's compositions, including 'Albatross' (1968), 'Man Of The World' (1968) and 'Oh Well' (1969). Fleetwood Mac albums featuring Green on Blue Horizon and Reprise include *Fleetwood Mac* (1968), *Mr Wonderful* (1968), *Blues Jam At Chess* (1969) and *Then Play On* (1969). Got into LSD and religion and left the band in 1970. Released solo albums on Reprise, PVK and other labels: *End Of The Game* (1970), *In The Skies* (1979), *Blue Guitar* (1981), *White Sky* (1982) and *Kolors* (1983). Also worked as a grave digger and joined a commune in Israel. One of the most influential British blues players of all time. Book: *Instant Peter Green* (IMP 1990).

Tiny GRIMES

Jazz guitarist. Born Lloyd Grimes in Newport News, Virginia on July 7, 1916. Played drums and piano before taking up the guitar at 25. Worked with Art Tatum and Charlie Parker during the '40s. Later played with a number of jazz notables such as saxophonist Coleman Hawkins, organist Milt Bruckner, and pianists Earl Hines and Lloyd Glenn. Featured on *The Guitar Album* (1971) on Columbia with a number of other players. Other recordings on Muse and Classic Jazz include *Profoundly Blue* (1973) and *Some Groovy Fours* (1974). Died on March 4, 1989.

Stefan GROSSMAN

Blues and ragtime revivalist. Born in Brooklyn, New York on April 16, 1945. Studied with the Rev. Gary Davis, Mississippi John Hurt, Son House and others. Acoustic fingerpicker. Worked with the Even Dozen Jug Band, The Fugs and Mitch Ryder in the '60s. Later published a number of books on ragtime guitar and instruction tapes with Happy Traum (Homespun Tapes). Formed Kicking Mule Records with Ed Denson and made a number of recordings including *How To Play Blues Guitar* (1966), *Aunt Molly's Murray Farm* (1969), *Ragtime Cowboy Jew* (1970), *Hot Dogs* (1972), *Memphis Jellyroll* (1974), *Bottleneck serenade* (1975), *Country Blues Guitar* (1977), *Thunder On The Run* (1980) and *Shining Shadows* (1988). Books include *Solos In Open Tunings*, *Fingerpicking Guitar Solos* and *Ragtime Guitar* (all published by Mel Bay). Regular columnist with *Guitarist* magazine during the '80s. Instruction video: *Bottleneck Blues Guitar* (Stefan Grossman's Guitar Workshop).

GUITAR SLIM

Blues singer and guitarist. Born Eddie Jones in Greenwood, Mississippi on December 10, 1926. Not much is known about his early years, although it is thought that he worked in local cottonfields. Had big hits in the '50s with singles 'The Things I Used To Do' and 'The Story Of My Life'. Also became well-known for his outrageous and spectacular live performances: wore purple, orange, green or blue suits, dyed his hair unusual colours; also used guitar leads up to 100 metres long, so that he could rush out of the venue and continue playing in the street, while walking over the tops of cars. Influenced players as diverse as Stevie Ray Vaughan and Frank Zappa. Recorded the album *The Things I Used To Do* (1954). Died of bronchial pneumonia in New York on February 7, 1959. Later compilation: *The Atco Sessions* (1987).

Arlo GUTHRIE

Folk singer/songwriter and guitarist. Born in Coney Island, New York on July 10, 1947. Eldest son of Woody (see below). Performed his father's songs in public at age 13. Became famous through 25 minute ballad/comedy song 'Alice's Restaurant Massacre' in 1967 (made into a film in 1969). Wrote a number of other humorous and optimistic songs. Worked with Pete Seeger, Joan Baez, John Sebastian and many others. Albums on Reprise include *Alice's Restaurant* (1967), *Arlo* (1968), *Washington County* (1970), *Hobo's Lullabye* (1972), *Last Of The Brooklyn Cowboys* (1973), *Arlo Guthrie* (1974), *Amigo* (1976), *Best Of Arlo Guthrie* (1977), *Outlasting The Blues* (1979) and *Power Of Love* (1981).

Woody GUTHRIE

Folk legend. Born Woodrow Wilson Guthrie in Okemah, Oklahoma on July 14, 1912. Father of Arlo Guthrie (above). Roadside performer at age 16, playing harmonica and guitar. Later worked with cousin Jack Guthrie, Pete Seeger, Leadbelly, Lee Hays and a number of others. Wrote nearly 1000 songs, including 'Pastures Of Plenty' and 'This Land Is Your Land'. Suffered from poor health during the '50s and '60s. Died of Huntington's Chorea (wasting

disease) in Queens, New York on October 3, 1967. His songs have been performed by son Arlo, Bob Dylan, Pete Seeger, Richie Havens, Judy Collins and many others. Compilations include *Library Of Congress Recordings* (1964), *This Land Is Your land* (1967), *Songs To Grow On* (1973), *Struggle* (1976), *Poor Boy* (1981) and *Columbia River Collection* (1988). Books include autobiography *Bound For Glory* and *Woody Guthrie - A Life* by Joe Klein.

Buddy GUY

Blues guitarist and singer. Born George Guy in Lettsworth, Louisiana on July 30, 1936. Started playing a home-made guitar at age 13. Influences included Lightnin' Hopkins and John Lee Hooker. Played with Big Poppa Tilley and Slim Harpo, before moving to Chicago in 1957. Won 'Battle Of The Blues' contest at the Blue Flame Club in 1958. High-octane vocals

Buddy Guy

combined with wild and penetrating guitar soon earned him a considerable reputation. Became house musician at Chess Records from 1960. Worked with Willie Dixon, Otis Rush and Junior Wells. R&B hit with Chess single 'Stone Crazy' in 1962. Albums include *A Man And His Blues* (1968), *This Is Buddy Guy* (1968), *Hold That Plane!* (1972), *I Was Walking Through The Woods* (1974), *Hot And Cool* (1978), *Got To Use Your House* (1979), *Dollar Done Fell* (1980), *DJ Play My Blues* (1982), *Ten Blue Fingers* (1985), *Breaking Out* (1988), *Damn Right, I've Got The Blues* (1991) and *The Complete Chess Studio Sessions* (1992). His many admirers include Eric Clapton, Jeff Beck and Jimmy Vaughan.

Steve **HACKETT**

UK rock guitarist and songwriter. Born on February 12, 1950. Joined Genesis in 1971 with Peter Gabriel (vocals), Tony Banks (keyboards), Mike Rutherford (bass) and Phil Collins (drums). His unique rock guitar style became an essential part of the band's unmistakeable sound on progressive albums such as *Nursery Cryme* (1971), *Foxtrot* (1972), *Selling England By The Pound* (1973), *The Lamb Lies Down On Broadway* (1974), *A Trick Of The Tail* (1976) and *Wind And Wuthering* (1977). Became dissatisfied with the band and left to go solo (for further information on Genesis see Mike RUTHERFORD). Debut album *Voyage Of The Acolyte* (1975) featured impressive 'Ace Of Wands'. Enjoyed moderate commercial success with further albums on Charisma, Virgin, Lamborghini and Start such as *Please Don't Touch* (1978), *Spectral Mornings* (1979), *Defector* (1980), *Cured* (1981), *Till We Have Faces* (1984) and *Momentum* (1988). Albums are a mixture of songs and atmospheric instrumentals. Also formed GTR with Steve Howe (guitar), Max Bacon (vocals), Phil Spalding (bass) and Jonathan Mover (drums). One of the more influential rock guitar players of the '70s.

Sammy **HAGAR**

Heavy metal guitarist and singer. Born in Monterey, California on October 13, 1947. Played in various San Bernadino Bands during the '60s. Worked with Montrose during the early '70s, before embarking on a solo career. Recorded a number of moderately successful albums and built up a reputation as a dynamic performer. Later collaborated with Neal Schon, Kenny Aaronson and Mike Shrieve as HGAS. Joined Van Halen in 1985 as David Lee Roth's replacement. Solo albums on Capitol and Geffen include *Nine On A Scale Of Ten* (1976), *Sammy Hagar 2* (1977), *Musical Chairs* (1978), *Street Machine* (1979), *Danger Zone* (1979), *Loud & Clear* (1980), *Standing Hampton* (1982), *Three Lock Box* (1983), *VOA* (1983), *Voice Of America* (1984), *Sammy Hagar* (1987) and *The Best Of Sammy Hagar* (1992). With Van Halen on Warner Brothers: *5150*

(1986), *OU812* (1988), *For Unlawful Carnal Knowledge* (1991) and *Van Halen Live: Right Here, Right Now* (1993).

Jim **HALL**

Jazz guitarist. Born James Stanley Hall in Buffalo, New York on December 12, 1930. Picked up the guitar at age 10. Played in local

Jim Hall

bars as a teenager. Moved to Cleveland, Ohio at age 16 and studied at the Cleveland Institute of Music. Became influenced by Charlie Christian, saxophonist Charlie Parker and pianist Bill Evans. Moved to Los Angeles and replaced Howard Roberts in Chico Hamilton's quintet in 1955. Took up classical lessons with Vincente Gomez. Later worked with Ella Fitzgerald, Sonny Rollins, Paul Desmond, Art Farmer, Ron Carter, Chet Baker, Steve Gadd and George Shearing. His sparse style, displaying harmonic and rhythmic subtlety, is widely respected. Solo albums on Pacific Jazz, Verve, Pausa, CTI, A&M Japan, Concord Jazz, Music Masters and Limelight include *Jazz Guitar* (1957), *Intermodulation* (1966), *In A Sentimental Mood* (1969), *Concierto* (1975), *Live In Tokyo* (1976), *Jim Hall's Three* (1986), *All Across The City* (1989), *Live At The Town Hall* (1991) and *Subsequently* (1992). Author of *Exploring Jazz Guitar* (Hal Leonard 1991).

Nicola HALL

UK classical virtuoso. Born in Ipswich, East Anglia on March 3, 1969. Started playing the guitar at around age 8. Studied at the Royal Northern College of Music and later with John Williams. Top prizewinner at the Polish International Competition (1986) and the Toronto Competition (1987). Also the first guitarist to be awarded the Royal Overseas League's Gold Medal (1989). Played for the Segovia Society in Madrid (1991) and at numerous festivals. Signed to Decca. Debut recording *Virtuoso Guitar Transcriptions* (1991) demonstrates her striking mastery of the instrument and features impressive transcriptions of Rachmaninov's 'Prelude in G minor' and Paganini's 'Caprice'. Other recordings include *Castelnuovo-Tedesco: Guitar Concerto No.1* (1993) and recitals of works by Bach, Walton and Rodrigo.

Stu HAMM

Rock bass virtuoso. Born in New Orleans on February 8, 1960. Started playing flute and oboe before switching to bass later at high school. Early influences included Chris Squire, Stanley Clarke and Jaco Pastorius. Studied at Berklee College of Music, where he met guitarist Steve Vai. Developed a solid and dextrous rock bass technique. Worked in various groups before moving to California to record on Vai's albums *Flexable* and *Leftovers* (Urantia/Relativity). Has since played bass with Joe Satriani and recorded a number of solo albums on Relativity Records, including *Radio Free Albemuth* (1988), *Kings Of Sleep* (1989) and *The Urge* (1991). Also featured on Adrian Legg's album *Mrs Crowe's Blue Waltz* (1992). Instruction video: *Slap, Pop & Tap For The Bass* (Hot Licks).

Kirk HAMMETT

Heavy metal player. Born in San Francisco, California on November 18, 1962. Started playing the guitar at age 15. Early influences included Ace Frehley, Jimi Hendrix, Pat Travers, Michael Schenker, Eddie Van Halen and several others. Studied with Joe Satriani. Joined Metallica in 1983 with James Hetfield (guitar, vocals), Clifford Lee Burton (bass, died in 1987) and Lars Ulrich (drums). Toured with Ozzy Osbourne, Twisted Sister and Motörhead and played at the Donington Monsters Of Rock Festival several times. Recordings on Music For Nations/Vertigo include *Kill 'Em All* (1983), *Ride The Lightning* (1984), *Master Of Puppets* (1986), *And Justice For All* (1988) and *Metallica* (1991). Highly respected lead guitarist and speed metal player.

Emmylou HARRIS

Country-rock singer/songwriter and bandleader. Born in Birmingham, Alabama on April 12, 1949. Initially a folk singer in New York's Greenwich Village. Sang mainly folk covers on commercially unsuccessful debut album: *Gliding Bird* (1969) on Jubilee. Formed a duo with Gram Parsons before releasing critically acclaimed *Pieces Of The Sky* (1975) on Reprise. Had considerable success with *Elite Hotel* (1976). Formed the Hot Band in the late '70s: members included guitarists Albert Lee and Ricky Skaggs. Later albums on Warner Bros/Reprise include *Luxury Liner* (1977), *Quarter Moon In A Ten Cent Town* (1978), *Blue Kentucky Girl* (1979), *Roses In The Snow* (1980), *Evangeline* (1981), *Cimmaron* (1981), *Last Date* (1982), *White Shoes* (1983), *The Ballad Of Sally Rose* (1985), *13* (1986), *Trio* (1987), *Bluebird* (1989), *Brand New Dance* (1990) and *At The Ryman* (1992). An outstanding writer/performer whose material has always been of a consistently high standard.

Steve HARRIS

Heavy metal bass player. Born in Leytonstone, London on March 12, 1957. Influenced by Deep Purple, Black Sabbath and bass players such as Mike Rutherford, Chris Squire and John Entwistle. Formed heavy metal band Iron Maiden in 1976 with Paul Di'Anno (vocals), Dennis Stratton (guitar), Dave Murray (guitar) and Clive Burr (drums). Stratton, Di'Anno and Burr were later replaced by a number of other players. The group revitalised the then stagnant heavy metal scene and became one of the foremost exponents of the New Wave Of British Heavy Metal (NWOBHM). Received good publicity from the music press, becoming very popular first in the UK and then worldwide. Albums on EMI include *Iron Maiden* (1980), *Killers* (1981), *Number Of The Beast* (1982), *Powerslave* (1984), *Somewhere In Time* (1986), *Seventh Son Of A Seventh Son* (1988), *No Prayer For The Dying* (1990), *Fear Of The Dark* (1992) and *A Real Live One* (1993).

George HARRISON

Rock/pop guitarist and singer/songwriter. Born in Liverpool, England on February 25, 1943.

Bought his first guitar at age 13. At school he met Paul McCartney, who introduced him to John Lennon c.1957. Joined Lennon's band the Quarrymen that year. The band eventually became the Beatles (see Paul McCARTNEY for more information on the Beatles). By 1970 the band had split up and Harrison had already completed his own project, a three-record set *All Things Must Pass* (1970) on the Beatles' Apple label. It featured the hit single 'My Sweet Lord', as well as contributions from Ringo Starr, Eric Clapton and Billy Preston. He brought the same musicians (and several more) together for the famous 'Concert For Bangladesh' in New York on July 31 (and August 1), 1971. Other solo albums on Apple and Warner Brothers include *Living In The Material World* (1973), *Dark Horse* (1974), *Cloud Nine* (1987) and *Live In Japan* (1992). Helped finance Monty Python's film *The Life Of Brian* in 1979 and set up his own successful company Handmade Films.

Jimmy HASLIP

Bass player born on December 31, 1951. Grew up in Long Island, New York. Started playing trumpet at school and switched to bass by the 8th grade. Had lessons with string bass player Ron Smith and was soon playing in bar bands. Moved to California and worked with Harvey Mandel, Tommy Bolin, Airto Moreira, Gino Vanelli and Robben Ford during the '70s. Met keyboardist Russel Ferrante while working on Ford's first album. They formed jazz-funk band the Yellowjackets with Marc Russo (sax, later replaced by Bob Mintzer) and Ricky Lawson (drums, later replaced by William Kennedy). Recordings became progressively more sophisticated with impressive atmospheric fusion albums on MCA and GRP such as *Four Corners* (1987), *Politics* (1989), *Greenhouse* (1991) and *Like A River* (1993).

Jeff HEALEY

R&B guitarist/singer. Born in Toronto, Canada on March 25, 1966. Blinded by eye cancer during infancy. Began teaching himself to play at age 3. Early influences included Robert Johnson, B.B.King, Freddie King and Eric Clapton. Developed an impressive and unorthadox lap-style blues guitar technique (plays with his left hand *over* the fingerboard). Debut Arista album *See The Light* (1988) features a version of the Freddie King classic 'Hideaway'. Later recorded *Hell To Pay* (1990), featuring contributions

from Mark Knopfler and George Harrison, and *Feel This* (1993). Appeared in 1989 Hollywood film *Roadhouse* (starring Patrick Swayze). One of the most original and respected blues-rock

Jeff Healey

players to emerge in the '80s (admirers include B.B.King, Gary Moore and the late Stevie Ray Vaughan).

Michael HEDGES

Acoustic guitar virtuoso. Noted for his solo performances. Born c.1953. Grew up in Oklahoma. Started learning piano, cello and clarinet. Later took up guitar as a teenager. Studied at Phillips University (Oklahoma) and at the Peabody Conservatory (Baltimore). Developed a style that is unique, spacious and melodic. Employs a number of two-handed techniques and uses unusual alternate tunings. Also plays 11- and 17-string harp guitars. Albums on Windham Hill include *Breakfast In The Field* (1982), critically acclaimed *Aerial Boundaries* (1984), *Watching My Life Go By* (1987), *Strings Of Steel* (1988) and *Taproot* (1991). Included in *Guitar Player* magazine's 'Gallery Of The Greats' (1992) after winning a number of acoustic categories.

Jonas HELLBORG

Electric bass virtuoso. Born in Gothenburg, Sweden on June 7, 1958. Started playing bass at age 12. Early influences included John Mayall, Jimi Hendrix, Cream and Led Zeppelin. Studied music theory extensively and developed his own advanced and unique bass style (solo chordal and slapping techniques). Toured as a solo act in Sweden and played at the Montreux Jazz Festival in 1981, where he met Billy Cobham, Michael Brecker and John McLaughlin. Joined McLaughlin's band the Mahavishnu Orchestra in 1983 and soon became widely recognised as an outstanding and highly original bass player. They recorded the albums *Mahavishnu* (1984) and *Adventures In Radioland* (1987). Also worked with Mick Jagger. Released solo albums on Day Eight: *Solobass*, *Axis* and *Elegant Punk*. Author of instruction books *Thumb Bassics On Electric Bass* (Music Sales) and *Chord Bassics* (Day Eight).

Scott **HENDERSON**

Jazz-rock virtuoso. Born in 1955. Grew up in West Palm Beach, Florida. Took up the guitar from an early age and played in local rock bands by the time he was 16. Early influences included Led Zeppelin, Deep Purple,

Scott Henderson

Mahavishnu Orchestra and a number of other bands. Studied at Florida Atlantic University with Bill Prince and then at the Guitar Institute of Technology in Hollywood with Joe Diorio (later taught there). Worked with Jeff Berlin (both featured on 1987 Passport fusion album *Players*), Jean-Luc Ponty, Joe Zawinul and Chick Corea's Elektric Band. Formed his own

progressive fusion band Tribal Tech with brilliant bass player Gary Willis and others. Henderson's style, incorporating a rich legato sustain and tasteful use of the tremolo arm, is instantly recognisable. Tribal Tech albums on Relativity include *Spears* (1986), *Dr.Hee* (1987), *Nomad* (1989), *Tribal Tech* (1991). Switched to Blue Moon for the more hard-hitting *Illicit* (1992) and *Face First* (1993). Instruction video: *Jazz Fusion Improvisation* (REH).

Jimi **HENDRIX**

Legendary blues/rock guitarist, singer and songwriter. Born James Marshall Hendricks in Seattle, Washington on November 27, 1942. Son of professional tap-dancers Al and Lucille Hendricks. Started playing acoustic guitar at age 10 and switched to electric a year later. By then he was already exposed to blues artists such as Muddy Waters and B.B.King through his father's record collection. Enlisted in the US army in 1959. A parachute jump went wrong, damaging his back and foot, and he was discharged 26 months later. Toured with a variety of acts in 1963/64 and soon earned a reputation as an outstanding sideman. He was left-handed and played a right-handed Fender Stratocaster upside down, with the order of the strings reversed. By 1965 he had worked with James Brown, Ike & Tina Turner, Little Richard, B.B.King, Wilson Pickett and the Isley Brothers. Formed his own band Jimmy James and the Blue Flames later that year. Chas Chandler (bass player with the Animals) was so impressed by Hendrix's playing he offered to bring him over to London. Chandler hastily introduced Hendrix to drummer Mitch Mitchell and guitarist/bass player Noel Redding: the Jimi Hendrix Experience was born. They were an immediate success in Europe and had the hit singles 'Hey Joe', 'Purple Haze' and 'The Wind Cries Mary' in 1967. Jimi's fame spread over to America when he played at the 1967 Monterey Pop Festival, on the recommendation of Paul McCartney. His use and control of distortion amazed the audience. Also set fire to his guitar on stage. Later on the same year the album *Are You Experienced?* (1967), one of the classic rock albums of all time, was released on Polydor. This was followed by the two albums *Axis: Bold As Love* (1968) and *Electric Ladyland* (1968). By 1969 the band had drifted apart and Hendrix formed the Band Of Gypsies with bassist Billy Cox and drummer Buddy Miles. They were not particularly successful and there was talk of reforming the Experience

Bob Baker/Redferns

Jimi Hendrix

which effectively came to nothing. Hendrix died in London on September 18, 1970. He was loaded with drugs and alcohol and had choked during his sleep. His death shook the music world. He was an exceptionally gifted guitar player who had expanded the instrument's range considerably. Included in *Guitar Player* magazine's 'Gallery Of The Greats' after being voted Best Rock Guitarist (1970) and for his lifetime achievement (1983). Compilations include *Smash Hits* (1968), *The Essential Jimi Hendrix* (1978), *The Singles Album* (1983), *Cornerstones* (1990) and *The Ultimate Jimi Hendrix* (1993).

James **HETFIELD**

Heavy metal guitarist/singer. Born on August 3, 1963. Grew up in Downey, California. Took piano lessons but soon switched over to the guitar. Early influences included Black Sabbath, Aerosmith and Motörhead. Formed Metallica in 1981 with drummer Lars Ulrich and others. First stable line-up included Kirk Hammett (guitar) and Clifford Lee Burton (bass), although the latter died when the band's bus overturned in 1987. Toured with Motörhead, Ozzy Osbourne and Twisted Sister. Played at the Donington Monsters Of Rock Festival several times. Recordings on Vertigo include *Kill 'Em All* (1983), *Ride The Lightning* (1984), *Master Of Puppets* (1986), *And Justice For All* (1988) and *Metallica* (1991).

Steve **HILLAGE**

UK rock guitarist. Born in England on August 2, 1951. Played in various bands with keyboardist Dave Stewart and others, before joining Gong in 1972. Played the Glastonbury Festival that year and later released psychedelic albums on Virgin such as *The Flying Teapot* (1973), *Angel's Egg* (1973) and *You* (1974). Left the band in 1975 to go solo: *Fish Rising* (1975) was strange, humorous and psychedelic; *L* (1976) was produced by Todd Rundgren and featured Utopia as the back-up band; *Green* (1978) was initially pressed on green vinyl and featured a superb guitar synthesiser sound. Other recordings include *Live Herald* (1979), *Open* (1979), *Rainbow Dome Musick* (1979) and *For To Next - And Not Or* (1983). Also Worked as a producer for Simple Minds and the Orb during the '80s. Formed ambient dance band System 7 with his former keyboardist Miquette Giraudy and others for Big Life recordings: *System 7* (1991) and *777* (1992).

Allan **HOLDSWORTH**

UK fusion virtuoso. Born in Bradford, Yorkshire in 1948. Started playing the guitar at age 17. Gigged with local bands. Developed a unique lead style characterised by rapid and enigmatic legato lines, combined with unusual tremolo effects and bizarre chord voicings. Became a sought after soloist, appearing on a number of impressive '70s fusion recordings such as *Believe It* (1975) with Tony Williams, *Bundles* (1975) with Soft Machine, *Enigmatic Ocean* (1977) with Jean-Luc Ponty, *UK* (1978) with UK and *One Of A Kind* (1979) with Bruford. Highly respected as unique and outstanding soloist, but wanted to spend more time on chordal work. Formed I.O.U. with Paul Carmichael (bass), Gary Husband (drums) and Paul Williams (vocals). Released their eponymously titled album independently in 1982. Later recorded various solo albums on Warner Brothers, Enigma, Intima and Cream including *Road Games* (1983), *Metal Fatigue* (1985), *Atavachron* (1986), *Sand* (1987), highly acclaimed *Secrets* (1989) and *Wardenclyffe Tower* (1992). The last four feature Holdsworth on SynthAxe (guitar synthesiser) as

Allan Holdsworth

well as electric guitar. An amazing guitarist, whose highly individual style has influenced countless other rock and jazz players. Other recordings include *Truth In Shredding* (1991) with Frank Gambale. Author of *Reaching For The Uncommon Chord* (21st Century). Instructional video: *Allan Holdsworth* (REH).

Buddy **HOLLY**

Legendary singer/songwriter and guitarist. Born Charles Hardin Holley in Lubbock, Texas on September 7, 1936. Formed C&W duo with schoolfriend Bob Montgomery; played at high school hops and performed regularly on KDAV Radio. Made several unsuccessful recordings for Decca in Nashville during 1956. Formed the Crickets with drummer Jerry Allison and bassist Larry Welborn. Travelled to Norman Petty's

Buddy Holly

recording studio in Clovis, New Mexico and recorded the hits 'That'll Be The Day', 'Oh Boy' and 'Peggy Sue' during 1957. These featured breakthrough techniques such as double-tracked vocals and overdubbing. Next year proved even more successful, with European and Australian tours and hits such as 'Rave On' and 'Think It Over'. Killed in a plane crash in Iowa on February 3, 1959. First from a country background to use a heavy R&B backbeat. A big influence on other pop musicians including the Beatles, the Hollies and many others. Albums on Coral and MCA include *The Chirping Crickets* (1958), *Buddy Holly* (1958), *The Buddy Holly Story* (1958) and *20 Golden Greats* (1978).

John Lee **HOOKER**

Blues singer/guitarist. Born in Clarksdale, Mississippi on August 22, 1917. Started singing gospel and blues. Moved to Detroit, where a record company talent scout spotted him playing in a club. Recorded many early R&B hits including 'Boogie Chillun' (1948), 'I'm In The Mood' (1951) and 'Dimples' (1956). His singing was accompanied by a driving open-tuned guitar and constant foot tapping. Played with Muddy Waters and Otis Spann. Influenced many later guitar players including Buddy Guy, John Mayall, Johnny Winter and Bo Diddley. His songs have been performed by the Doors, the Allman Brothers Band, George Thorogood, Robert Cray, Bonnie Raitt, the Yardbirds, J.Geils Band and many others. Albums include

John Lee Hooker

The Folk Blues Of John Lee Hooker (1959), *Hooker 'N' Heat* (1971), *John Lee Hooker - 20 Blues Greats* (1985), *The Healer* (1989), *Boogie Awhile* (1990), *More Real Folk Blues: The Missing Album* (1991), *Mr Lucky* (1991), *Simply The Truth* (1992) and *Boom Boom* (1992).

Lightnin' HOPKINS

Country-blues guitarist and singer. Born Sam Hopkins in Centreville, Texas on March 15, 1912. Grew up in Leona, Texas. Learned the blues from Blind Lemon Jefferson. Moved to Houston in the late '20s. Performed in local clubs. Went to the West Coast in the mid-'40s and made several recordings with pianist Wilson Smith for Aladdin Records. Earned his nickname from his fast picking on those sessions. Later worked with Taj Mahal, Barbara Dane and Sonny Terry. Made many radio, TV and festival appearances since the '60s. His poetic vocal style was supplemented by irregular and compulsive guitar playing. Recordings include *The Roots Of Lightnin' Hopkins* (1959), *Down South Summit Meeting* (1960) and *The Great Electric Show And Dance* (1968). Died on January 30, 1982. Later compilations include *Lightnin' Hopkins* (1991),

The Complete Aladdin Recordings (1992) and *Sittin' In With Lightnin' Hopkins* (1992).

Son HOUSE

Blues singer/guitarist. Born Eddie James House Jr. in Riverton, Mississippi on March 21, 1902. Became a Baptist pastor before turning to music in the late '20s. Served a year in jail for manslaughter (self-defence) in 1928. Worked with Charley Patton in 1929. Recorded for the Library of Congress in 1941. Worked outside music during 1948-64. Played at the Newport Folk Festival in 1964 and Carnegie Hall in 1965. Suffered from poor health during the '70s and '80s. Died in Detroit, Michigan on October 19, 1988. His own style was characterised by powerful vocals and driving bottleneck guitar. A highly influential bluesman. Recordings on Blue Goose, Edsel and Travellin' Man include *Real Delta Blues* (1974), *Death Letter* (1990) and *The Complete Library Of Congress Sessions* (1990).

Steve HOWE

UK rock guitarist. Born in London on April 8, 1947. Played in Tomorrow during the '60s, before replacing guitarist Peter Banks in Yes. Played on Atlantic albums *The Yes Album* (1971), *Fragile* (1971), *Close To The Edge* (1972), *Yessongs* (1973), *Tales From Topographic Oceans* (1973) and *Relayer*

Steve Howe

(1974), before recording solo album *Beginnings* (1975). Continued with Yes on *Going For The One* (1977), *Tormato* (1978) and *Drama* (1980). Left to form 'supergroup' Asia with Geoff Downes (keyboards), John Wetton (bass)

and Carl Palmer (drums). Recordings on Geffen include *Asia* (1982), *Alpha* (1983) and *Astra* (1985). Also teamed up with ex-Genesis guitarist Steve Hackett for Arista recording *GTR* (1986). Formed a band with other Yes veterans Jon Anderson, Rick Wakeman and Bill Bruford during the late '80s. However they were unable to use the original band name (owned by other members of the group) and released *Anderson, Bruford, Wakeman, Howe* (1989). The two quartets merged in 1991 for a world tour and album *Union* (1991). Later Howe solo album: *The Grand Scheme Of Things* (1993) on Roadrunner. His unique 'classical-rock' style was a major influence on other players including Steve Morse. Included in *Guitar Player* magazine's 'Gallery Of The Greats' after being voted Best Overall Guitarist (1977-1981).

HOWLIN' WOLF

Blues guitarist and singer. Born Chester Burnett in West Point, Mississippi on June 10, 1910. Picked up the guitar as a boy, influenced by Charley Patton. Developed a harsh and powerful blues style. Learned harmonica from Sonny Boy Williamson. Worked in cotton fields and played at weekend dances during the '30s. Moved to West Memphis, Arkansas in 1948 and formed a band with Junior Parker, James Cotton, Willie Steel and others. Impressed Sam Phillips of Sun Records, who recorded the band and leased the tapes out to Chess Records. Moved to Chicago and signed to Chess in 1952. Gained a large following with songs such as 'Smoke Stack Lightning', 'Little Red Rooster' and 'Evil'. Albums on Chess, Rolling Stones and other labels include *Howlin' Wolf* (1962), *This Is Howlin' Wolf's New Album. He Doesn't Like It. He Didn't Like His Electric Guitar At First Either* (1969), *London Sessions* (1971) and *Change My Way* (1975). Influenced players such as Johnny Winter, Eric Clapton and Jimmy Page. Died of cancer in Hines, Illinois on January 10, 1976. Later compilations include *His Greatest Hits* (1986) and *Howlin' For My Baby* (1987).

Mississippi John HURT

Blues guitarist and singer. Born in Carroll County, Mississippi on July 3, 1893. Started playing the guitar at age 10. Self-taught. Developed a complex fingerpicking style and a unique brand of gentle folk-influenced blues. 'Discovered' by Okeh Records in 1928.

Recorded a number of traditional songs for the label, before returning to farming for 35 years. Re-discovered in 1963 and recorded Piedmont album *Mississippi John Hurt: Folk Songs & Blues* (1963). Also recorded for the Library of Congress. Appeared at the Newport Folk Festival in 1963 and 1964. Influenced many musicians including Bonnie Raitt and John Sebastian. Died after a heart attack on November 2, 1966. Other recordings include *Worried Blues* (1964), *Blues At Newport* (1965), *Best Of Mississippi John Hurt* (1965), *Last Sessions* (1966), *Avalon Blues* (1982), *Shake That Thing* (1986) and *Monday Morning Blues* (1987).

Chrissie HYNDE

Singer/songwriter and rhythm guitarist. Born in Akron, Ohio on September 7, 1951. Attended Kent State University at the time the National Guard fired upon anti-Vietnam protesters. Moved to the UK and wrote for *New Musical Express,* before forming The Pretenders with

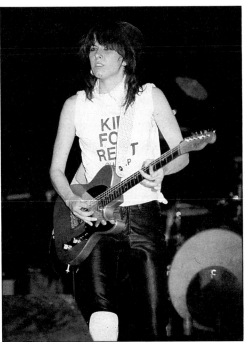

Mark Weiss/Idols

Chrissie Hynde

James Honeyman-Scott (guitar), Pete Farndon (bass) and Martin Chambers (drums). Signed to Warner Brothers and released an eponymous UK chart-topping album in 1980. One of the most successful new-wave bands of the '80s, although Honeyman-Scott and Farndon both died of drug overdoses during 1982-83. They were replaced by a number of other players. Hit singles include 'Brass In Pocket' (1979), 'I Go

To Sleep' (1981) and a cover of Sonny & Cher's 'I Got You Babe' (1985) with UB40. Albums include *Pretenders* (1980), *Learning To Crawl* (1984), *Get Close* (1986), *The Singles* (1987) and *Packed* (1990).

Tony IOMMI

Rock guitarist. Born in Birmingham, England on February 19, 1948. Left-handed. Early influences included blues and jazz players.

Mark Weiss/Idols

Tony Iommi

Worked as a typewriter repairer. Accidently cut off the ends of his 2nd and 3rd fingers while operating a faulty guillotine. Made his own plastic finger-tips. Formed Black Sabbath (named after a Dennis Wheatley book) in 1969 with old schoolfriends John 'Ozzy' Osbourne (vocals), Terence 'Geezer' Butler (bass) and Bill Ward (drums). Signed to Vertigo and First album *Black Sabbath* (1970) bore the band trademarks of Iommi's heavily distorted and devastatingly powerful riffs, along with

Osbourne's manic vocals. Encouraged black magic image with lyrics about madness, death and distruction. Considerable success with the follow up *Paranoid* (1970). Their brand of doom-laden rock with satanic overtones was readily accepted on both sides of the Atlantic. Other early recordings include *Volume 4* (1972), *Sabbath Bloody Sabbath* (1974) and *Technical Ecstasy* (1977). Osbourne left to go solo in 1979. Later Sabbath releases on Vertigo and IRS include *Heaven And Hell* (1980), *Seventh Star* (1986), *Headless Cross* (1989), *Tyr* (1990) and *Dehumaniser* (1992). Considered by many to be the father of the heavy metal riff. Instructional video: *Tony Iommi* (Star Licks).

Ike ISAACS

Jazz player. Born in Rangoon, Burma on December 1, 1919. Started playing the guitar at age 14. Studied chemistry at Rangoon University and graduated in 1942. Spent some time in India before moving to London in 1946 to pursue a career in music. Played in the Bomber Command Band and was later featured regularly on the BBC radio programme *Guitar Club*. Later played guitar with Ted Heath's band and worked extensively in television and radio studios, before joining the Stephane Grappelli quartet in 1975. Became a regular columnist with *Crescendo*. Recordings include *I Like Ike* (Morgan) and *I Love Paris* (Chapter One). Author of instruction book *Jazz Guitar School* (IMP). Also a highly respected teacher.

Sharon ISBIN

Classical virtuoso. Born in Minneapolis, Minnesota on August 7, 1956. Started playing guitar at age 9. Studied with Aldo Minella, Jeffrey Van and Sophocles Papas. Later with Oscar Ghiglia at the Aspen Music Festival in Colorado. Played for Segovia and Julian Bream.

Won first prize in the International Guitar Competition in Toronto (1975), the Munich International Competition (1976) and the Queen Sofia International Competition in Madrid (1979). Since then she has performed extensively, taught at the Manhattan School of Music and made several recordings on Pro Arte and Virgin including *Dances For Guitar* (1984), *J.S.Bach: Complete Lute Suites* (1989) *Guitar Works* (1990) and latin *Estrada Do Sol* (1991).

Ernie ISLEY

Soul/rock guitarist. Born in Cincinatti, Ohio on March 7, 1952. Started learning drums at age 12, before switching over to guitar. His older brothers O'Kelly, Rudolph and Ronald had already formed the Isley Brothers in the late '50s. Ernie joined the group around 1969. Their hit single 'That Lady' (T-Neck) in 1973 was punctuated by his spacey sustained soloing, as were several of their later hits. His syncopated rhythm guitar playing also became a band trademark. Isley Brothers albums on T-Neck featuring Ernie include *3+3* (1973), *Live It Up (1974), The Heat Is On* (1975), *Harvest For The World (1976), Go For Your Guns (1977),* a compilation *Forever Gold (1977), Showdown* (1978), *Go All The Way* (1980), *Grand Slam* (1981), *The Real Deal* (1982) and *Between The Sheets* (1983). On Warner Bros: *Masterpiece* (1985).

J

Anthony JACKSON

Electric bass virtuoso. Born in New York City on June 23, 1952. Started learning the piano at age 5. Picked up guitar and bass in his early teens. Concentrated on bass from age 16. Within a year he was playing in New York clubs. Graduated from high school in 1971 and moved to Philadelphia a year later. There he recorded on Billy Paul's 'Me And Mrs Jones' and a number of other hits. His exceptional and innovative bass playing, along with his distinctive full sound, brought in work with many top musicians including Chick Corea, Paul Simon, The O'Jays, Roberta Flack, Eric Gale and many others. With Steely Dan on *Gaucho* (1980). Joined Steve Khan's fusion band Eyewitness, featuring heavily on recordings such as *Casa Loco* (1983) and *Blades* (1985). With Al Di Meola on *Elegant Gypsy* (1977), *Casino* (1978), *Electric Rendezvous* (1982), *Tirami Su* (1987) and *Kiss My Axe* (1991). Joined fusion trio Protocol with guitarist Ray Russell and drummer Simon Phillips. They released *Force Majeure* (1993). Plays a six-string contrabass guitar.

Michael Gregory JACKSON

Jazz-rock player. Born in New Haven, Connecticut on August 28, 1953. Started taking acoustic guitar lessons at age 7 and received his first electric instrument at 9. Early influences included Eric Clapton, Jimi Hendrix, Johnny Winter, Wes Montgomery and classical music. Played in various rock and blues bands while in his teens. Later worked with Anthony Braxton, Oliver Lake and Leo Smith. Formed his own band, the Michael Gregory Jackson Band. Solo albums on Bija, Improvising Artists and Enja include *Clarity* (1976), *Karmonic Suite* (1978) and *Cowboys, Cartoons & Assorted Candy* (1982).

James JAMERSON

Legendary Motown bassist. Born in South Carolina in 1938. Grew up in Detroit. Learnt upright bass at high school and studied at Wayne University. Became influenced by jazz bass players such as Ray Brown and Paul Chambers. Worked with Yusef Lateef, John Lee Hooker and Washboard Willie in the late '50s. Played bass guitar with Jackie Wilson in 1961. Joined the Motown House band with Earl Van Dyke/Joe Hunter (piano) and Berry Benjamin (drums). Their groovy style combined with previously unheard of recording techniques constituted the 'Motown Sound': a strong drum beat (accentuated with tambourine) with a driving up-front bass. They recorded with many artists including Diana Ross & The Supremes, Four Tops, Stevie Wonder, Marvin Gaye, Martha Reeves and many others. Jamerson later became addicted to alcohol and spent some time in various sanatoriums. Died of a heart problem in 1983. Influenced many other major bass players including Nathan East, Mark Egan, Stanley Clarke and Pino Palladino. Included in *Guitar Player* magazine's 'Gallery Of The Greats' (1985) for his lifetime achievement.

Elmore JAMES

Blues guitarist and singer. Born in Richland, Mississippi on January 27, 1918. Made a guitar out of a lard can at age 12. Self-taught. Became influenced by Robert Johnson. Bought a National guitar at age 19 and started playing locally. Developed a hard-driving slide guitar style that inspired B.B.King, Eric Clapton, Johnny Winter, George Thorogood and many others. Heart condition diagnosed while in the US Navy in the mid-'40s. Appeared on *Sonny Boy's King Biscuit Time* (KFFA Radio, Arkansas) in 1947. Had hits with 'Dust My Broom' (1952), 'I Believe' (1953) and 'The Sky Is Crying' (1960). Health problem exacerbated by heavy drinking. Died after a heart attack in Chicago on May 24, 1963. Albums (mainly compilations) include *Blues After Hours* (1961), *Original Folk Blues* (1964), *To Know A Man* (1969), *The Legend Of Elmore James* (1970), *All Them Blues* (1976), *One Way Out* (1980), *The Best Of Elmore James* (1981), *Red Hot Blues* (1983), *Greatest Hits* (1987), *Dust My Broom* (1990) and *King Of The Slide Guitar* (1992).

Bert JANSCH

Folk-influenced guitarist/singer. Born in Glasgow, Scotland on November 3, 1943. Initially influenced by early bluesmen such as Big Bill Broonzy as well as folk musicians. Developed a unique folk-baroque style. Made a number of recordings for Transatlantic during the '60s, including *Bert Jansch* (1965), *It Don't Bother Me* (1966) and *Jack Orion* (1966). Formed Pentangle in 1967 with John Renbourn (guitar, sitar, vocals), Jacqui McShee (vocals), Danny Thompson (bass) and Terry Cox (drums). Their music was an innovative blend of folk and jazz (see John RENBOURN for more information on Pentangle). Other Jansch recordings on numerous labels include *Nichola* (1967), *Lucky Thirteen* (1969), *Rosemary Lane* (1971), *LA Turnaround* (1974), *A Rare Conundrum* (1978), *Avocet* (1979), *Heartbreak* (1981), *From The Outside* (1985), *Leather Launderette* (1988), *The Gardener: Essential Bert Jansch 1965-71* (1992) and *Three Card*

Bert Jansch

Brian Shuel/Redferns

Trick (1993). Influenced artists as diverse as Gordon Giltrap, Led Zeppelin and Nic Jones.

Blind Lemon JEFFERSON

Blues pioneer. Born blind during the summer of 1897. Youngest of seven children. Suffered from obesity from an early age. Picked up the guitar as a teenager and taught himself. One of the first blues artists to record, making his debut in 1925 under the name Deacon Bates, although this was a religous record. By 1926 Jefferson was recording under his own name. It was raw, uncompromising and unlike anything heard before. His most popular songs included 'Pneumonia Blues' and 'Black Snake Blues'. Died on the streets of Chicago in December 1929, under mysterious circumstances (some say he froze to death). Compilation albums include *King Of The Country Blues* (1985) and *The Complete Blind Lemon Jefferson* (1991).

Jerry JEMMOTT

Session bass ace. Grew up in South Bronx, New York. Became interested in the bass at age 10 after hearing Paul Chambers play on Miles

J

Davis records. Played his first professional gig at age 12. Built up an impressive technique, earning the nickname 'Fingers'. Later became widely recognised as master of the 'turnaround'. Worked with King Curtis on *Memphis Soul Stew* (1971) and Roberta Flack on *Killing Me Softly* (1973). Also sessioned and performed with B.B.King, Wilson Pickett, Aretha Franklin, Freddie King and many others. His many admirers included the late Jaco Pastorius, who as a youngster used to see Jemmott play regularly.

Antonio Carlos **JOBIM**

Legendary composer/guitarist. Born in Rio de Janeiro, Brazil on February 2, 1927. One of the first to blend the Brazilian samba with laid-back jazz to form the bossa nova. Wrote a number of classic songs including 'Desafinado', 'Insensatez (How Insensitive)', 'Corcovado' and 'One Note Samba'. The music was popularised in the US by the Stan Getz/Charlie Byrd album *Jazz Samba* (1962). Another song 'The Girl From Ipanema' (sung in English by Astrud Gilberto) reached the US Top 5 in 1964. Jobim's songs have been covered by Frank Sinatra, Ella Fitzgerald, Miles Davis, Dionne Warwick, Gene Lees, Sergio Mendes, Sarah Vaughan, Eliane Elias, Stan Getz and many others. Various compilations on Discovery and Polydor include *The Wonderful World Of Antonio Carlos Jobim* (1986) and *Compact Jazz: Antonio Carlos Jobim* (1990). A much respected and highly influential composer.

Alphonso **JOHNSON**

Jazz/fusion bassist. Born in Philadelphia, Pennsylvania c.1951. Started playing double bass and trombone, before taking up the bass guitar in 1968. Developed a unique and fluid style. Worked with Horace Silver, Woody Herman, Chuck Mangione and Chet Baker in the early '70s. Joined fusion band Weather Report in 1974, playing on CBS/Columbia albums such as *Mysterious Traveller* (1974) and *Black Market* (1975). Later worked with Billy Cobham, Flora Purim, the Crusaders, Freddie Hubbard, Arthur Blythe, Carlos Santana and many others. One of the first generation of virtuoso electric bass soloists, along with Stanley Clarke, Jaco Pastorius and Percy Jones.

Eric **JOHNSON**

Rock guitarist. Born in Austin, Texas on August 17, 1954. Started learning piano from age 5 and took up guitar by the time he was 11. Early influences included the Ventures, Jimi Hendrix, Wes Montgomery and Django Reinhardt. By the time he was 16 he had a considerable reputation as a lead guitarist in Austin. Formed a fusion group the Electromagnets in 1974. They recorded the album *The Electromagnets* (EGM), which is now a collector's item. The band broke up after four years and Eric formed his own group. Also worked with Steve Morse, Carole King, Christopher Cross and many others. His outstanding rock leadwork is highly melodic and expressive. Blends rock with folk, jazz and country. Recordings on Reprise and Capitol include *Tones* (1986) and *Ah Via Musicom* (1990). Author of instruction video *Total Electric Guitar* (Hot Licks 1990). Voted Best Overall Guitarist in *Guitar Player* (1991).

James Cumpsty/Music Maker

Eric Johnson

Lonnie **JOHNSON**

Legendary blues/jazz player and singer. Born Alonzo Johnson in New Orleans on February 8, 1889. Learned guitar and violin as a child. Left school in 1902 to work in music. Often performed with brother James 'Steady Roll' Johnson in New Orleans clubs and theatres. Toured the United States and Europe in 1917, but returned to find that a flu epidemic had killed off most of his family. Moved to St.Louis and won a talent contest organised by Okeh records. Later worked with Louis Armstrong, Duke Ellington, Eddie Lang and many others.

Made a large number of recordings up until the time of his death in Toronto on June 16, 1970. Albums include *Blues By Lonnie Johnson* (Bluesway/ Prestige), *Bluebird Blues* (RCA) and *Mr. Trouble* (Folkways). A pioneer of jazz and blues guitar, along with Eddie Lang. Influenced many later players including Charlie Christian, T-Bone Walker, Kenny Burrell, Barney Kessel, B.B.King, Jim Hall and Joe Pass.

Robert JOHNSON

Blues legend. Born in Hazlehurst, Mississippi on May 8, 1911. First took up harmonica. Bought a guitar and taught himself while still in his teens. Heavily influenced by Son House and Lonnie Johnson. Story has it that he disappeared for a while when he was younger and suddenly came back a much better guitar player (some believe that he "went down to the crossroads" and made a pact with the devil). Excelled at interpreting the songs of others: considered to be the first real blues performance artist. Died in Greenwood, Mississippi on August 16, 1938 under mysterious circumstances: an early report claimed that he had been stabbed but many felt that he had been poisoned by the jealous husband of a woman he was seeing. Compilations on CBS/ Sony include *King Of The Delta Blues Singers* and *Robert Johnson: The Complete Recordings*. His songs have also been performed by Cream, the Rolling Stones, John Mayall and many others. Included in *Guitar Player* magazine's 'Gallery Of The Greats' (1987) for his lifetime achievement. Book: *Searching For Robert Johnson* by Peter Guralnick.

Wilko JOHNSON

UK rock guitarist. Born John Wilkinson in 1947. Grew up in Southend, Essex. Played in various local bands during the '60s. Became influenced by Mick Green of Johnny Kidd and the Pirates. Formed Dr Feelgood in 1971 with Lee Brilleaux (vocals, harmonica), John 'Sparko' Sparks (bass) and 'Bandsman' Howarth (drums, later replaced by John 'The Big Figure' Martin). Developed into a manic R&B act, with Brilleaux bellowing into the microphone and Wilko playing his Telecaster like a machine-gun. Became popular on the London pub-club circuit. Albums include *Down By The Jetty* (1975), *Malpractice* (1975), *Stupidity* (1976) and *Sneaking Suspicion* (1977). Johnson left after a row in 1977 and formed his own band the Solid Senders.

Recordings on Virgin and Jungle include *Solid Senders* (1978) and *Barbed Wire Blues* (1988).

Brian JONES

Rock guitarist. Born in Cheltenham, Gloucester, England on February 28, 1942. Met Mick Jagger and Keith Richards at Alexis Korner's blues club in London during the early '60s. They formed the Rolling Stones (named after a Muddy Waters song). Jones played on several hits including 'Satisfaction', 'Paint It Black' and 'Jumping Jack Flash' during the '60s (see Keith RICHARDS for more information on the Rolling Stones). Arrested for drug offences in 1967. His drug addiction problem became so bad he left the band in 1969. Drowned in his swimming pool on July 3, 1969.

Darryl JONES

US bass player. Born in Chicago on December 11, 1961. Started learning drums at age 8 and picked up bass a year later. Studied music theory at high school and played upright bass in the orchestra. Early influences include Earth, Wind & Fire, James Brown and Stanley Clarke. Played locally with Phil Upchurch and Ramsey Lewis. Gained a considerable reputation as a solid bass player with a feel for a groove. Worked with Miles Davis on the Columbia albums *Decoy* (1984) and *You're Under Arrest* (1985). Also with Sting on A&M recording *The Dream Of The Blue Turtles* (1985) and John Scofield's *Still Warm* (1986) on Gramavision.

Percy JONES

UK fusion bassist. Born in Llandrindod Wells, Wales on December 3, 1947. Started playing the bass at age 15. Studied electronics at the University of Liverpool. Moved to London during the early '70s and got into session work. Formed Brand X with John Goodsall (guitar), Robin Lumley (keyboards) and Phil Collins (drums, also with Genesis). Debut album on Charisma *Unorthadox Behaviour* (1975) highlighted Jones' highly individual fluid fretless bass style. There were a number of personnel changes and other band members included keyboardist Peter Robinson, percussionist Morris Pert and drummers Chuck Burgi, Mike Clarke and Frank Katz. Another bassist John Giblin was also featured on some tracks. Recordings on Charisma and Ozone include *Masques* (1978), *Product* (1979), *Do They Hurt?* (1980) and *XCommunication* (1992).

Solo albums on Hot Wire include *Propeller Music* (1990) and *Cape Catastrophe* (1990).

Steve **JONES**

UK rock/punk guitarist. Born in England on May 3, 1955. Grew up in West London. Joined punk band the Swankers (later Sex Pistols) c.1975 with Glen Matlock (bass, later replaced by Sid Vicious) and Paul Cook (drums). Chelsea shop-owner Malcolm McLaren became the band's manager and recruited vocalist Johnny Rotten (born John Lydon). Signed to EMI for hit single 'Anarchy In The UK' (1976), although the label dropped them after the band gained notoriety through swearing on TV and vomiting in public. A&M took them on but cancelled within a week. Signed to Virgin for 'God Save The Queen' (1977) and 'Pretty Vacant' (1977). The grossness of Rotten and Vicious was complemented by the raw, solid sound of Jones. Albums include *Never Mind The Bollocks - Here's The Sex Pistols* (1977) and *The Great Rock'N'Roll Swindle* (1978, also film). Rotten quit in 1978 and Vicious died of a heroin overdose on February 2, 1979. The group soon disbanded. They were the most significant British punk band and influenced many others. Jones later worked with Iggy Pop

Sex Pistols

on A&M recordings *Blah Blah Blah* (1986) and *Instinct* (1988). Solo albums on MCA include *Mercy* (1987) and *Fire And Gasoline* (1989).

Stanley Jordon

Stanley **JORDAN**

Jazz guitarist. Born in Chicago, Illinois on July 31, 1959. Started playing piano at age 6, before switching to the guitar at 11. Early influences included Jimi Hendrix, George Benson and Wes Montgomery. Studied theory and composition at Princeton University. Wanted to play the guitar like a keyboard and developed a revolutionary technique with both hands on the fingerboard. Expanded the instrument's range by being able to play melodies, chords and bass lines independently with each hand. Worked with Quincy Jones, Dizzie Gillespie, Wynton Marsalis and many others. Played at the Montreux Jazz Festival in 1985. Uses specially-prepared (ultra-low action) electric guitars tuned in fourths (E, A, D, G, C, F). Debut recording: *Touch Sensitive* (Tangent 1983). Switched to Blue Note for *Magic Touch* (1985), produced by Al Di Meola. Later Blue Note recordings include *Standards* (1986) and *Cornucopia* (1990).

K

Brij Bhushan **KABRA**

Indian classical 'slide-guitarist'. Born in
Jodhpur, Rajasthan in 1937. Studied geology
and business administration. Became interested
in the guitar after hearing traditional Indian
music being played on an electric Hawaiian
guitar. Also influenced by virtuoso sarod player
Ali Akbar Khan. Developed a unique and
formidable technique through years of intensive
practice. Worked with many musicians,
including santur player Shivkumar Sharma and
percussionist Zakir Hussain, and has recorded
several albums including *The Evening Mood*
(EMI India), *Two Raga Moods On Guitar*
(World Pacific) and *Raga Puriya Alap*
(Celluloid). Plays Indian ragas on lap-style
guitar.

Henry **KAISER**

Experimental guitarist. Born in Oakland,
California in 1952. Grandson of famous
industrialist Henry J. Kaiser. Influences
included Albert Collins, Hubert Sumlin, Jerry
Garcia and Derek Bailey (experimental
guitarist). Worked with Herbie Hancock, Fred
Frith, Bill Frisell, Ali Akbar Khan (sarod player)
and many others. A versatile guitarist who has
worked on many unusual and diverse projects
such as bizarre cover versions, free-
improvisations, warped blues pieces and
electronic experimentation. Albums on
Metalanguage, Minor Music, SST and Reckless
include *Protocol* (1979), *Aloha* (1982),
Marrying For Money (1986), *Devil In The
Drain* (1987), *Those Who Know History Are
Doomed To Repeat It* (1988) and *Heart's
Desire* (1990). Also teamed up with John
French, Fred Frith and Richard Thompson for
recordings on Rhino and Demon: *Live, Love,
Larf & Loaf* (1987) and *Invisible Means*
(1990).

Paul **KANTNER**

Rock player. Born in San Francisco on March
19, 1941. Early influences included Elvis
Presley, Gene Vincent and the Beatles. Founding
member of Jefferson Airplane with Grace Slick
(vocals), Marty Balin (vocals), Jorma Kaukonen
(guitar), Jack Casady (bass) and Spencer
Dryden (drums). Recordings on RCA include
Jefferson Airplane Takes Off (1966),
Surrealistic Pillow (1967), *After Bathing At
Baxters* (1967), *Bless Its Pointed Little Head*
(1969) and *Volunteers* (1970). Kantner solo
albums include *Blows Against The Empire*
(1970) and *Sunfighter* (1971). The band formed
the Grunt Record company and continued with
Bark (1971) and *Long John Silver* (1973).
Kaukonen and Casady left and the band was
renamed Jefferson Starship in 1974, with
newcomers Craig Chaquico on guitar and Pete
Sears on bass. Further Starship albums featuring
Kantner include *Dragon Fly* (1974), *Red
Octopus* (1975), *Spitfire* (1976), *Earth* (1978),
Winds Of Change (1982) and *Nuclear Future*
(1984). Left the band in 1985, but later
reformed Jefferson Airplane with Kaukonen,
Slick, Balin and Casady in 1989.

Mick **KARN**

UK bass player. Born on July 24, 1958. Started
learning mouth organ, violin and bassoon
before switching to bass at age 16. Self-taught.
Also sculptor. Joined a local band, which
eventually became Japan. Developed an original
fluid fretless bass style, which was heavily
featured in the band's later compositions.
Recordings on Ariola and Virgin include
Adolescent Sex (1979), *Obscure Alternatives*
(1979), *Quiet Life* (1980), *Gentlemen Take
Polaroids* (1980), *Tin Drum* (1981) and
compilation *Assemblage* (1981). After Japan
split in the early '80s, he formed Dali's Car with
vocalist Peter Murphy (ex-Bauhaus). Solo
albums on Virgin and CMP including *Titles*
(1982), *Dreams Of Reason Produce Monsters*
(1987) and *Bestial Cluster* (1993). Also worked
with Midge Ure and many others.

Jorma **KAUKONEN**

Blues/rock player. Born in Washington DC on
December 23, 1940. Started learning piano and
violin from an early age and switched to guitar
at age 16. Influences included Blind Blake and
the Rev. Gary Davis. Played in acid rock band
Jefferson Airplane in the late '60s (see Paul

KANTNER for further information on Jefferson Airplane). Left the band in 1972 to play full-time in Hot Tuna (initially Hot Shit). Albums on RCA and Grunt include *Electric Hot Tuna-Live* (1972), *The Phosphorescent Rat* (1974) and *Yellow Fever* (1975). Solo recordings on Grunt, RCA and Relix include *Quah*, *Jorma*, *Barbecue King* and *Too Hot To Handle*. Reformed Jefferson Airplane in 1989 with Slick, Kantner, Balin and Casady. They released *Jefferson Airplane* (1989) on Epic. Instruction video: *The Acoustic Guitar Of Jorma Kaukonen* (Homespun 1991). His style combines R&B with folk.

Carol **KAYE**

Session bass legend. Born in Everett, Washington on March 24, 1935. Family moved to Los Angeles when she was 6. Started learning the guitar at age 13 and was teaching others to play the instrument within a year. Played bebop in LA nightclubs during the late '50s. Introduced to session work by entrepreneur Bumps Blackwell in 1958 and soon started playing bass. By 1965 she was the premier session bassist in LA, working with top artists such as Phil Spector, Elvis Presley, the Beach Boys and the Monkees. Bass and guitar credits on '60s hits include 'You've Lost That Lovin' Feelin'' (Righteous Bros), 'Good Vibrations' (Beach Boys), 'River Deep, Mountain High' (Ike & Tina Turner), 'Spanish Eyes' (Al Martino), 'I Was Made To Love Her' (Stevie Wonder), 'Get Ready' (Temptations), 'Homeward Bound' (Simon & Garfunkel) and many more. Her solid 'pick-style' sound influenced many other musicians. Also worked on film and TV music such as *Hawaii 5-O*, *Mission Impossible*, *McCloud*, *Streets Of San Francisco*, *Bonanza* and *The Addams Family*. Formed her own publishing company in 1969 and wrote numerous bass instruction books. Later concentrated mainly on teaching and giving seminars. Instructional videos: *Carol Kaye - Electric Bass* and *Bass II: More Music Reading Plus Theory*.

Barney **KESSEL**

Jazz guitarist. Born in Muskogee, Oklahoma on October 17, 1923. Started playing the guitar at age 12. Self-taught. Became the only white player in a local all-negro band at age 14. Met Charlie Christian in 1939. Moved to California in 1942. Appeared in Lester Young's film 'Jammin The Blues' in 1944. Worked with

Barney Kessel

Charlie Parker, Oscar Peterson, Benny Goodman, Artie Shaw and many others. Won jazz polls in *Downbeat*, *Melody Maker*, *Metronome* and *Esquire* in the '50s. Later gave seminars and wrote for *Guitar Player* magazine. Toured extensively and made many recordings on Contemporary, Emerald, Black Lion and Concord including *Let's Cook* (1957), *On Fire* (1965), *Swinging Easy* (1967), *Feeling Free* (1969), *Summertime In Montreux* (1973), *Barney Plays Kessel* (1975), *Jelly Beans* (1981), *Solo* (1983), *Spontaneous Combustion* (1987) and *Kessel Plays Standards* (1989). Instructional videos on Rumark: *Progressive Concepts* and *Chord-Melody Style*.

Steve **KHAN**

Jazz/fusion guitarist and session ace. Born in Los Angeles, California in 1947. Started off as a drummer and took up guitar at age 20. Early influences include Wes Montgomery, Kenny Burrell and Albert King. Recorded several solo albums for Columbia including *Tightrope* (1977), *The Blue Man* (1978) and compilation *The Best Of Steve Khan* (1980), before forming all-star fusion band Eyewitness with Anthony Jackson (bass), Steve Jordan (drums) and Manolo Badrena (percussion, effects). Albums on Antilles and Passport include *Eyewitness* (1981), *Casa Loco* (1983) and *Blades* (1985). Duo album with keyboardist Rob Mounsey: *Local Colour* (1987). Also worked with George Benson, Larry Coryell, Billy Cobham, Bill

Connors, Michael Brecker, Donald Fagen, Steely Dan, James Brown, Billy Joel, Danny Gottlieb and Aretha Franklin. His unique style fuses elements of bebop and rock. Highly respected teacher and author of *The Wes Montgomery Guitar Folio* (Gopam Enterprises) and *Pat Martino - The Early Years* (CCP Belwin 1991).

Albert KING

Blues guitarist and singer. Born Albert Nelson in Indianola, Mississippi on April 25, 1923. Taught himself to play a home-made guitar at an early age. Influences included Lonnie Johnson and T-Bone Walker. Moved to Chicago and made his first recordings in the early '50s. Within a decade he was recognised as being one of the most dynamic blues artists. His raw vocals and hard, biting leadwork inspired countless other bluesmen and guitar players. Albums on King, Stax, Fantasy and other labels include *The Big Blues* (1962), *Born Under A Bad Sign* (1967), *King Of The Blues Guitar* (1968), *Years Gone By* (1969), *Lovejoy* (1971), *I'll Play The Blues For You* (1972), *I Wanna Get Funky* (1974), *Albert* (1976), *Albert Live* (1977), *King Albert* (1977), *New Orleans Heat* (1979), *San Francisco '83* (1983), *I'm In The Phone Booth, Baby* (1984), *Blues At Sunrise* (1988), *Let's Have A Natural Ball* (1990) and *Red House* (1991). Also played on Gary Moore's *Still Got The Blues* (1990). Died after a heart attack in Memphis, Tennessee on December 21, 1992. Videos include *Maintenance Shop Blues* (Yazoo 1993).

B.B.KING

Blues legend. Born Riley B. King in Itta Bena, Mississippi on September 16, 1925. Worked on a plantation from age 8. Given a guitar as part of his wages when he was 14. Early influences included gospel music and blues players such as Lonnie Johnson, Blind Lemon Jefferson and T-Bone Walker, as well as jazzers like Charlie Christian and Django Reinhardt. Moved to Memphis in 1948 and worked as a disc jockey for WDIA radio station, where he was nicknamed "Blues Boy From Beale Street" (later shortened to B.B.). Started recording for the Bullet label in 1949 and soon matured into an outstanding blues performer. Became famous for his 'singing' blues lines, as well as being a pioneer of across-the-string vibrato and note bending techniques. A fight broke out at one of his concerts in Twist, Arkansas in 1949. The

building caught fire and everyone including King rushed out. He suddenly realised he had left his guitar inside and managed to rescue it just before the building collapsed. He named the guitar 'Lucille', after the girl who was reputedly the cause of the fight, and has always given that name to his current guitar. Has favoured Gibson ES335s since 1958. Albums on ABC, MCA and other labels include *The Blues* (1960), *King Of The Blues* (1961), *Blues In My Heart* (1962), *Mr Blues* (1963), the classic *Live At The Regal* (1965), *The Soul Of B.B.King* (1966), *Blues Is King* (1967), *Lucille* (1968), *Indianola Mississippi Seeds* (1970), *Live In Cook County Jail* (1971), *Guess Who* (1972),

B.B.King

Best Of B.B.King (1973), *Lucille Talks Back* (1975), *Midnight Believer* (1978), *Take It Home* (1979), *Love Me Tender* (1982), *Blues'N'Jazz* (1983), *Six Silver Strings* (1985), *Do The Boogie* (1989), *Live At The Apollo* (1991), *My Sweet Little Angel* (1992) and *Blues*

Summit (1993). Also worked with Miles Davis, Ray Charles, U2 and many others. Inspired many top guitarists including Eric Clapton, Duane Allman, Roy Buchanan, Duane Eddy, Jimmy Vaughan and Mike Bloomfield. One of the most influential guitar players of all time. Included in *Guitar Player* magazine's 'Gallery Of The Greats' after being voted Best Electric Blues Player (1970-1974). Also Grammy Award (1987) for Lifetime Achievement. Instructional videos include *Blues Master I, II & III* (REH/DCI).

Earl **KING**

Blues guitarist, singer and pianist. Born Earl Johnson in New Orleans, Louisiana on February 7, 1934. Started playing guitar at age 14. Recorded his first single 'Have You Gone Crazy?' in 1953. Had a number of hits including 'Don't Take It So Hard' (1955), 'Always A First Time' (1962) and 'Trick Bag' (1962). Played with B.B.King, Guitar Slim, Junior Parker, Professor Longhair, Roomful of Blues and many others. Recordings on Pathe, Black Top and other labels include *Trick Bag* (1962), *New Orleans Rock'N'Roll* (1977), *Street Parade* (1981), *Glazed* (1986), *Soul Bag* (1987) *and Sexual Telepathy* (1990). Influenced many other musicians including Jimi Hendrix, Little Richard, Lloyd Price and Dr John.

Freddie **KING**

Blues player. Born in Gilmer, Texas on September 3, 1934. Picked up the guitar at age 6. Moved to Chicago when he was 16. Early influences included Robert Johnson, Lightnin' Hopkins, Muddy Waters, Jimmy Rogers and B.B.King. Had a number of hits during the '60s, including 'HideAway', 'Lonesome Whistle Blues' and 'I'm Tore Down'. Worked with Howlin' Wolf, Muddy Waters and Little Walter (harmonica player). Noted for his percussive attack and distorted tone. Albums on Cotillion, Shelter and RSO include *Let's Hide Away And Dance Away* (1961), *Boy-Girl-Boy* (1962), *Freddie King Is A Blues Master* (1969), *My Feeling For The Blues* (1970), *Getting Ready* (1971), *Texas Cannonball* (1972), *Woman Across The Water* (1973), *Burglar* (1974) with Eric Clapton and *Larger Than Life* (1975). Suffered from poor health in his final years (heart condition and ulcers) and died in Dallas on December 28, 1976. A number of compilations of early material were later released, including *Takin' Care Of Business* (1985) on Charly and *Live In Nancy 1975 Vol. I* (1988) on Concert.

Mark **KING**

UK rock/funk bassist and singer. Born on October 20, 1958. Grew up on the Isle of Wight. Early influences included Stanley Clarke and fusion bands such as the Mahavishnu Orchestra. Developed an original and formidable funk bass technique of his own. Formed Level 42 in 1980, with Mike Lindup (keyboards), Boon Gould (guitar) and Phil Gould (drums). Keyboardist Wally Badarou also contributed regularly as co-writer and co-producer. Initially played jazz-funk songs and instrumentals, driven by King's innovative bass

Mark King

grooves. Later recorded more mainstream pop albums with bass still prominent. Toured almost constantly and earned a reputation as an outstanding live act. Hits include 'Love Games' (1981), 'The Chinese Way' (1982), 'Hot Water' (1984) and 'Something About You' (1985). Gould brothers left during 1987 and were replaced by Alan Murphy (guitar) and Gary Husband (drums). Albums on Polydor include *Level 42* (1981), *The Early Tapes* (1982), *The Pursuit Of Accidents* (1982), *Standing In The Light* (1983), *True Colours* (1984), Mark King solo album *Influences* (1984), *World Machine* (1985), *Running In The Family* (1987) and

Staring At The Sun (1988). Switched to RCA for *Guaranteed* (1991) with Allan Holdsworth on guitar, following the death of Alan Murphy.

Earl **KLUGH**

Jazz-influenced guitarist. Born in Detroit on September 16, 1953. Started learning piano but switched to acoustic nylon-string guitar at age 10, after hearing Bob Dylan and other folk singers. Later influences included Chet Atkins, George Benson, Wes Montgomery, Charlie Byrd and George Van Eps. Worked with Yusef Lateef at age 16. Also with George Benson and Chick Corea's Return To Forever by the time he was 20. Developed a sparse, melodic, easy-listening style, which can be heard on any of his albums on Blue Note including *Earl Klugh* (1976), *Living Inside Your Love* (1976), *Finger Paintings* (1977). On Liberty: *Crazy For You* (1981). On Warner Brothers: *Soda Fountain Shuffle* (1985), *Life Stories* (1986), *Whispers And Promises* (1989), *Solo Guitar* (1989) and *The Earl Klugh Trio* (1991).

Mark **KNOPFLER**

Rock guitarist, singer/songwriter. Born in London, England on August 12, 1949. Started working as a journalist and teacher. Became influenced by Bob Dylan and J.J.Cale. Formed Dire Straits in 1977 with David Knopfler (guitar, later replaced), John Illsley (bass) and Pick Withers (drums, later replaced). Named after their financial status at the time. Developed an intimate R&B sound, punctuated by Knopfler's fluid guitar work. Charlie Gillett played a demo version of their 'Sultans Of Swing' on his BBC radio show. Signed to Vertigo. Their reputation grew with the release of debut album *Dire Straits* (1978), but the big break came with the release of a more polished version of 'Sultans Of Swing' in 1979. It reached the Top 10 on both sides of the Atlantic and album sales soared. More success followed with further recordings on Vertigo including *Communique* (1979), *Making Movies* (1980), *Love Over Gold* (1982), *Alchemy* (1984), *Brothers In Arms* (1985), compilation *Money For Nothing* (1988) and *On Every Street* (1991). Guitar playing became more sparse and lyrical on later recordings. Headlined at the Nelson Mandela Tribute in Wembley (1988). Knopfler recorded scores for films such as *Local Hero* (1983) and *Cal* (1984). Teamed up with Chet Atkins for *Neck & Neck* (1990) on Columbia. Also sessioned

Mark Knopfler

with Steely Dan, Van Morrison, Bryan Ferry, Phil Everly and many others. A highly successful and respected guitarist.

Alexis **KORNER**

Blues guitarist. Born in Paris on April 19, 1928. Moved over to to England. Started off playing skiffle and traditional jazz. Became inspired by Muddy Waters. Opened the London Blues and Barrelhouse Club in 1955 with Cyril Davies. They formed their own R&B band Blues Incorporated in 1961. The original band line-up was Alexis Korner (guitar), Cyril Davies (harmonica), Art Woods (vocals) and Charlie Watts (drums). Later members included Jack Bruce, Ginger Baker, Long John Baldry and Graham Bond. Korner also did a lot of work for TV in the mid '60s and later formed the blues bands Free At Last, New Church, CCS and Snape. Influenced a whole generation of guitarists in the UK and is generally regarded as the father of British R&B. Died of lung cancer on January 1, 1984. Recordings include *Alexis Korner's Blues Incorporated* (1964), *Sky High* (1966), *I Wonder Who* (1967), *What's That Sound I Hear?* (1969), *Alexis* (1971), *Mr Blues* (1974), *Get Off My Cloud* (1975), *Just Easy* (1978), *Me* (1979), *The Party Album* (1980) and *Juvenile Delinquent* (1984).

Paul KOSSOFF

Blues/rock player. Born in London on September 14, 1950. Started learning classical guitar and was playing electric by the time he was 16. Influenced by Eric Clapton, Peter Green, B.B.King and Otis Redding. Formed the rock band Free in 1968 with Paul Rodgers (vocals), Andy Fraser (bass) and Simon Kirke (drums). They had hits in the early '70s with 'Wishing Well' and 'All Right Now'. Kossoff's raw, expressive guitar enhanced the band's reputation. Albums on Island include *Tons Of Sobs* (1968), *Free Live* (1971), *Free At Last* (1972), *Heartbreaker* (1973) and compilation *All Right Now* (1991). The band split in 1973 and Kossoff formed another band Back Street Crawler. Suffered from ill health and died of a heart attack (thought to be drug related) on March 19, 1976.

Leo KOTTKE

Folk guitarist and singer/songwriter. Born in Athens, Georgia on September 11, 1945. Started playing the guitar at age 11. Became influenced by folk-blues singers such as Mississippi John Hurt. Developed an impressive acoustic guitar style. Wrote many songs with ironic lyrics and built up a cult following. Recorded many albums on Takoma (for John Fahey), Capitol, Chrysalis and Private Music: *Twelve String Blues* (1969), *Circle Around The Sun* (1970), *Mudlark* (1971), *6 And 12-String Guitar* (1971), *Greenhouse* (1972), *Ice Water* (1973), *My Feet Are Smiling* (1973), *Dreams And All That Stuff* (1974), *Chewing Pine* (1975), *Leo Kottke* (1976), *Burnt Lips* (1978), *Balance* (1979), *Live In Europe* (1980), *Guitar Music* (1981), *Time Step* (1983), *Regards From Chuck Pink* (1988), *My Father's Place* (1989), *That's What* (1990), *Great Big Boy* (1991) and *Essential Collection* (1991).

Ritchie KOTZEN

Heavy metal guitarist. Born c.1971. Grew up in Birdsboro, Pennsylvania. Started playing the piano before switching over to the guitar at age 7. Formed a band during his teens and developed his own advanced lead guitar technique. Impressed Mike Varney, who signed him to Shrapnel Records for instrumental solo album *Ritchie Kotzen* (1989), highlighting the guitarist with Stuart Hamm (bass) and Steve Smith (drums). Second album *Fever Dream* (1990) featured Danny Thompson (bass) and Atma Anur (drums) as well as Kotzen on guitar

and vocals. Later recorded *Electric Joy* (1991). Joined heavy metal band Poison and played guitar on Capitol recording *Native Tongue* (1993), although he left the band after various disagreements (replaced by Blues Saraceno). Author of instruction video *Rock Chops* (REH).

Carl KRESS

Jazz guitarist. Born in Newark, New Jersey on October 20, 1907. Joined the Paul Whiteman Orchestra in 1926. Also performed with Bix Beiderbecke, Frankie Trumbauer, Miff Mole and the Dorsey Brothers in the late '20s. Worked extensively on American radio. Formed guitar duos with Eddie Lang and Dick McDonough in the early '30s. Co-founder of the Onyx jazz club in New York. Highly respected as a pioneering rhythm player. Used unorthadox tuning (B flat, F, C, G, A, D). Collapsed and died during a duo performance with guitarist George Barnes in Reno, Nevada on June 10, 1965. Recordings included *Pioneers Of Jazz Guitar* (Yazoo).

Robbie KRIEGER

Rock guitarist. Born in Los Angeles, California on January 8, 1946. Learned flamenco guitar at high school. Later studied at University of California in Santa Barbara, where he gigged as a folk guitarist for a while. Traded his classical guitar in for a Gibson SG electric after seeing Chuck Berry play in Santa Monica. Also became influenced by blues, jazz and Indian classical music. Met keyboard player Ray Manzarek and singer Jim Morrison. They formed psychedelic band the Doors (named after Aldous Huxley's book 'The Doors Of Perception') in 1965. The band had considerable success with classic rock albums on Elektra such as *The Doors* (1967), *Strange Days* (1968) and *L.A. Woman* (1971). Morrison died of a heart attack in a bath (probably drug related) on July 3, 1971. Krieger left the group in 1972 to form the Butts Band and has since recorded solo albums including *Robbie Krieger And Friends* (Blue Note), *Versions* (Passport) and *No Habla* (I.R.S.).

Alexandre **LAGOYA**

Classical guitarist. Born in Alexandria, Egypt on June 21, 1929. Started playing guitar at age 8. Gave more than 500 concerts as a teenager. Studied at the Ecole Normale De Musique in Paris and later with Segovia in Siena. Met another virtuoso Ida Presti in 1950. They married two years later and formed a guitar duo, commissioning new works from composers such as Mario Castelnuovo-Tedesco and Joaquin Rodrigo. The duo gave many highly acclaimed performances and made several recordings including *Music For Classic Guitar* (Nonsuch) and *Masters Of The Guitar - Volume One* (RCA). Presti suddenly fell ill and died in 1967 and Lagoya eventually embarked on a new solo career five years later. Recordings include *The Spanish Guitar* (Columbia) and *Viva Lagoya* (Phillips).

Bireli **LAGRENE**

Jazz guitarist. Born in Saverne, France on September 4, 1966. Parents were gypsies. Picked up guitar at age 5 and was playing improvisations in the style of Django Reinhardt by the time he was 7. Recorded his debut album *Routes To Django* (1980) for Antilles at age 13. His playing was so good many people considered him to be Reinhardt reincarnated. Recorded several other albums, each one showing a further maturation of his playing. On Antilles, Austrophon Diepholz and Jazzpoint: *Down In Town* (1983), *Bireli Swing 81* (1983) and critically acclaimed *Bireli Lagrene Ensemble Live Featuring Vic Juris* (1984). Signed to Blue Note for fusion album *Inferno* (1988). Later albums on Blue Note: *Acoustic Moments* (1990) and *Standards* (1992). Also worked with Jaco Pastorius, Larry Coryell, Al Di Meola, Miroslav Vitous and many others.

Sonny **LANDRETH**

Slide guitarist. Born in Canton, Mississippi. Grew up in Lafayette, Louisiana. Started playing guitar at age 13 and was soon playing slide. Early influences included Clarence White, Robert Johnson, Chet Atkins, Clifton Chenier and Ry Cooder. Joined John Hiatt's band (recorded on 1988 album *Slow Turning*), and also worked with Albert Lee and Jo-El Sonnier (Cajun). Developed an advanced, expressive and unique glass slide technique (blends notes made by his slide with ones fingered behind it). Recordings on Blues Unlimited, Epic and Zoo/Praxis include *Blues Attack* (1981), *Way Down Louisiana* (1985), and *Outward Bound* (1992).

Shawn **LANE**

Rock/fusion virtuoso. Born in Memphis, Tennessee on March 21, 1963. Took up the guitar at age 9 (also learned to play drums, bass and keyboards) and toured with southern-rock band Black Oak Arkansas by the time he was 14. Influences included John McLaughlin, Pat Metheny, Allan Holdsworth, Ray Gomez and Lenny Breau. Later studied classical music and jazz. Worked with Willie Nelson, Kris Kristofferson, Waylon Jennings, Johnny Cash, Frank Gambale and a number of others. His formidable, exciting and highly expressive technique can be heard on his Warner Brothers instrumental tour de force *Powers Of Ten* (1992). Admirers include Eric Johnson, Kirk Hammett, Vernon Reid, George Lynch and columnist Mike Varney. Instructional videos on REH: *Power Licks* and *Power Solos*.

Eddie **LANG**

Jazz guitar pioneer. Born Salvatore Massaro in Philadelphia, Pennsylvania on October 25, 1902. His father made fretted instruments. Started learning violin from an early age and later switched to guitar. By the early '20s Lang was playing banjo-guitar in Philadelphia and Atlantic City clubs. Joined the Mound City Blue Blowers in 1924 for a European tour and various recordings. Later worked with violinist Joe Venuti (an old schoolmate), Adrian Rollini's Big Band, Bix Beiderbecke, Lonnie Johnson, Benny Goodman, Ella Fitzgerald, Paul Whiteman and Bing Crosby. Died after a tonsillectomy operation on March 26, 1933. Paved the way for later guitarists such as Charlie

Christian, Django Reinhardt, George Van Eps and Tal Farlow. Compilations on Yazoo and Rounder include *Jazz Guitar Virtuoso* (1988) and *Troubles, Troubles* (1988). Included in *Guitar Player* magazine's 'Gallery Of The Greats' (1985) for his lifetime achievement.

Andy LATIMER

UK rock guitarist, singer/songwriter and flautist. Born in Guildford, Surrey in 1949. Played in local bands before forming Camel in 1971 with Peter Bardens (keyboards), Doug Ferguson (bass) and Andy Ward (drums). Supported Wishbone Ash and Barclay James Harvest and recorded debut album *Camel* (1973) on MCA. Switched to Decca/Deram for *Mirage* (1974). Big break came with instrumental concept album *The Snow Goose* (1975), based on a story by Paul Gallico. It reached the UK Top 30. Fused rock music with classical and folk. Ferguson left (replaced by ex-Caravan bassist Richard Sinclair) after *Moonmadness* (1976). Two more albums followed, *Rain Dances* (1977) and *Breathless* (1978), before Bardens left to work with Van Morrison and pursue a solo career. There have been a number of personnel changes since then and other albums on Decca include *I Can See Your House From Here* (1979), *Nude* (1981), *The Single Factor* (1982), *Stationary Traveller* (1983) and *Pressure Points* (1984). Also compilation on Castle: *Collection* (1986).

LEADBELLY

Blues and folk guitarist. Also singer/songwriter. Born Huddie William Ledbetter in Mooringsport, Louisiana c.1889. Grew up in Texas. Played guitar, harmonica and accordion by the time he was 15. Heavily influenced by Blind Lemon Jefferson. Entertained in the street and at dances. A violent man who reputedly had a knife scar circling his neck from ear to ear. Sentenced to 30 years imprisonment in 1916 for murdering a man in New Boston, Texas. Entertained the cons and staff in jail and was pardoned after 7 years. Sentenced to another 10 years for attempted murder in 1930. Discovered in Angola State Prison, Louisiana by Alan and John Lomax, who recorded him for the Library of Congress. Released from prison in 1934. Moved to New York City in 1937 and played at clubs and political rallies. Worked with Woodie Guthrie, Pete Seeger and Burl Ives at a concert for migrant workers in 1940. His distinctive style featured powerful vocals, backed by his expressive acoustic 12-string guitar. Collected and composed a large number of folk-blues songs over the years, including 'The Midnight Special' and 'Pick A Bale Of Cotton'. Died in New York City on December 6, 1949. A year later The Weavers had a No.1 hit with his song 'Goodnight Irene'. Compilation recordings include *Sings Folk Songs* (1968), *Leadbelly* (1970), *Alabama Bound* (1990) and *King Of The 12-String Guitar* (1991).

Albert LEE

Country guitar legend. Born in Herefordshire, England on December 21, 1943. Early influences included Buddy Holly, Ricky Nelson, Speedy West, James Burton and Jimmy Bryant. Worked with Jackie Lynton, Chris Farlowe and Head, Hands & Feet during the '60s. Later with Jerry Lee Lewis, Joe Cocker, Emmylou Harris

Albert Lee

and Eric Clapton in the '70s. Recorded critically acclaimed A&M album *Hiding* (1979), which boasted an outstanding version of a traditional song 'Country Boy'. His superb picking and fluent sound soon earned him considerable respect in country music circles. Often used slapback echo with lead runs to get an effect that sounds as though notes are bouncing off one another. Later recordings on A&M and MCA include *Albert Lee* (1983), the highly-acclaimed instrumental album *Speechless* (1986) and *Gagged But Not Bound* (1988).

Also with Jackson Browne, Dave Edmunds, the Everly Brothers and many others during the '80s. Main guitars include a Fender Telecaster, a Gibson gut-string acoustic and a special 'Albert Lee' model built for him by Ernie Ball Music Man. Instruction videos: *Albert Lee* (Star Licks) and *Advanced Country Guitar* (REH). Included in *Guitar Player* magazine's 'Gallery Of The Greats' after being voted Best Country Player (1981-1985). One of the most influential country guitar players of all time.

Alvin LEE

Rock guitarist. Born in Nottingham, England on December 19, 1944. Formed Ten Years After (originally the Jaybirds) in the late '60s with Leo Lyons (bass), Chick Churchill (keyboards) and Ric Lee (drums). Played a rock-influenced R&B, propelled by Lee's speedy guitar style. Performed at the Woodstock Festival in 1968. Set a new trend by not releasing a single with their first album. Recordings on Decca and Chrysalis include *Ten Years After* (1967), *Undead* (1968), *Watt* (1970), *A Space In Time* (1972) and *Positive Vibrations* (1974). The band split up in 1974 and reformed in 1978 as Ten Years Later. Alvin Lee solo projects on Chrysalis and Sequel include *In Flight* (1974), *Pump Iron!* (1975), *Saguitar* (1976), *Rocket Fuel* (1978), *Ride On* (1979), *Free Fall* (1980), *RX-5* (1981), *Detroit Diesel* (1986) and *Zoom* (1992).

Geddy LEE

Rock bass player/singer. Born in Willowdale, Ontario on July 29, 1953. Son of Polish immigrants. Grew up in Toronto. Started playing bass at age 14 after trying various other instruments. Became influenced by rock bass players such as Jack Bruce, John Entwistle and Chris Squire. Formed the band Rush with guitarist Alex Lifeson in 1968 (see Alex LIFESON for more information about Rush). By the late '70s Rush had become one of the most popular rock bands and Geddy had earned a considerable reputation as an exciting, solid and dextrous rock bass player. Debut album on Moon Records: *Rush* (1974). On Mercury: *Caress Of Steel* (1975), *Fly By Night* (1975), *2112* (1976), *Exit...Stage Left* (1976), *A Farewell To Kings* (1977), *Hemispheres* (1978), *Permanent Waves* (1980), *Moving Pictures* (1981), *Signals* (1982). On Vertigo: *Grace Under Pressure* (1984), *Power Windows* (1985), *Hold Your Fire* (1987). On Atlantic: *Presto* (1989) and *Roll The Bones* (1991).

Adrian LEGG

UK acoustic virtuoso. Born in Hackney, London on May 16, 1948. Played oboe for the local school orchestra. Later took up the guitar at around age 18. Influences included folk music and blues-influenced guitar players such as Lonnie Mack. Worked with Irish and country bands, before performing solo. Also involved in instrument research and development from the mid-'70s onwards. Albums on Making Waves and Relativity/Roadrunner labels include *Technopicker* (1983), *Fretmelt* (1984), *Lost For Words* (1986), *Guitars And Other Cathedrals* (1990), *Guitar For Mortals* (1991) and *Mrs Crowe's Blue Waltz* (1992). Hot Licks instructional videos: *Beyond Acoustic Guitar* and *Finger Picking & Open Tunings*. Author of books including *Customising Your Electric Guitar* and *The All Round Gigster*. An impressive, versatile and original player.

David LEISNER

Classical guitarist. Born in Los Angeles on December 22, 1953. Started learning folk guitar and switched to flamenco. Studied at Wesleyan University in Connecticut and also with John Duarte in England. Won a silver medal at the Toronto Guitar Competition. Began teaching at Amherst College in Massachusetts and has since specialised in unusual and rare works for the guitar, including some by 19th-Century Hungarian virtuoso Johann Kaspar Mertz and early guitarists Giulio Regondi and Simon Moliter. Recordings include *Works Of Johann Kaspar Mertz and Mauro Giuliani* (Titanic Records).

LEMMY

Rock bass player and vocalist. Born Ian Kilminster in Stoke, England on December 24, 1945. Son of a vicar. Played in local bands before moving to London and working as a roadie for Jimi Hendrix. Joined Hawkwind in 1971, playing bass on United Artists albums such as *Doremi Fasolatido* (1972) and *Space Ritual* (1973). Sacked from the band in 1975 after being busted for drugs. Formed heavy metal band Motörhead. First stable line-up included 'Fast' Eddie Clarke (guitar) and Phil 'Philthy Animal' Taylor (drums). Music was uncompromisingly heavy (and loud), appealing to both heavy metal and punk audiences. Recorded sledgehammer metal albums on Chiswick and Bronze: *Motörhead* (1977), *Overkill* (1979), *Ace Of Spades* (1980) and *No*

Sleep Till Hammersmith (1981). Clarke left in 1982 and was replaced by Brian Robertson (ex-Thin Lizzy), who was in turn replaced by Michael 'Wurzel' Burston and Philip Campbell, to make the band a four-piece. Later recordings

Lemmy

on Roadrunner and Epic include *Rock'N'Roll* (1987), *No Sleep At All* (1988), *1916* (1991) and *The Best Of...* (1992).

John LENNON

Legendary UK singer/songwriter and rhythm guitarist. Born in Liverpool, England on October 9, 1940. Became influenced by Buddy Holly, the Everly Brothers and Chuck Berry. Formed the Quarrymen while still at school. They became The Moondogs, the Silver Beatles and eventually the Beatles (see Paul McCARTNEY for more information on the Beatles). They split up in 1970, after a number of disagreements. Lennon had already made several recordings with his wife Yoko Ono (as the Plastic Ono Band) on the Beatles' Apple label by then. *Imagine* (1971) topped the US and UK charts, the title track being one of his most memorable songs. Other albums on Apple and Geffen include *Walls And Bridges* (1974), *Shaved Fish* (1975) and *Double Fantasy* (1980). Also author of a number of poems, stories and cartoons. Shot dead by crazed fan Mark

Chapman outside New York's Dakota Building on December 8, 1980. Thus ended the rumours of a possible Beatles reunion. One of the most influential songwriters of all time.

Joaquin LIEVANO

Fusion/rock player. Born in Bogota, Colombia in 1953. His family moved to New York while he was young. Picked up guitar at age 12. Influences included the Beatles, Cream, Jimi Hendrix and John McLaughlin. Played in several bands before working with Jean-Luc Ponty, Tom Coster, Angela Bofill and Narada Michael Walden. Can be heard on the Jean-Luc Ponty recordings *Cosmic Messenger* (1978), *Taste For Passion* (1979), *Jean-Luc Ponty Live* (1979) and *Civilised Evil* (1980). With Tom Coster: *T.C.* (1982) on Fantasy. Later worked on solo projects and formed new age band Zazen with bassist Andy West (ex-Dixie Dregs) and others.

Alex LIFESON

Canadian rock guitarist. Born in Fernie, British Columbia on August 27, 1953. Grew up in Toronto. Picked up the guitar at age 12. Mainly self-taught, although he did study some classical guitar later. Early influences included Jimi Hendrix, Eric Clapton and Jimmy Page. Formed the band Rush with bassist Geddy Lee and drummer John Rutsey in 1968. The band spent six years gigging in bars and small venues in the Toronto area, before recording their first album *Rush* (1974) for Moon Records. Rutsey left just before their first US tour that year and was replaced on drums by Neil Peart. Lifeson had his own unique melodic heavy-rock style by then. The new power-trio achieved considerable success as they developed their own special blend of rock using bass pedals, synthesizers and extra percussion instruments, in addition to their intricate guitar/bass/drums line-up. One of the most influential rock bands of the '70s and '80s (see Geddy LEE for Rush discography).

David LINDLEY

Steel guitar virtuoso. Born in San Marino, California in 1944. Took up acoustic guitar and banjo at age 14. Won the Topanga Canyon banjo competition for five consecutive years. Became inspired by steel guitarist Freddie Roulette. Formed an eclectic band called Kaleidoscope and experimented with Eastern music in the late '60s. They recorded several unusual albums for Epic, including *Side Trips* (1967) and *Incredible Kaleidoscope* (1969). Later worked with Ry Cooder, Linda Ronstadt, Little Feat, America, Warren Zevon, Jackson Browne, Joe Walsh and many others. Solo albums on Asylum include *El-Rayo-X* (1981), *Win This Record* (1982) and *Mr.Dave* (1985). Well-known for his outstanding lap steel and session playing.

Nils LOFGREN

Rock guitarist and singer/songwriter. Born in Chicago, Illinois on June 21, 1951. Grew up in Washington DC. Started playing accordion and switched to guitar after hearing the Beatles and the Rolling Stones. Became heavily influenced by Jimi Hendrix. Recorded with a band called The Dolphin at age 16 and soon formed another band called Grin. Earned a reputation as an exciting and acrobatic performer and worked with Neil Young, Stephen Stills and Bruce Springsteen. Recorded several albums on A&M including *Nils Lofgren* (1975), *Cry Tough* (1976), *Night After Night* (1977) and *Nils* (1979). Later albums on MCA, Columbia and Rykodisc include: *Wonderland* (1983), *Flip* (1985), *Silver Lining* (1990) and *Crooked Line* (1992). Plays a raw blues-influenced rock. Hot Licks instructional video: *Electric & Acoustic Rock Guitar* (1992).

Mundell LOWE

Jazz guitarist. Born in Laurel, Mississippi on April 21, 1922. Played the guitar from an early age. Worked with a New Orleans country band at age 14. Moved to Nashville in 1939. Joined the Pee Wee King Band and appeared on the Grand Ole Opry radio show. Worked with Ray McKinley, Mary Lou Williams, Red Norvo and Ellis Larkins during the late '40s. Joined NBC staff in 1950. Wrote many TV themes for ABC, including 'Hawaii Five-0' and 'I Dream Of Jeannie' in the '60s. Recordings on Riverside, Camden, Famous Door and Pausa include *Mundell Lowe Quartet* (1955), *The Mundell Lowe Trio* (1956), *TV Themes* (1959), *California Guitar* (1974) and *Transit West* (1983).

Steve LUKATHER

Rock player and studio ace. Born in Los Angeles on October 21, 1957. Given an acoustic guitar on his seventh birthday. Started playing electric at age 10. Early influences included Jimi Hendrix and Eric Clapton. Took lessons with Jimmy Wyble while at high school. Played in a number of bands before becoming a session player. His tasteful rock soloing and versatility brought live and studio work with Hall & Oates, Diana Ross, Lee Ritenour, Joni Mitchell, Michael Jackson, Barbra Streisand and many others. Formed the band Toto with other session musicians Jeff Porcaro (drums), Steve Porcaro (keyboards), David Paich (keyboards), David Hungate (bass) and Bobby Kimball (vocals). Had big hits with 'Rosanna' and 'Africa' in 1982. Albums on Columbia/CBS include *Toto* (1979), *Hydra* (1980), *Turn Back* (1981), *Toto IV* (1982), *Farenheit* (1986), *The Seventh One* (1988) and compilation *Toto Past To Present* (1990). Solo album on Fish Kitten: *Lukather* (1991). Instruction video: *Steve Lukather* (Star Licks). Included in *Guitar Player* magazine's 'Gallery Of The Greats' after being voted Best Studio Guitarist (1985-1989).

George LYNCH

Heavy metal guitarist. Born in Spokane, Washington. Grew up in Los Angeles. Picked up the electric guitar at age 15. Influenced greatly by heavy rock bands of the '70s. Played in several local bands. Joined Dokken in the early '80s, with Don Dokken (vocals), Juan Croucier (bass, later replaced by Jeff Pilson) and Mick Brown (drums). Enjoyed considerable success as a live act. Released atmospheric hard-rock albums on Carrere and Elektra: *Breaking The Chains* (1982), *Tooth And Nail* (1984), *Under Lock And Key* (1986) and *Beast From The East* (1988). Split up in 1988 and Lynch formed Lynch Mob. Recordings on Elektra include *Wicked Sensation* (1990) and *Lynch Mob* (1992). A much-admired melodic soloist with an advanced fingertapping technique. Instruction video: *George Lynch* (REH).

Steve LYNCH

Heavy rock player. Born c. 1955. Grew up in Seattle, Washington. Started playing bass and switched to guitar at age 15. Early influences included Jimi Hendrix, Jeff Beck and Eddie Van Halen. Studied with Don Mock in Seattle and then later at the Guitar Institute of Technology in Hollywood. Developed an advanced two-handed tapping technique. Formed the band Autograph with Steve Plunkett (vocals, guitar), Steve Isham (keyboards), Randy Rand (bass) and Keni Richards (drums). Delivered a brand of melodic AOR with pop crossover appeal.

Recordings on RCA include *Sign In Please* (1984) and *That's The Stuff* (1985). Instruction video: *Two-Handed Guitarist* (REH).

Phil **LYNOTT**

Rock bass player, singer/songwriter. Born in Dublin, Ireland on August 20, 1951. Played

Phil Lynott

with Black Eagles, Orphanage and Skid Row during the '60s. Formed Thin Lizzy in 1969

with Eric Bell (guitar) and Brian Downey (drums). Breakthrough came with a reworking of traditional song 'Whiskey In The Jar', which reached the UK Top 10 in 1973. Bell left in 1974 and was replaced by Gary Moore, who was in turn replaced by guitar super-duo Scott Gorham and Brian Robertson, making a four-piece band. The combination of the double lead guitar sound and Lynott's distinctive vocal delivery clicked: they had a big hit with 'The Boys Are Back In Town' in 1976 and went on to become one of the most popular rock bands of the late '70s. Later guitar players included Gary Moore again and Snowy White. Accused of bad taste over hit single 'Killer On The Loose' (released during the search for the Yorkshire Ripper in 1980). Disbanded in 1984. Lynott died of a drugs overdose on January 4, 1986. Thin Lizzy albums on Decca and Vertigo include *Thin Lizzy* (1971), *Shades Of A Blue Orphanage* (1972), *Night Life* (1974), *Jailbreak* (1976), *Johnny The Fox* (1977), *Live And Dangerous* (1978), *Black Rose* (1979), *Chinatown* (1980), *Renegade* (1981) and *Thunder And Lightning* (1983). Lynott solo albums include *Solo In Soho* (1980) and *The Phil Lynott Solo Album* (1982).

M

Tony **MacALPINE**

Rock guitarist. Also classically-trained pianist. Born in Springfield, Massachusetts on August 29, 1960. Started studying piano at age 5 and took up guitar during his late teens. Studied music at Hartt College in Bloomfield. Developed an advanced classically-influenced rock technique. Sent a tape in to Mike Varney, who was impressed and included the guitarist in his 'Spotlight' column (Aug 1985) in *Guitar Player* magazine. Debut Shrapnel/Roadrunner recording *Edge Of Insanity* (1986) featured Billy Sheehan (bass) and Steve Smith (drums). Later albums on Vertigo include *Maximum Security* (1987) and more mainstream *Eyes Of The World* (1990). Also formed Project Driver with Rudy Sarzo (bass), Robert Rock (vocals) and Tommy Aldridge (drums). Instruction video: *Guitar Lessons* (DCI).

Mario **MACCAFERRI**

Italian guitarist/luthier. Born in Bologna, Italy on May 20, 1900. Started learning to play and make guitars at age 11 with guitarist/luthier Luigi Mozzani. Later studied classical guitar at the Academy in Siena (received highest honours there in 1926). One of the first classical players to use a thumbpick. Set up a contract with Selmer to market his cutaway guitars in the early '30s (one famous client was Django Reinhardt). Also made 9-string 'harp-guitars' with bass strings off the fretboard. Later set up his own company Mastro Industries in New York in the late '30s (later based in Louisville, Kentucky). Also constructed violins and was working on a line of new plastic instruments at the time of his death in Stamford, Connecticut on April 16, 1993.

Lonnie MACK

Blues-rock player and singer/songwriter. Born in Indiana, 1941. Started learning guitar at 5. Played country music in bars as a teenager. Became influenced by Scotty Moore and other rock'n'roll guitar players. Had a hit with an instrumental version of Chuck Berry's 'Memphis' (Fraternity) in 1963. Its original sound featured his electric guitar put through a Leslie organ cabinet. One of the first players to fuse blues and country music into a rock format. Worked with James Brown, Freddie King and the Doors. His fiery playing influenced many younger guitarists such as Mike Bloomfield, Eric Clapton and Stevie Ray Vaughan. Dropped out of the music business for a while in the early '70s to drive a truck and operate an outdoor music park. Recordings on Elektra, Capitol and Alligator include *The Wham Of That Memphis Man* (1963), *Glad I'm In The Band* (1969), *Whoever's Right* (1970), *The Hills Of Indiana* (1971), *Home At Last* (1977), *Lonnie Mack With Prismo* (1978), *Strike Like Lightning* (1985) and *Second Sight* (1986).

Yngwie MALMSTEEN

Heavy metal virtuoso. Born in Sweden on June 30, 1963. Given an acoustic guitar on his fifth birthday but wasn't interested until he saw Jimi Hendrix on the TV a couple of years later. Also became influenced by Ritchie Blackmore and classical composers such as Bach and Paganini. Played in local teenage bands, doing cover versions of Deep Purple and Jimi Hendrix songs. Practiced up to nine hours a day and also took lessons on classical guitar. Played in a group called Powerhouse for a couple of years before forming his own band Rising Force in 1978. Appeared in Mike Varney's Spotlight column in *Guitar Player* (Feb 1983). Moved to the States to join heavy metal band Steeler in Hollywood. They recorded the album *Steeler* (1983) on Shrapnel, before Malmsteen left to join Alcatrazz with singer Graham Bonnett and others. The band became a successful live act and released *No Parole From Rock And Roll* and *Live Sentence* (both 1984), before Malmsteen quit to work on his own classically orientated heavy metal projects with Rising Force. Albums on Polydor include *Rising Force* (1984), *Marching Out* (1985) *Trilogy* (1986), *Odyssey* (1988), *Eclipse* (1990) and *Fire & Ice* (1992). Instructional video: *Yngwie Malmsteen* (REH). His melodic solos are improvised and usually include ultra-fast scales/arpeggios, neo-classical passages and heavy use of the tremolo arm. An outsanding rock guitarist whose formidable soloing influenced thousands of other players.

Yngwie Malmsteen

Mark Weiss/Idols

Harvey MANDEL

Blues player. Born in Detroit on March 11, 1945. Began learning guitar as a teenager. Early influences included the Ventures, Buddy Guy, Eric Clapton and B.B.King. Started playing in black ghetto clubs in Chicago. Played with Charlie Musselwhite's Southside Band in the mid-'60s. Worked with Canned Heat and John Mayall during the late-'60s and early-'70s. Solo albums include *Christo Redentor* (1968), *Righteous* (1969), *Games Guitars Play* (1970), *Electric Progress* (1971), *The Snake* (1972), *Shangrenade* (1973), *Feel The Sound Of Harvey Mandel* (1974) and *The Best Of Harvey Mandel* (1975). Featured on the Rolling Stones album *Black & Blue* (1975). His fluent and melodic playing can also be heard on work by Ron Carter, Jimmy Witherspoon and Dewey Terry.

Phil **MANZANERA**

UK rock guitarist. Born Philip Targett-Adams in London on January 31, 1951. Formed rock group Quiet Sun during the early '70s. Worked as a roadie for Bryan Ferry's group Roxy Music and eventually joined them as a guitarist. They became one of the most original and successful pop bands of the '70s. Albums on Island (later Virgin) include *Roxy Music* (1972), *For Your Pleasure* (1973), *Stranded* (1973), *Country Life* (1974), *Siren* (1975), *Manifesto* (1979), *Flesh & Blood* (1980) and *Avalon* (1982). Also re-formed Quiet Sun for *Mainstream* (1975) and joined Brian Eno (ex-Roxy synthesist) and others for *801 Live* (1975). Collaborated with Andy Mackay (Roxy saxophonist) and singer James Wraith on *The Explorers* (1984). Solo albums on Island (later Virgin) include *Diamond Head* (1974), *Listen Now* (1977), *Primitive Guitars* (1982) and *The Golden Scarab* (1992). Also worked extensively on TV/film music and as a session guitarist.

Joe **MAPHIS**

Country flatpicking pioneer. Born in Suffolk, Virginia on May 12, 1921. Began playing guitar at age 11. Also learned piano. Early influences included Maybelle Carter and Riley Puckett. Played in his father's dance band the Railsplitters. Moved south to Fredericksburg, Virginia to play with Blackie Skiles and the Lazy K Ranch Boys (often featured on WFVA Radio). Later worked with Merle Travis, Ricky Nelson, Johnny Bond and Grandpa Jones. Often performed with wife Rosie Lee (singer) as a duo. An impressive picker who influenced Larry Collins, Barbara Mandrell and many others. Recordings on various labels include *Fire On The Strings* (1957), *Hootenanny Star* (1964), *The Amazing Joe Maphis* (1965), *King Of The Strings* (1965), *Gospel Guitar* (1970), *Dim Lights, Thick Smoke* (1975), *Grass'N'Jazz* (1977), *Boogie Woogie Flat Top Guitar Pickin' Man* (1978) and *Flat Picking Spectacular* (1982). Died in Nashville, Tennessee on June 27, 1986.

Bob **MARLEY**

Reggae legend. Singer/songwriter and guitarist. Born Nesta Robert Marley in St. Anne's, Jamaica on February 6, 1945. Son of English serviceman and a local woman. Grew up in Trenchtown, a Kingston slum. Early influences included local blue beat and ska musicians, as well as Fats Domino, Elvis Presley and The Drifters. Cut his first single 'One More Cup Of Coffee' in 1961 with Leslie Kong. Formed The Wailers with Bunny Livingstone and Peter Tosh. Had unprecedented success for reggae band. Notable songs include 'Jamming', 'No Woman No Cry' and 'I Shot The Sheriff' (later a hit for Eric Clapton). Awarded a Third World Peace Medal in 1978 for his intervention in West Indian politics. Died of cancer in Miami, Florida on May 11, 1981. The most influential reggae artist of all time: popularised Rastafarianism and introduced the rock audience to reggae music. Albums on Trojan and Island include *African Herbsman* (1973), *Natty Dread* (1975), *Rastaman Vibration* (1976) and compilation *Legend* (1984).

Johnny **MARR**

Rock guitar player. Born on October 31, 1963. Grew up in Manchester, England and started

The Smiths (Johnny Marr far right)

Peter Ashworth/Idols

playing guitar seriously at around age 13. Diverse influences included Motown songwriters, Pentangle, Nils Lofgren and many others. Formed British indie band The Smiths with Steven Morrissey (vocals), Andy Rourke (bass) and Mike Joyce (drums) in 1982. Marr's unique and uncluttered rhythm work became an essential part of the band's sound (along with Morrissey's enigmatic lyrics/vocals). UK hits with 'Heaven Knows I'm Miserable Now' (1984), 'Panic' (1986) and 'Sheila Take A Bow' (1987). Albums on Rough Trade include *The Smiths* (1984), *Hatful Of Hollow* (1984), *Meat Is Murder* (1985), *The Queen Is Dead* (1986) and compilation *The World Won't Listen*

(1987). Left the band in 1987 and has since worked with Talking Heads, Paul McCartney, Brian Ferry, the Pretenders and on his own Electronic project.

Barry **MARTIN**

UK rock guitarist. Born in Southend on November 25, 1953. Started playing the guitar at age 20. Influenced largely by rock with elements of blues and country music. Brief stint with the Kursaal Flyers in 1977. Spent some time working in A&R, record distribution and as a radio DJ. Formed raunchy blues-rock band the Hamsters in 1988 with Dave Bronze (bass) and Alan Parish (drums). Used the pseudonym 'Snail's-Pace Slim'. Toured extensively and earned a reputation as one of the best live acts in the UK. Albums on On The Beach Records and Rocking Rodent Recordings include Hendrix tribute *Electric Hamsterland* (1990), *Hamster Jam* (1991) and *The Hamsters* (1993). Video: *Burnin' Vermin* (1991). All are distributed by Pinnacle in the UK. Regular contributions to *Guitarist* magazine.

Pat **MARTINO**

Jazz and fusion guitarist. Born Pat Azzara in Philadelphia, Pennsylvania on August 25, 1944. Started playing the guitar at an early age. Influences included Eddie Lang, Django Reinhardt and Wes Montgomery. Played in R&B bands with Willis Jackson and Brother Jack McDuff during the early '60s and worked in the studio, before eventually forming his own band in 1967. News of his amazing technique and complex bebop improvisations soon spread around the jazz world. Winner of a Jazz Critics' Poll in *Downbeat* (1969). Recorded several critically-acclaimed albums for Prestige, Cobblestone and Muse including *El Hombre* (1967), *The Visit* (1972), *Footprints* (1981) and *We'll Be Together Again* (1981). Suffered from an aneurism on the brain (dilation of blood vessel), and a period of inactivity followed during the early '80s. Later involved in work with Apple Macintosh computers and Synclavier synthesizers. A number of his solos have been analysed in Steve Khan's book *Pat Martino: The Early Years* (CCP Belwin 1991). A gifted and exciting player.

John **MARTYN**

Singer/songwriter and guitar player. Born in Glasgow, Scotland in 1948. Performed on the UK folk club circuit as a teenager during the '60s. Developed an eclectic low-key style that won admirers from folk, rock, jazz and pop circles. Recordings on Island have featured collaborations with Phil Collins, Eric Clapton, Robert Palmer, Stevie Winwood, Paul Kossoff, Ralph McTell and others: *London Conversation* (1967), *The Tumbler* (1968), *Stormbringer* (1970), *Bless The Weather* (1971), *Solid Air* (1973) featuring classic song 'May You Never', *Sunday's Child* (1975), *One World* (1977), *Grace & Danger* (1980), *Sapphire* (1984), *Piece By Piece* (1986), *Foundations* (1988), *The Apprentice* (1990), *Cooltide* (1991), *Couldn't Love You More* (1992) and *No Little Boy* (1993).

Hank **MARVIN**

Legendary pop guitarist. Born Brian Rankin in Newcastle, England on October 28, 1941. Started playing the instrument at a young age. Formed a guitar duo with Bruce Welch (born Bruce Cripps, 1941) while still in his teens. They travelled to London in 1958 and played at the 2I's coffee bar in Soho. Met singer Cliff Richard and formed the Shadows (originally the Drifters). Original line-up was Hank Marvin (guitar), Bruce Welch (guitar), Jet Harris (bass) and Tony Meehan (drums). Secured a deal with EMI in 1959 and released two unsuccessful

Hank Marvin

singles, before they recorded the guitar-driven instrumental 'Apache' in 1960. It went to the top of the UK charts and stayed there for six weeks. Further hits included 'Kon Tiki' (1961), 'Wonderful Land' (1962) and 'Foot Tapper' (1963). All featured simple, hummable melodies played by a twangy-tremolo guitar. It became the Hank Marvin trademark and influenced many younger players. Later had a hit with the more mellow 'Don't Cry For Me, Argentina' (1979). The band also continued to back Cliff Richard in the studio and on the stage for many years, although there were several personnel changes. Compilation albums on EMI and Polydor include *The Shadows: 20 Golden Greats* (1977), *String Of Hits* (1979), *Moonlight Shadows* (1986). Later Marvin recording on Parlophone: *Into The Light* (1992).

Brian MAY

UK rock guitarist. Born in Hampton, Middlesex on July 19, 1947. Grew up in nearby Feltham.

James Cumpsty/ Music Maker

Brian May

Started learning ukulele-banjo at age 8 and was strumming a guitar within a year. Early influences included Lonnie Donegan, Buddy

Holly, the Shadows, Eric Clapton, B.B.King, Jeff Beck and Jimi Hendrix. Made his own guitar at age 17. Studied physics at Imperial College (London University). Formed the group Smile with vocalist Tim Staffell and drummer Roger Taylor. When Smile broke up in 1970, May and Taylor formed a new band Queen with Freddie Mercury (Staffell's flatmate and singer with Wreckage). Bass player John Deacon was later recruited through an advert in the music press. The band secured a record deal with EMI and released their debut album *Queen* (1973). It was not an initial success, although it later went gold. The next albums *Queen II* and *Sheer Heart Attack* (both 1974) were considerably more successful, largely because of the singles 'Seven Seas Of Rhye', 'Killer Queen' and 'Now I'm Here'. The big break came with *A Night At The Opera* (1975), boasting the epic hit 'Bohemian Rhapsody'. Mercury's extravagance and May's unique guitar sound (beautiful tone and rich multi-tracked lines), supplemented by quasi-operatic vocal arrangements and an innovative video production, proved to be extremely successful. It topped the UK singles chart for 9 weeks and was a major hit in the US. Recorded many other successful albums including *A Day At The Races* (1977), *Jazz* (1978), *The Game* (1980), *The Works* (1984), *A Kind Of Magic* (1986), *The Miracle* (1989) and *Innuendo* (1991), before Mercury died of AIDS-related illness in 1991. May also recorded *Star Fleet* (1984) and *Back To The Light* (1992). He used the same home-made guitar for all of the Queen recordings and concerts and employed an English sixpence piece (old currency) as a pick. A highly original and influential rock player.

John MAYALL

UK blues bandleader, writer and producer. Born in Macclesfield, Cheshire on November 29, 1933. Grew up in Manchester. Became interested in blues at age 13. Formed his first group Powerhouse Four while at college in 1955. Moved to London in 1963 and formed the first Bluesbreakers band with Bernie Watson (guitar), John McVie (bass) and Peter Ward (drums). There were many personnel changes over the years. Outstanding recordings on Decca include *Bluesbreakers With Eric Clapton* (1965) with Clapton on guitar and *A Hard Road* (1966) with Peter Green. The most influential British blues band of the '60s. Other albums on various labels include *Crusade* (1967), *Blues Alone* (1967), *Bare Wires* (1968),

Looking Back (1969), *Empty Rooms* (1970), *USA Union* (1970), *Memories* (1971), *Jazz Blues Fusion* (1972), *Movin' On* (1973), *The Latest Edition* (1975), *Notice To Appear* (1976), *Lots Of People* (1977), *Blues Roots* (1978), *Bottom Line* (1979), *Road Show Blues* (1981), *Last Edition* (1983), *Chicago Line* (1988), *A Sense Of Place* (1990) and *Wake Up Call* (1993).

Paul McCartney

Paul **McCARTNEY**

Legendary singer/songwriter and bassist. Also producer and multi-instrumentalist. Born James Paul McCartney in Liverpool, England on June 18, 1942. Met John Lennon at school. Joined Lennon's band the Quarrymen c.1957. They bacame the Moondogs, the Silver Beatles and eventually the Beatles. Influences included the Everly Brothers, Buddy Holly, Chuck Berry and Elvis Presley. By 1960 the line-up also included George Harrison (guitar), Stuart Sutcliffe (bass guitar) and Pete Best (drums). Gained considerable experience by gigging regularly in Liverpool and Hamburg. Developed their own style, the 'Liverpool Sound'. Sutcliffe left in 1961, before manager Brian Epstein secured a deal with EMI's George Martin. Pete Best was replaced by Ringo Starr on drums. Debut single 'Love Me Do' (1962) caused a stir,

but the big break came with best-sellers 'Please Please Me', 'She Loves You' and 'I Wanna Hold Your Hand' (all 1963). They brought a fresh sense of melody, harmony and rhythm to the charts. Beatlemania swept the UK in 1963 and the rest of the world followed suit a year later. More success followed with classics such as 'Can't Buy Me Love' (1964), 'Yesterday' (1965), 'All You Need Is Love' (1967) and 'Hey Jude' (1968). Albums on Parlophone and Apple include *A Hard Day's Night* (1964), *Rubber Soul* (1965), *Revolver* (1966), *Sergeant Pepper's Lonely Hearts Club Band* (1967), *Abbey Road* (1969) and *Let It Be* (1970). Also made a number of films. They were a self-contained unit and composed all of their own material (such bands later became the norm, rather than the exception). The most influential pop group ever. Split up in 1970, after a number of disagreements. McCartney and wife Linda had already recorded *McCartney* on the Beatles Apple label earlier that year. They followed it up with *Ram* (1971). Formed Wings with Linda (keyboards), Denny Laine (guitar) and Denny Seiwell (drums). Albums include *Red Rose Speedway* (1972), the critically acclaimed *Band On The Run* (1973) and *Wings At The Speed Of Sound* (1976). McCartney was presented with a special rhodium disc in 1979 for selling more than 200 million albums. Later solo recordings on Fame and Parlophone include *McCartney II* (1980), soundtrack for his film *Give My Regards To Broad Street* (1984), Russian release *Choba B CCCP* (1989), *Flowers In The Dirt* (1989) and *Off The Ground* (1993). Also duets with Michael Jackson and Stevie Wonder. Classical collaboration with Carl Davis: *Liverpool Oratorio* (featuring singer Kiri Te Kanawa). One of the most influential singer/songwriters of all time. Books include *Paul McCartney: The Biography* by Chet Flippo.

Dick **McDONOUGH**

Jazz guitarist. Born in 1904. Grew up in New York City. Started playing the banjo before taking up the guitar at age 21. Developed an impressive and versatile technique which earned him considerable respect in jazz circles. Worked extensively in radio and recording studios. Formed an impressive guitar duo with Carl Kress. Also performed with Red Nichols, Benny Goodman and the Dorsey Brothers. Later suffered from a drinking problem and collapsed at NBC Studios in New York. Died of a ruptured ulcer on May 25, 1938. Recordings include *Pioneers Of Jazz Guitar* (Yazoo) and *Dick McDonough And Carl Kress* (Jazz Archives).

John McLAUGHLIN

UK fusion pioneer. Born near Doncaster, England on January 4, 1942. Started learning the piano at age 9 and switched to the guitar by the time he was 12. Early influences included Django Reinhardt, Tal Farlow, Jim Hall and Barney Kessel. Also became inspired by classical composers such as Debussy and Bartok. Worked with the Graham Bond Organisation and Brian Auger during the mid-'60s before recording his first album *Extrapolation* (1969) for Polydor. By then McLaughlin's formidable technique and highly expressive playing had

John McLaughlin

Fin Costello/Redferns

earned him a considerable reputation as a virtuoso guitarist, leading to work with drummer Tony Williams and appearances on the Miles Davis albums *In A Silent Way* (1969) and *Bitches Brew* (1969). Recorded two more solo albums *Devotion* (1970) and the acoustic *My Goals Beyond* (1971). Formed the Mahavishnu Orchestra (name influenced by guru Sri Chimnoy) which featured McLaughlin on electric guitar with Jerry Goodman (violin), Rick Laird (bass), Jan Hammer (keyboards), and Billy Cobham (drums). Signed to CBS and received public and critical acclaim with *The Inner Mounting Flame* (1972), *Birds Of Fire* (1973), and the live *Between Nothingness And Eternity* (1973). The band's dazzling virtuosity (high-energy solos from McLaughlin, Hammer and Goodman) and emotional impact also

broke through to rock audiences. However, they split up and McLaughlin recorded *Love, Devotion, Surrender* (1973) with Carlos Santana. He then re-formed the Mahavishnu Orchestra with various line-ups for *Apocalypse* (1974), *Visions Of The Emeralds Beyond* (1975) and *Inner Worlds* (1976). These featured impressive musicians such as Jean-Luc Ponty (violin) and Narada Michael Walden (drums), as well as some extraordinary ring-modulated guitar solos. Joined the Eastern acoustic band Shakti with Indian musicians including L.Shankar (violin) and Zakir Hussain (tabla), playing a Gibson acoustic fitted with a scalloped neck and drone strings. They made recordings such as *Shakti With John McLaughlin* (1976) and *Natural Elements* (1977). Also recorded a solo album *Electric Guitarist* (1978) with top jazz musicians including Chick Corea, Stanley Clarke, Billy Cobham and Tony Williams. Formed the One Truth Band, to record *Electric Dreams* (1979), before teaming up with Al Di Meola and Paco de Lucía to make an acoustic guitar trio. They gave many outstanding performances and recorded highly acclaimed *Friday Night In San Francisco* (1981). Switched to Warner Brothers. Further solo albums followed: *Belo Horizonte* (1981) and *Music Spoken Here* (1982). Then two more Mahavishnu albums, with emphasis on guitar synthesis on *Mahavishnu* (1985) and electric guitar on *Adventures In Radioland* (1987) on Relativity. Later recordings on JMT and Verve include acoustic trio *Live At The Royal Festival Hall* (1990) and *Que Alegria* (1992). Also worked with pianist/keyboardist Katia Labeque. McLaughlin is a highly respected and innovative guitarist who has inspired, and will continue to inspire, countless guitar players and other musicians worldwide. Included in *Guitar Player* magazine's 'Gallery Of The Greats' (1991) after winning the Jazz, Overall and Acoustic categories.

Blind Willie McTELL

Blues guitarist and singer. Born blind in Thompson, Georgia on May 5, 1901. Played the guitar from an early age. Developed a soft and poetic Piedmont blues style. Also played harmonica, accordion and violin. Performed at various locations in the South. Made a number of recordings from 1927, including 'Statesboro Blues' and and 'Georgia Rag'. Worked at a drive-in restaurant in Atlanta during the late '40s. Later became a preacher. Died in

Midgeville, Georgia on August 19, 1959.
Compilation albums include *Early Years*
(Charly), *Trying To Get Home* (Biograph),
Doing That Atlanta Strut (Yazoo) and *Library
Of Congress Recordings* (Melodeon).

Lydia **MENDOZA**

Tex-Mex singer/songwriter and guitarist. Born
in Houston, Texas on May 31, 1916. Started
playing guitar at age 12. Her earliest and
biggest influence was her mother, who was also
a musician. She sang 'corridos' (song-stories),
love songs and played with various bands and
orchestras. Reputedly the greatest Tex-Mex
artist in the genre, with an astounding voice.
Nicknamed 'The Lark Of The Border'.
Recordings include *La Gloria de Texas*
(Arhoolie), *Una Voz y una Guitarra* (Azteca),
50 Years With Lydia Mendoza (DLB) and
Lydia Mendoza: First Recordings 1928-38
(Folklyric).

Pat **METHENY**

Guitarist/composer. Born in Lee's Summit,
Missouri, on August 12, 1954. Started playing
guitar at around age 13. Early influences
included Wes Montgomery, Kenny Burrell, Jim
Hall and Jimmy Raney. Studied at the
University of Miami. Taught improvisation at
Berklee and joined Gary Burton's band at age
19. Stayed with Burton for three years before
embarking on solo career. Signed To ECM.
Debut album *Bright Size Life* (1976) featured
bass genius Jaco Pastorius and drummer Bob
Moses. The second album *Watercolours* (1977)
included keyboardist Lyle Mays and drummer
Danny Gottlieb. Formed the Pat Metheny
Group with Mays, Gottlieb and bass player
Mark Egan. The first two band albums *Pat
Metheny Group* (1978) and *American Garage*
(1980) were successful, both commercially and
artistically. Metheny had forged a new earthy
and mellow jazz sound, incorporating elements
from bebop, folk and rock. Egan left the band
and was replaced by Steve Rodby in 1981.
Other Metheny Group albums on ECM and
Geffen include *Offramp* (1982), double live
album *Travels* (1983), *First Circle* (1984), *Still
Life Talking* (1987), *Letter From Home* (1989)
and another live recording *The Road To You*
(1993). With Lyle Mays: *As Falls Wichita, So
Falls Wichita Falls* (1981). With bassist Dave
Holland and drummer Roy Haynes: *Question
And Answer* (1990). Also recorded a more
radical and experimental project with Ornette

Pat Metheny

Coleman: *Song X* (1986). Solo albums on ECM
and Geffen include *New Chautauqua* (1979)
and *Secret Story* (1992). Used many guitars,
including a Gibson ES-175, the Coral Electric
Sitar, various Ovation acoustics and a guitar-
controlled Synclavier synthesizer. Metheny is an
unusually gifted and innovative
guitarist/composer, well known for his unique
sound and complex jazz phrasing. Included in
Guitar Player magazine's 'Gallery Of The
Greats' after being voted Best Jazz Guitarist
(1982-1986).

Vladimir **MIKULKA**

Czechoslovakian classical virtuoso. Born in
Prague on December 11, 1950. Started playing
guitar at age 13. Studied at the State
Conservatory in Prague two years later. Won
the International Competition for Guitar in
Paris in 1969. Later conducted numerous
International Master Classes and performed at
International Music Festivals in Paris, Rome
and Helsinki. Made several outstanding
recordings on Supraphon and BIS including
Compositions By J.S.Bach (1982), a six-
movement work by Stepan Rak *The Prince's
Toys* (1986) and *Iberoamerican Guitar Music*
(1987).

Marcus **MILLER**

Bass session ace. Born in Brooklyn, New York on June 14, 1959. Started learning clarinet at age 10 and picked up bass by the time he was 13. Inspired by Robert Bell, Stanley Clarke, Alphonso Johnson and Jaco Pastorius. Started working professionally in New York clubs after school. Hired by saxophonist Bobbi Humphrey in 1977 and soon had a reputation as an outstanding bass player. Worked with David Sanborn on *Hideaway* (1980), *Voyeur* (1981) and *As We Speak* (1982). With Miles Davis on *We Want Miles* (1982) and *Tutu* (1986). Also with Lenny White, Aretha Franklin, Elton John, Luther Vandross, Donald Fagen, Spyrogyra and Earl Klugh. Major exponent of thumb-style funk bass guitar. Solo albums on Warner Brothers include *Suddenly* (1983), *Marcus Miller* (1984) and *Jamaica Boys* (1987). On Dreyfus: *The Sun Don't Lie* (1993).

Steve Miller

Steve **MILLER**

Blues-rock player and songwriter. Born in Milwaukee, Wisconsin on Nov 5, 1943. Grew up in Texas. Started learning guitar at an early age with Les Paul and Mary Ford. Took lessons in lead guitar with T-Bone Walker and was playing with Jimmy Reed before he was 20. Formed his own band the Steve Miller Band in 1966 with Boz Scaggs (guitar, an old school mate), Lonnie Turner (bass), Jim Peterman

(keyboards) and Tim Davis (drums). There have been several variations in the line-up since then. Albums on Capitol include *Children Of The Future* (1968), *Grave New World* (1969), *Your Saving Grace* (1969), *Number Five* (1970), *Recall The Beginner* (1972), *The Joker* (1973), *Fly Like An Eagle* (1976), *Book Of Dreams* (1977), *Abracadabra* (1982), *Italian X-Rays* (1984) and *Living In The 20th Century* (1986). On Sailor: *Wide River* (1993).

June **MILLINGTON**

Rock guitarist and singer. Born in Manilla, Phillippines in 1949. Moved to California in 1961. Studied music at the University of California. Formed the band Fanny (originally called Wild Honey) with sister Jean Millington (bass), Nickey Barclay (keyboards) and Alice de Buhr (drums) in 1969. They were the first successful all-female rock band. Albums on Reprise include *Fanny* (1970), *Charity Ball* (1971), *Fanny Hill* (1972) and *Mother's Pride* (1973). Also worked with Barbra Streisand in 1970. Left the band in 1973 and reunited later with her sister Jean to record duo album *Ladies On The Stage* (1978) on United Artists. Has since worked as a producer and founded Fabulous Records.

John **MILLS**

UK classical player. Born in Kingston-Upon-Thames, Surrey on September 13, 1947. Started playing guitar at age 9. Studied at the Royal College of Music in London (1966-69) and took part in Master Classes given by Segovia in Spain (1968). Later gave many recitals and master classes worldwide. Appeared several times on radio and television in the UK during the '70s. Author of *The John Mills Guitar Tutor* (Musical New Services). Recordings include *20th Century Guitar Music* (Guitar) and *Five Centuries Of Classical Guitar* (Discource).

Joni **MITCHELL**

Singer/songwriter and guitarist. Also pianist and painter. Born Roberta Joan Anderson in McLeod, Alberta, Canada on November 7, 1943. Studied art at the Alberta College of Art in Calgary. Became interested in folk music and started learning guitar from a Pete Seeger instruction record. Moved to Toronto in 1964; started writing folk songs and playing local coffee bars. Developed a frank lyric style that

Joni Mitchell

with Howard Roberts and others. Later director
and producer for REH instructional videos
(artists as diverse as Joe Pass, Robben Ford,
Yngwie Malmsteen, Steve Morse, Shawn Lane,
Joe Diorio and Jerry Donahue). Books on REH
and Musicians Institute Publications: *Artful
Arpeggios* (1977), *Hot Licks* (1979), *Ten*
(1983) and *Fusion Hot Lines* (1986). REH
instructional video: *The Blues - From Rock To
Jazz* (1989). Solo recordings on Wolf and DDD:
Mock I (1979) and *Speed Of Light* (1993). A
gifted player and highly respected teacher.

Wes **MONTGOMERY**

Legendary jazz guitarist. Born John Leslie
Montgomery in Indianapolis, Indiana on March
6, 1925. Started playing the guitar at age 19,
after hearing Charlie Christian records. Taught
himself and developed his own unique style.
Obtained an unusually mellow sound by

Wes Montgomery

was soon to gain considerable critical acclaim.
Married and divorced folk singer Chuck
Mitchell during 1965-66. Moved to New York
and made her first recordings, before eventually
settling in California. Later songs were more
eclectic. Albums on Reprise, Asylum and Geffen
include *Songs To A Seagull* (1968), *Clouds*
(1969), *Ladies Of The Canyon* (1970), *Blue*
(1971), *For The Roses* (1972), *Court And
Spark* (1974), *Miles Of Aisles* (1975), *Hissing
Of The Summer Lawns* (1975), *Hejira* (1976),
Don Juan's Reckless Daughter (1978), *Mingus*
(1979), *Shadows Of Light* (1980) with Pat
Metheny and Jaco Pastorius, *Wild Things Run
Fast* (1982), *Dog Eat Dog* (1985), *Chalk Mark
In A Rain Storm* (1988) and *Night Ride Home*
(1991). Her songs have also been covered by
Judy Collins, Gordon Lightfoot, Fairport
Convention and many others. Inducted into
Canada's Juno Hall Of Fame in 1981 by Prime
Minister Pierre Trudeau. One of the most
original and significant singer/songwriters to
emerge from the '60s.

Don **MOCK**

Fusion virtuoso, teacher, producer and director.
Born in Port Angeles, Washington in 1950.
Grew up in Seattle. Picked up the guitar at age
12. Influences included Jimi Hendrix, Eric
Clapton, George Benson, John McLaughlin and
Wes Montgomery. Played in local bands and
started teaching around 1972. Started the
Guitar Institute of Technology (GIT) in 1977

picking notes with his thumb instead of a
plectrum. Also added unison octaves and
chords to melodies. Toured with Lionel
Hampton in the late '40s, before performing
with his brothers Monk (bass) and Buddy
(vibes/piano) as the Montgomery Brothers.
Formed a trio with Melvin Rhyne (organ) and
Paul Parker (drums). Worked during the day
while playing Indianapolis clubs at night. Also
with the Wynton Kelly Trio and the John
Coltrane Sextet. Cannonball Adderley heard

Montgomery play and was so impressed he recommended that Riverside Records sign him up immediately. The result was some of the finest jazz recordings ever made, including *The Incredible Jazz Guitar Of Wes Montgomery* (1960), *So Much Guitar* (1961) and *Full House* (1962). Quickly became the most popular and frequently recorded jazz guitarist of the early-'60s. Later made more commercial recordings for Verve such as *Tequila* (1966). Received awards from many jazz magazines including *Downbeat*, *Billboard* and *Playboy*. Also a Grammy for best instrumental jazz performance in 1967. Died after a heart attack on June 15, 1968. One of the most influential guitarists of all time. Included in *Guitar Player* magazine's 'Gallery Of The Greats' (1986) for his lifetime achievement. Books include biography: *Wes Montgomery* by Adrian Ingram (Ashley Mark 1985).

Ronnie **MONTROSE**

Rock player. Born in 1947. Picked up guitar at age 17. Early influences included Jimi Hendrix and Eric Clapton. Formed the band Montrose in 1973, with Sammy Hagar (vocals), Bill Church (bass) and Denny Carmassi (drums). The impressive debut Warner Brothers rock album *Montrose* (1974) featured some raunchy guitar playing. The band underwent several personnel changes and two more albums were released: *Paper Money* (1974) and *Jump On It* (1976). Formed another band called Gamma and then went solo. Later recordings on Passport, Enigma, Road Runner and IRS include *Territory* (1986), *Mean* (1987), *Speed Of Sound* (1988), *The Diva Station* (1990) and *Mutatis Mutandis* (1991). Also worked with Van Morrison, Boz Scaggs, Herbie Hancock, Edgar Winter and Kathi MacDonald. Produced projects by Jeff Berlin, Heathen, Wrath and others.

Christy **MOORE**

Irish folk legend. Born Christopher Andrew Moore in Dublin, Ireland on May 7, 1945. Started with local groups. Played in folk clubs around Ireland and the UK during the '60s. Formed folk group Planxty in the early '70s. They recorded *Planxty* (1972), *Cold Blow And A Rainy Night* (1974), *After The Break* (1979), *The Woman I Loved So Well* (1980), *Timedance* (1981) and *Words And Music* (1982). Solo albums feature soulful (often political) songs: *Paddy On The Road* (1969), *Prosperous* (1971), *Whatever Tickles Your*

Fancy (1975), *Christy Moore* (1976), *The Iron Behind The Velvet* (1978), *Live In Dublin* (1978), *The Spirit Of Freedom* (1983), *The Time Has Come* (1983), *Ordinary Man* (1985), *Nice'N'Easy* (1985), *Voyage* (1989), *Unfinished Revolution* (1986), *Smoke And Strong Whiskey* (1991), compilation *The Christy Moore Collection* (1991) and *King Puck* (1993).

Gary **MOORE**

Rock guitarist. Also singer/songwriter. Born in Belfast, Northern Ireland on April 4, 1952. Started playing the guitar at age 11. Joined Skid

Gary Moore

Row at age 16 with Phil Lynott (guitar, vocals), Brendan Shields (bass) and Noel Bridgeman (drums). Lynott soon left to form Thin Lizzy. Skid Row continued for a while as a three-piece, recording CBS albums *Skid Row* (1970) and *Thirty Four Hours* (1971). Formed the Gary Moore Band and recorded *Grinding Stone* (1973). Joined Thin Lizzy in 1974 and played some guitar on Vertigo album *Night Life* (1974), before leaving after personality clashes (he was replaced by Scott Gorham and Brian Robertson). Joined Colosseum II in 1976 with Jon Hiseman and others for exciting fusion albums on Bronze and MCA including *Strange New Flesh* (1976) and *Electric Savage* (1977). Recorded solo album *Back On The Streets* (1978) before rejoining Thin Lizzy for *Black*

Rose (1979). Left the band halfway through a US tour and formed heavy metal band G-Force with Tony Newton (vocals), Willie Dee (bass) and Mark Nauseef (drums). They had limited success with *G-Force* (1980). Later went solo with albums on Ten and Virgin: *Corridors Of Power* (1982), *Victims Of The Future* (1984) and *Run For Cover* (1985). The latter featured the hit 'Out In The Fields', a powerful anti-war anthem recorded with Phil Lynott. Celtic influence prominent in *Wild Frontier* (1987) and *After The War* (1989). Then mainstream blues with *Still Got The Blues* (1990, also featuring Albert King) and *After Hours* (1992). Also worked with Andrew Lloyd Webber, Greg Lake, Gary Boyle and Rod Argent. His blues-influenced lead style combines fast hammer-on/pull-off passages with lyrical melodies. Highly respected as a rock and blues guitarist.

Oscar **MOORE**

Jazz guitarist. Born in Austin, Texas on December 25, 1916. Played acoustic guitar from a young age. First professional performance with his brother at age 18. Took up electric guitar at around the same time as Charlie Christian. Joined the Nat King Cole Trio in 1939 with Cole (piano, vocals) and Wesley Prince (bass). They originally had a drummer, but he didn't show up for a concert and they decided they didn't need one. The band enjoyed considerable success as performers and appeared in several Hollywood films, before Moore left in 1949 to play in a West Coast band called The Three Blazers. Won jazz polls in magazines such as *Downbeat* and *Metronome*. Died in Las Vegas on October 8, 1981. A big influence on later jazz players.

Scotty **MOORE**

Rock guitar pioneer. Born Winfield Scott Moore in Gadsden, Tennessee on December 27, 1931. Started playing the guitar from an early age, influenced by hillbilly music. Later inspired by jazz and country giants such as Tal Farlow, Barney Kessel, Merle Travis and Chet Atkins. Moved to Memphis and formed a hillbilly band called the Starlight Wranglers. Sam Phillips (Sun Records) introduced them to Elvis Presley in 1954 and they recorded two songs with him: 'That's All Right Mama' and 'Blue Moon Of Kentucky'. The two tracks were released as a single and played on Memphis radio within days of the recording session. It caused a local sensation and Presley was soon gigging

throughout the United States. Signed to RCA. Big break came with 'Heartbreak Hotel' (1956): topped the US charts and was a worldwide hit. Presley's charisma and Moore's exciting guitar licks proved to be a successful combination. More hits followed: 'Hound Dog' (1956), 'Love Me Tender' (1956), 'All Shook Up' (1957) and 'Jailhouse Rock' (1957). The band split up in 1958 and Moore later worked with Thomas Wayne, Dale Hawkins and Billy Swan (also made several other appearances with Presley). Solo album on Epic: *The Guitar That Changed The World* (1964). Presley albums on RCA featuring Moore include *Elvis Presley* (1956), *Elvis* (1956) and *Christmas Album* (1957). Included in *Guitar Player* magazine's 'Gallery Of The Greats' (1992) for his lifetime achievement.

Vinnie **MOORE**

Heavy metal player. Born in 1965. Picked up the guitar from an early age and was playing competently by the time he was 12. Early influences included Ritchie Blackmore, Jimi Hendrix and Al Di Meola. Studied jazz. Impressed Mike Varney, who introduced the guitarist to heavy metal band Vicious Rumours. They released *Soldiers Of The Night* (1985) on Shrapnel, before Moore left to pursue a solo career. Recorded neo-classical rock instrumental albums for Shrapnel/Roadrunner: *Mind's Eye* (1986) and *Time Odyssey* (1988). Later more mainstream *Meltdown* (1991) on Relativity. Also toured with Alice Cooper in 1991. Voted Best New Talent in *Guitar Player* magazine's readers poll (1987). Outstanding rock player with impressive technique. Instruction video: *Advanced Lead Techniques* (Hot Licks).

Jorge **MOREL**

Classical guitarist. Born Jorge Scibona in Buenos Aires, Argentina on May 9, 1931. Studied at the University of Musical Studies in Buenos Aires. Played a guitar duet with his teacher Pablo Escobar on a radio programme when he was 16. Later developed his own latin-influenced style. Transcribed and performed music by Bernstein, Gershwin, Lennon & McCartney and many others. Recordings on Guitar Masters include *Virtuoso South American Guitar* (1981), *Jorge Morel Plays Broadway* (1982), *Latin Impressions* (1983) and *The Art Of Jorge Morel* (1991). A number of his arrangements are notated in the book

74

39ff1a62e9704bbaaf48b4a52c88e4c6

Classical Guitar Solos - Bernstein & Gershwin (Ashley Mark). Video: *In Performance* (1987 Frets X Frame).

Van **MORRISON**

Legendary singer/songwriter. Born George Ivan Morrison in Belfast, Northern Ireland on August 31, 1945. Played guitar, saxophone and harmonica by the time he was 13. Early influences included Muddy Waters, John Lee Hooker and Ray Charles. Toured with the Monarchs before forming Them in 1963. Had hits with 'Baby Please Don't Go' and 'Here Comes The Night' in the mid-'60s. The band split in 1966 and Morrison went to America to work with producer Bert Berns: had instant success with US Top 10 hit 'Brown Eyed Girl' (1967). Berns died of a heart attack the same year. Then came critically acclaimed Warner Brothers album *Astral Weeks* (1968). Later recordings on Warners and Polydor include *Moondance* (1970), *Tupelo Honey* (1971), *St Dominic's Preview* (1972), *It's Too Late To Stop Now* (1974), *Wavelength* (1978), *Common One* (1980), *Inarticulate Speech Of The Heart* (1983), *Avalon Sunset* (1989), *The Best Of Van Morrison* (1990) and *Too Long In Exile* (1993). His songs are a unique blend of R&B, folk and soul.

Steve **MORSE**

Rock composer and virtuoso guitarist. Born in Hamilton, Ohio, on July 28, 1954. Grew up in Michigan before moving to Georgia in his teens. Early influences included the Allman Brothers and the Mahavishnu Orchestra. Studied music at the University of Miami. There he formed a rock ensemble called the Dixie Dregs (formerly Dixie Grits) with fellow students Andy West (bass), Rod Morgenstein (drums), Allen Sloan (violin) and Steve Davidowski (keyboards). After graduation the band relocated to Augusta, Georgia and gigged regularly. Recorded their first album *Freefall* (1977) on Capricorn. Davidowski left a year later and was replaced by Mark Parrish on keyboards for the albums *What If* (1978) and *Night Of The Living Dregs* (1979), before he was in turn replaced by another keyboardist T-Lavitz. The new line-up switched to Arista and recorded *Dregs Of The Earth* (1980), before shortening their name to the Dregs. Two more recordings followed: *Unsung Heroes* (1981) and *Industry Standard* (1982). The latter featured violinist/guitarist Mark O'Connor and singer Alex Ligertwood.

Steve Morse

The band's instrumental fusion of rock, country, bluegrass, jazz and classical music earned them Grammy nominations and considerable respect as virtuosic performers. Morse's compositions were tight and inventive. The Dregs split in 1982 and later the more guitar orientated Steve Morse Band was formed with Jerry Peek (bass) and Rod Morgenstein (drums). They recorded Elektra albums *The Introduction* (1984) and *Stand Up* (1985), before Morse temporarily worked as an airline pilot, joined the rock band Kansas for a spell and recorded the solo album *High Tension Wires* (1989) on MCA. Reformed the Steve Morse Band with Dave La Rue (bass) and Van Romaine (drums), recording raw instrumental rock albums such as *Southern Steel* (1991) and *Coast to Coast* (1992). Later Dregs live reunion released as *Bring 'Em Back Alive* (1992). Highly versatile guitar player with formidable picking technique. His rock lead style often combines mixolydian runs with tasteful bends and artificial harmonics. Equally impressive on classical guitar. Instruction videos for Hot Licks and REH. Included in *Guitar Player* magazine's 'Gallery Of The Greats' after being voted Best Overall Guitarist (1982-1986) and Best Country Guitarist (1986).

MUDDY WATERS

Blues legend. Born McKinley Morganfield in Rolling Fork, Mississippi on April 4, 1915. Playing in a nearby muddy creek earned him his nickname. His mother died when he was 3 and so he went to live with his grandmother on Stovall's plantation. Started playing harmonica at age 13 and guitar at 17. Worked in the local cottonfield for 50 cents a day. Developed a blues style influenced by Son House, Blind Blake, Blind Lemon Jefferson and Robert Johnson. In 1941 two members of the Library of Congress (Alan Lomax and John Work) travelled to Mississippi in search of Robert Johnson. However Johnson was dead by then and locals pointed them towards Muddy Waters. A few recordings were made in 1941/42 including 'Country Blues' and 'I Be's Troubled'. Moved to Chicago in 1943 and

David Redfern/Redferns

Muddy Waters

picked up electric slide guitar later. Worked in a paper mill and drove a truck during the day, while playing blues at parties and clubs at night. Recorded hits for the Chess label in the late '40s and early '50s, including 'She Moves Me' and 'Hoochie Coochie Man'. Formed one of the best and most popular Chicago blues bands which included Little Walter (harmonica), Elgin Evans (drums), Jimmy Rogers (guitar) and Willie Dixon (bass). Helped evolve the acoustic Delta-blues style into the more electric Chicago South Side sound. Often combined moody vocals with raw single-note phrases. Continued playing and recording up until the '80s. Died peacefully in his sleep in Chigaco on April 30, 1983. One of the most influential blues performers. Albums on Muse, Chess, Blue Sky and other labels include *Muddy Waters At Newport* (1960), *Folk Singer* (1964), *Sings Big*

Bill Broonzy (1964), *Down On Stovall's Plantation* (1966), *Mud In Your Ear* (1967), Grammy-winner *They Call Me Muddy Waters* (1971), *Can't Get No Grindin'* (1973), *Hard Again* (1977), *I'm Ready* (1978), *Live* (1980), *King Bee* (1980) and 6LP/3CD box set *Muddy Waters* (1989). Included in *Guitar Player* magazine's 'Gallery Of The Greats' (1992) for his lifetime achievement.

Dave **MURRAY**

UK heavy metal guitarist. Born on December 23, 1955. Formed Iron Maiden in the late '70s with Steve Harris (bass), Dennis Stratton (guitar, later replaced by Adrian Smith and Janick Gers), Paul Di'Anno (vocals, later replaced by Bruce Dickinson) and Clive Burr (drums, later replaced by Nicko McBrain). Named after medieval instrument of torture. Became foremost of the second generation heavy metal bands. Staged spectacular live shows and recorded a number of best-selling albums on EMI including *Iron Maiden* (1980), *Killers* (1981), *Number Of The Beast* (1982), *Powerslave* (1984), *Somewhere In Time* (1986), *Seventh Son Of A Seventh Son* (1988), *No Prayer For The Dying* (1990), *Fear Of The Dark* (1992) and *A Real Live One* (1993).

Neil **MURRAY**

UK bass player. Born in Edinburgh, Scotland on August 27, 1950. Took up the electric bass at age 17. Influences included Jack Bruce and Tim Bogert. Studied graphic design in London. Played with fusion bands Colosseum II and National Health, before joining David Coverdale's heavy metal band Whitesnake in 1977. They recorded *Trouble* (1978), *Love Hunter* (1979), *Ready An' Willing* (1980), *Live In The Heart Of The City* (1980), *Come An' Get It* (1981) and *Saints & Sinners* (1982). Played at Amnesty International's *Secret Policeman's Other Ball* (1981) with Eric Clapton and Jeff Beck. Left Whitesnake in '82 and joined Gary Moore for *Corridors Of Power* (1982) and *Victims Of the Future* (1984). Rejoined Whitesnake for *Slide It In* (1984) and *Whitesnake* (1987). Also with Japanese metal band Vow Wow and Black Sabbath recording *Tyr* (1990). Played at the 'Guitar Legends' concert in Seville (1991) with Steve Vai, Brian May and others. Later on May's album *Back To The Light* (1992). A tasteful and powerful fingerstyle rock bass player.

N

Bill **NELSON**

UK rock guitarist, singer/songwriter and producer. Born in Wakefield, Yorkshire on December 18, 1948. Worked in local bands Global Village and Gentle Revolution, before forming unique rock group Be-Bop Deluxe in 1972. Enjoyed limited success with Harvest albums *Axe Victim* (1974), *Futurama* (1975), *Sunburst Finish* (1976), *Modern Music* (1976), *Live! In The Air Age* (1977) and *Drastic Plastic* (1978). Set up his own label Cocteau Records. Later issued a number of more experimental solo recordings, including *Sound On Sound* (1979), *Quit Dreaming And Get On The Beam* (1981), *Map Of Dreams* (1987) and *Blue Moons And Laughing Guitars* (1992). Also produced a number of other bands.

Rick **NELSON**

Rock singer/guitarist. Born Eric Hilliard Nelson in Teaneck, New Jersey on May 8, 1940. Son of Ozzie Nelson (bandleader) and Harriet Hilliard (singer). Appeared on his parents' radio show at age 8. Called himself Ricky Nelson and had a hit with a version of Fats Domino's 'I'm Walkin'' (1957). Other hits (often rockabilly style) during the late '50s and early '60s include 'Believe What You Say' (1958), 'Poor Little Fool' (1958), 'Never Be Anyone Else But You' (1959), 'Travelin' Man' (1961) and 'Young World' (1962). His band featured guitarist James Burton (later with Elvis Presley). Shortened name to Rick during the early '60s and switched to country-rock. Later albums include *Country Fever* (1967), *Rick Sings Nelson* (1971), *Windfall* (1974), *Intakes* (1977), *Playing To Win* (1981), *Rockin' With Ricky* (1984) and *The Best Of Rick Nelson* (1985). Died in a plane crash near De Kalb, Texas on December 31, 1985. Compilation: *The Best Of Ricky Nelson* (1991) on Capitol. Books include *Ricky Nelson* by Joel Selvin.

Rick **NIELSEN**

Rock guitarist/singer. Born in Rockford, Illinois on December 22, 1946. Played in various high school bands before forming Fuse with bassist Tom Peterson in the late '60s. The band became Cheap Trick with the addition of Bun E. Carlos (drums) and Robin Zander (guitar, vocals) during the early '70s. Earned a reputation as an exciting and unusual live act, with Nielsen playing multiple guitars in oddball costume, Zander and Peterson becoming teeny heart-throbs and seedy Carlos at the back. Albums on Epic include *Cheap Trick* (1977), *In Color* (1977), *Heaven Tonight* (1978), *Dream Police* (1979), *Live At The Budokan* (1979), *All Shook Up* (1980), *One On One* (1982), *Next Position Please* (1983), *Standing On The Edge* (1985), *The Doctor* (1986), *Lap Of Luxury* (1988) and *Busted* (1990). Compilations: *Cheap Trick - The Collection* (1991) and *Greatest Hits* (1992).

Jimmy **NOLEN**

Funk rhythm pioneer. Born in Kansas City on April 3, 1934. Picked up the guitar at age 14. Became influenced by T-Bone Walker and started playing blues. Moved over to R&B by the '50s. Joined forces with James Brown and soon became well-known for his tight rhythm grooves on songs such as 'I Got You (I Feel Good)' and 'Papa's Got A Brand New Bag'. Stayed with Brown for nearly 20 years. Died of a heart attack on December 18, 1983. Considered by many to be the father of funk guitar. Influenced players as diverse as Nile Rodgers, Jimi Hendrix, Jeff Beck and Keith Richards. Recordings include James Brown compilations such as *The Best Of James Brown* (Polydor), and 4 disc set *Startime* (Polydor). Included in *Guitar Player* magazine's 'Gallery Of The Greats' (1991) for his lifetime achievement.

Ted **NUGENT**

Rock guitarist. Born in Detroit, Michigan on December 13, 1948. Started playing guitar at age 9 and was playing lead guitar in a rock and roll band by the time he was 12. Early influences were Chuck Berry, Lonnie Mack and Keith Richards. Formed a band called the Amboy Dukes in 1965. They recorded many albums on Mainstream, Polydor and Edsel including *Journey To The Center Of Your Mind* (1968), *Survival Of The Fittest* (1970) and *Tooth, Fang And Claw* (1974), before Nugent decided on a solo career. Made many successful recordings on Epic, Atlantic and WEA including *Ted Nugent* (1975), *Free For All* (1976), *Cat Scratch Fever* (1977), *Penetrator* (1984), *Little Miss Dangerous* (1986) and *If You Can't Lick 'Em...Lick 'Em* (1988). Became infamous for playing very loud gigs ("If it's too loud, you're too old!"). Formed heavy metal band Damn Yankees in 1989. They recorded *Damn Yankees* (1990) and *Don't Tread* (1992) on Warner Brothers.

Right: Ted Nugent

Mike **OLDFIELD**

UK composer and multi-instrumentalist. Born in Reading, Berkshire on May 15, 1953.

Marc Marnie/Redferns

Mike Oldfield

Formed a folk duo with elder sister Sally at age 14. They released an acoustic album *Sallyangie* (1968) on Transatlantic. Worked for Kevin Ayers during 1970-71. Made a demo tape of an ambitious 50 minute composition consisting of folk, rock and classical melodies. Hawked the tape around many UK record companies. It was eventually taken up by Richard Branson's recently opened Virgin label. The project was re-recorded at Branson's Manor Studio in 1972, with Oldfield playing 21 different instruments himself (requiring more than 1000 overdubs), in addition to a few other musicians. The result was the critically acclaimed *Tubular Bells* (1973). It became the second-biggest selling album of the decade and won a Grammy. *Hergest Ridge* (1974) was more of the same, while *Ommadawn* (1975) included Celtic and African elements. *Orchestral Tubular Bells* (1975) was performed by the Royal Philharmonic Orchestra and conducted by David Bedford. Later Virgin recordings include *Incantations* (1978), *Five Miles Out* (1982), *Crises* (1983), *Killing Fields Soundtrack* (1984), *Islands* (1987) and *Heaven's Open* (1991). Switched to Warner Brothers for *Tubular Bells II* (1992). Virgin compilation: *The Best Of Mike Oldfield* (1993).

Mary **OSBORNE**

Jazz player. Born in Minot, North Dakota in 1921. Started playing ukulele at age 4 before switching to guitar by the time she was 9. Heavily influenced by Charlie Christian. Worked with the Winifred McDonald trio, pianist Mary-Lou Williams and Coleman Hawkins. Also worked extensively in the studio and for radio. Married trumpeter Ralph Scaffidi in 1946. Moved to New York in the late '40s and formed her own trio. Studied classical guitar with Albert Valdes Blain. Moved to California in 1968 and formed a quartet. Continued playing and teaching up until the time of her death in 1992. Recordings include *Now's The Time* (Halcyon) and *Now And Then* (Stash).

P

Jimmy **PAGE**

Rock guitar legend. Born in Heston, London on January 9, 1944. Started playing guitar at age 14. Early influences included Scotty Moore, James Burton and B.B.King. Studied at art college before working extensively as a session guitarist in London. Played up to 3 sessions a day, recording with artists as diverse as The

Jimmy Page (left) with Les Paul

Who, Tom Jones and Joe Cocker. Joined the Yardbirds in 1966 and played alongside Jeff Beck. The band split up in 1968 and Page formed heavy-rock group Led Zeppelin with Robert Plant (vocals), John Paul Jones (bass) and John Bonham (drums). They proved to be one of the most original and successful bands of all time, recording rock classics such as 'Whole Lotta Love' and 'Stairway To Heaven'. Albums on Atlantic include *Led Zeppelin* (1969), *Led Zeppelin II* (1969), *Led Zeppelin III* (1970), *Led Zeppelin IV* (1971) and *Houses Of The Holy* (1973). These recordings featured some highly original and exciting riffs, as well as some earthy acoustic playing. The band formed their own Swansong label and continued with *Physical Graffiti* (1975), *Presence* (1976), *The Song Remains The Same* (1976), *In Through The Out Door* (1979) and *Coda* (1982). Page was fascinated by the occult and the works of Aleister Crowley. Some felt the group was jinxed after Plant's son died from a stomach infection and the band suffered injuries in a car crash. The bad luck continued when Bonham was found dead in a bed at Page's house in 1980, having choked after a massive binge. The band split later that year and Page embarked on solo career. Composed music for the film *Death Wish II* (1982). Formed another rock group the Firm and had moderate success in the mid '80s with Atlantic and Warner Brothers albums *The Firm* (1985) and *Mean Business* (1986). Also solo album *Outrider* (1988) on Geffen. Later remastered Led Zeppelin's back catalogue for Atlantic compilation *Remasters* (1990). Included in *Guitar Player* magazine's 'Gallery Of The Greats' (1990) for his lifetime achievement. Jimmy Page and Led Zeppelin influenced countless other guitar players and bands throughout the '70s, '80s and '90s. Books include *Led Zeppelin: A Celebration* by Dave Lewis.

Pino **PALLADINO**

Bass session ace. Born in Cardiff, Wales on October 17, 1957. Took up the classical guitar at around age 14. Switched to electric bass at

17. Influences included James Jamerson, Jaco Pastorius, Anthony Jackson and Marcus Miller. Started with local bands and TV work. Moved to London and joined Jools Holland's group in the early '80s for *Jools Holland & The Millionaires* (1981). Also with Gary Numan on *I Assassin* (1982), before joining Paul Young's band. Big break came with Young's chart-topping version of Marvin Gaye's 'Wherever I Lay My Hat' (1983). It featured the bass as the main instrument: a beautiful fluid tone reminiscent of Pastorius. Palladino's reputation as an outstanding bass player soon grew and brought work with Don Henley, Elton John, Pete Townshend and many others. Albums with Paul Young: *No Parlez* (1983), *The Secret Of Association* (1985), *Between Two Fires* (1986), *Other Voices* (1990) and *The Crossing* (1993). With Eric Clapton: *Journeyman* (1989). With Phil Collins: *But Seriously...* (1989). One of the UK's premier bass players.

Sophocles **PAPAS**

Classical guitar pioneer and teacher. Born in Epirus, Greece on December 18, 1893. Started learning mandolin in Cairo, Egypt before emigrating to the United States in 1914. Settled in Washington DC and took lessons with William Foden. Gained recognition from performing guitar on a local radio station in Washington. Became friends with Segovia. Began teaching and established the Sophocles Papas Guitar Shop (which still exists). Well-known pupils have included Sharon Isbin, Larry Snitzler and Charlie Byrd. Became president of the Columbia Music Company. Died in Washington DC on February 26, 1986. An outstanding player and teacher who influenced generations of classical players.

Christopher **PARKENING**

Classical virtuoso. Born in Brentwood, California in 1947. Started playing guitar at age 11. Studied with Celedonio and Pepe Romero. Later attended a Segovia Master Class at the University of California at Berkley (selected as a soloist when the Master Class was broadcasted on television). Premiered Castelnuovo-Tedesco's 'Second Concerto in C for Guitar and Orchestra' in 1966. Gave many recitals and made several recordings for Angel including *Parkening Plays Bach*, *Parkening And The Guitar* and *Christopher Parkening Album*. Went into temporary retirement (moved to a ranch in Montana to raise horses and fish for

trout) for 6 years. Later returned to the major concert circuit and recorded further Angel albums including *Simple Gifts* (1987) and *Pleasures Of Their Company* (1987, nominated for a Grammy Award). Later compilation: *The Christopher Parkening Collection* (1993). Author of several highly-rated classical guitar transcription books.

Andy **PARTRIDGE**

UK singer/songwriter and rock guitarist. Born in Swindon, Wiltshire on December 11, 1953. Formed XTC (originally Helium Kidz) in 1976 with Colin Moulding (bass) and Terry Chambers (drums). Keyboardists John Perkins and Barry Andrews came and went. Emerged with the UK punk scene but had a unique style that was more sophisticated, with intelligent and humorous lyrics. Received critical and cult acclaim with hits 'Making Plans For Nigel' (1979), 'Sgt Rock' (1981) and 'Senses Working Overtime' (1982), but never a huge commercial success. Albums on Virgin all feature Partridge's choppy rhythm playing and unusual chord progressions: *White Music* (1978), *Go2* (1978), *Drums And Wires* (1979), *Black Sea* (1980), *English Settlement* (1982), *Mummer* (1983), *The Big Express* (1984), *Skylarking* (1986), *Oranges And Lemons* (1988) and *Nonsuch* (1992). They also made a number of recordings under the pseudonym Dukes Of Stratosphear.

Joe **PASS**

Jazz guitarist. Born Joseph Anthony Passalaqua in New Brunswick, New Jersey on January 13, 1929. Picked up the guitar at age 9. Played in

Joe Pass

David Redfern/Redferns

wedding and dance bands by the time he was 14. Worked with saxophonist Tony Pastor while still at school. Moved to New York to become involved in the bebop scene but became addicted to drugs. Arrested several times and incarcerated, before undergoing rehabilitation at the Synanon Foundation in California in 1961. Stayed there for three years, during which time he recorded with other musicians undergoing rehabilitation. The result was *Sounds Of Synanon* (1962) on Pacific Jazz. The critics were impressed and Pass won the *Downbeat* New Star Award in 1963. Later worked extensively in the studio and played with Julie London, Les McCann, George Shearing, Benny Goodman, Norman Granz, Oscar Peterson, Ella Fitzgerald, Count Basie, Dizzie Gillespie, Herb Ellis and many others. Became famous for his exceptional single-note work and later extended his range by performing unaccompanied. His beautiful technique and sound made him the most influential jazz player since Wes Montgomery. Recordings on Discovery, MPS and Concord include *The Living Legends* (1969), *Intercontinental* (1970), *Jazz/Concord* (1973). On Pablo: *Virtuoso* (1973), *Virtuoso 2* (1976), *Virtuoso 3* (1977), *Live At Montreux* (1977), *Northsea Lights* (1979), *Eximious* (1982), *Live At Long Beach College* (1984), *Whitestone* (1985) and *Appassionato* (1991). Instruction videos: *Jazz Lines* (REH) and *The Blue Side Of Jazz* (Hot Licks).

Jaco **PASTORIUS**

Legendary bass player. Born in Morristown, Pennsylvania on December 1, 1951. Grew up in

Jaco Pastorius

Fort Lauderdale, Florida. Took up bass as a teenager. Also played drums, piano, saxophone and guitar. His debut solo album *Jaco Pastorius* (1975) caused a stir when it was released. He was soon playing with top names in jazz and rock including Pat Metheny, Al Di Meola, and Joni Mitchell. Joined fusion band Weather Report with keyboardist Joe Zawinul and saxophonist Wayne Shorter in 1976. His unique bass playing became an essential component of the band's sound on Columbia recordings such as *Heavy Weather* (1977), *Mr.Gone* (1978), *8.30* (1979), *Night Passage* (1980) and *Weather Report* (1981). Formed his own band Word Of Mouth and quit Weather Report in 1982. A manic-depressive, he spent his final years as a destitute alcoholic. Died in Fort Lauderdale on September 22, 1987, after being severely beaten, while trying to enter a night club from which he had been banned. A supremely gifted and revolutionary player, whose unique style incorporated a lilting fretless legato, formidable jazz licks, complex harmonics and brutal distortion tones. Redefined the role of the bass in modern music. Later releases on Timeless, Big World and Sound Hills include *Jazz Street* (1989), *Live In N.Y.C.* (1990) and *Holiday For Pans* (1993). Included in *Guitar Player* magazine's 'Gallery Of The Greats' after being voted Best Jazz Bass Player (1982-1986).

John **PATITUCCI**

Jazz and fusion bass player. Born in Brooklyn, New York on December 22, 1959. Started learning bass at age 11. Played in local bands at age 12. Learned string bass at high school. Also studied with Charles Siani in San Francisco and Barry Lieberman of the Los Angeles Philharmonic. Jazz influences included Ron Carter, Eddie Gomez and Stanley Clarke. Started doing session and gig work in LA and was soon working with Larry Carlton, Victor Feldman and Manhattan Transfer. Joined Chick Corea's Elektric Band in the mid-'80s with Corea (keyboards), Dave Weckl (drums) and Scott Henderson (guitar, later replaced by Carlos Rios and Frank Gambale). Albums on GRP include *The Chick Corea Elektric Band* (1986), *Light Years* (1987), *Eye Of The Beholder* (1988), *Inside-Out* (1990) and *Beneath The Mask* (1991). Patitucci solo albums on GRP include *John Patitucci* (1988), *On The Corner* (1989) and *Sketchbook* (1990). Instructional video: *Electric Bass* (DCI 1989). Highly respected on both electric and acoustic bass, for his solid foundation work and exceptional soloing abilities.

Charley **PATTON**

Blues pioneer. Born in Edwards, Mississippi in April 1891. Considered himself to be more of an entertainer than a blues singer and developed an extroverted and humorous style. His repertoire included 'Down The Dirt Road Blues', 'Pony Blues' and 'Mississippi Boll Weevil Blues'. Made a number of recordings for Paramount and Vocalion before his death (chronic heart condition) in Indianola, Mississippi on April 28, 1934. One of the most influential early delta blues performers. Recordings include *Founder Of The Delta Blues* (Yazoo), *Bottleneck Guitar Pioneer* (Herwin) and *Remaining Titles 1929-34* (Wolf).

Les **PAUL**

Legendary guitarist and inventor. Born Lester Polfus in Waukesha, Wisconsin on June 9, 1916. Played the guitar and harmonica from an early age. Self-taught. Initially performed country music and jazz under the names Rhubarb Red and Les Paul respectively. Moved to New York and formed the Les Paul Trio in the late '30s. Appeared regularly on the Fred Waring Show (NBC Radio) in 1941. Broke his right elbow in a serious car crash in 1941 and the doctor (a Les Paul fan) set it at an angle so he could continue playing the guitar. Took an interest in electronics and built the first multi-track studio in 1946; went on to make recordings of an unprecedented quality. Also built his first solid-body guitar and took it to the Gibson guitar company the same year. Eventually they accepted it, and in 1952 the Gibson Les Paul was issued, complete with sustaining pickups. It went on to be one of the most famous and popular guitar designs, later used by players as diverse as Jimmy Page, Pete Townshend and Al Di Meola. Married Mary Ford in 1949. They had hits with 'Mocking Bird Hill' and 'How High The Moon' during the '50s. Later recorded albums on London and RCA such as *Les Paul Now* (1968) and Grammy-winning country album *Chester & Lester* (1978), with his old friend Chet Atkins. Compilations include the 4-CD set *Les Paul: The Legend And The Legacy* (1991) on Capitol. Included in *Guitar Player* magazine's 'Gallery Of The Greats' after being voted Best Jazz Guitarist (1972), Best Pop Guitarist (1978, 1979) and for his lifetime achievement (1984).

Paco **PEÑA**

Traditional flamenco player. Born in Córdoba, Spain in 1942. Started playing guitar at a young age. Gave his first professional performance at age 12 and played in local folk groups as a teenager. Soon he was accompanying top flamenco singers and dancers. Achieved global acclaim, after he visited London in the early '60s and was asked to record for Decca, who were amazed by his playing. Albums include *Art Of Flamenco*, *La Guitarra Flamenca* and *Paco Peña Live*. In 1982 he founded the Centre Of Flamenco (Andalucia), which hosts the annual Festival Internacional De La Guitarra, featuring classical and flamenco artists such as John Williams, Benjamin Verdery and Eduardo Falu. Later recordings on Nimbus include *Azahara* (1989), *Leyenda* (1990) with Inti-Illimani/John Williams and *Misa Flamenca* (1990). Included in *Guitar Player* magazine's 'Gallery Of The Greats' after being voted Best Flamenco Guitarist (1986-1990).

Carl **PERKINS**

Singer/songwriter/guitarist. Born in Lake County, Tennessee on April 9, 1932. His father gave him a home-made guitar when he was 4 and soon Carl was entertaining his classmates at school. Picked up electric guitar and won a local talent contest at age 14. Influenced by local country and blues musicians. Teamed up with brothers Jay and Clayton to form the Perkins Brothers Band. Later wrote and recorded 'Blue Suede Shoes', but was unable to promote it due to a serious car accident in 1956. The song was a massive hit for Elvis Presley later that year. Perkins' songs were also covered by artists as diverse as Johnny Cash and the Beatles. Albums include *Whole Lotta Shakin'* (1958), *Blue Suede Shoes* (1969), *My Kind Of Country* (1974), *Carl Perkins Show* (1976), *The Class Of '55* (1986), *Born To Rock* (1990), *Friends, Family & Legends* (1992) and *The Best Of Carl Perkins* (1993).

Joe **PERRY**

Heavy-rock guitarist. Born in Boston, Massachusetts on September 10, 1950. Formed Aerosmith with Steven Tyler (vocals), Brad Whitford (guitar), Tom Hamilton (bass) and Joey Kramer (drums). Signed to Columbia/CBS for albums such as *Aerosmith* (1973), *Toys In The Attic* (1975) and the platinum-selling *Rocks* (1976). Left in 1979 to form the Joe Perry project: *Let The Music Do The Talking*

(1980), *I've Got The Rock'N'Rolls Again* (1982) and *Once A Rocker, Always A Rocker* (1983) featured some interesting and unpredictable riffs, but lacked the fire of his original group, which he rejoined in 1984. Aerosmith then switched to Geffen and had considerable commercial success with later albums such as *Done With Mirrors* (1985),

William Hames/Idols

Joe Perry

Permanent Vacation (1987), *Pump* (1989), compilation *Gems* (1988) and *Talk This Way - The Interview* (1992). Also teamed up with Run DMC in 1986 for unexpected version of Aerosmith classic 'Walk This Way'. An impressive hard-rock act.

Tom **PETTY**

Rock singer/guitarist. Born in Gainsville, Florida on October 20, 1953. Early influences included The Animals and James Brown. Played in local bands such as the Epics and Mudcrutch, before forming the Heartbreakers with Mike Campbell (guitar), Benmont Tench (keyboards), Ron Blair (bass) and Stan Lynch (drums). Successfully bridged the gap between traditional rock and new-wave with albums such as *Tom Petty And The Heartbreakers* (1977) on Shelter. On MCA: *Damn The Torpedoes* (1979), *Southern Accents* (1985), *Let Me Up - I've Had Enough* (1987), *Full Moon Fever* (1989) and *Tom Petty & The Heartbreakers - Greatest Hits*

(1993). Also worked with Stevie Nicks and Del Shannon. Formed the Travelling Wilburys with Bob Dylan, George Harrison, Jeff Lynne and Roy Orbison.

Bucky **PIZZARELLI**

Jazz guitarist. Born John Pizzarelli in Paterson, New Jersey on January 9, 1926. Started playing the guitar at age 9. Joined Vaughan Monroe's dance band at age 17. Worked with bands such as the Three Sins and the Les Egbert Band during the '50s. Involved in studio work during the '60s. Started playing a 7-string guitar, after seeing George Van Eps perform at a New York club in 1967. Formed a successful guitar duo with George Barnes. Also worked with Joe Venuti, Bob Wilber, Slam Stewart and Zoot Simms. Recordings include *Midnite Mood* (1960), *Green Guitar Blues* (1972), *Nightwings* (1975), *Soprano Summit II* (1977), *2 Times 7 = Pizzarrelli* (1980), *Love Songs* (1982), *Swinging Sevens* (1984) and *Solo Flight* (1986).

Andy **POWELL**

UK rock guitarist. Born February 8, 1950. Early influences included the Yardbirds and the Allman Brothers. Joined Wishbone Ash in 1969 with Ted Turner (guitar), Martin Turner (bass) and Steve Upton (drums). Developed a progressive rock sound, driven by the twin guitars of Powell (playing a Gibson Flying V guitar) and Turner. Built up a loyal following on the UK club circuit and signed to MCA. *Wishbone Ash* (1970) and *Pilgrimage* (1971) were well received. *Argus* (1972) was considered to be their best. Ted Turner left after *Live Dates* (1974) and was replaced by Laurie Wisefield on guitar. Other notable albums of the '70s include *There's The Rub* (1974) and *New England* (1976). Martin Turner left in 1980, replaced by John Wetton, Trevor Bolder and Robin Spense. The original line-up got together for an instru-mental album *Nouveau Calls* (1988) on IRS.

Ida **PRESTI**

Classical virtuoso. Born Yvette Ida Montagnon in Suresnes, France on May 31, 1924. Started learning piano at age 5 and switched over to guitar a year later. Gave her first public recital at age 8. Studied with Mario Maccaferri for two years and was the first guitarist invited to play at the Societe des Concerts du Conservatoire de Paris. Later toured extensively and earned a reputation as an outstanding guitarist. Met another classical virtuoso Alexandre Lagoya in 1952. They married a year later and formed an impressive classical duo. Performed all over the world and made several recordings including *Concertos Pour Deux Guitares* and *Musique Espagnole Pour Deux Guitares* (both Philips). Ida suddenly became ill while preparing for a concert in New York and died soon afterwards on April 24, 1967.

PRINCE

Singer/songwriter. Also multi-instrumentalist and producer. Born Prince Rogers Nelson in Minneapolis, Minnesota on June 7, 1958. Son of a jazz pianist and singer. Self-taught on guitar, piano and drums. Formed a band called Grand Central (later Champagne) at high school. Guitar influences included Carlos Santana and Jimi Hendrix. Signed a lucrative deal with Warner Brothers while still in his teens. Produced and played all of the instruments on first album *For You* (1978). It featured the US soul hit 'Soft And Wet'. Many other albums, prolifically recorded, include *Prince* (1979), *Dirty Mind* (1980), *1999* (1982), *Purple Rain* (1984), *Around The World In A Day* (1985), *Parade* (1986), *Sign 'O' The Times*

Mark Weiss/Idols

Prince

(1987), *Lovesexy* (1988), *Graffiti Bridge* (1990), *Diamonds And Pearls* (1991), *Symbol* (1992). Each of these spawned hit singles. Highly talented guitarist, although best known as one of the most original and flamboyant pop performers. Successfully fuses rock music with soul. Winner of Grammy and Academy awards.

Robert **QUINE**

Rock guitar player. Born in Akron, Ohio on Dec 30, 1942. Earliest influences included Django Reinhardt, Gene Autry and Jimmy Wakely. Picked up an acoustic guitar at age 15 and taught himself to play from Chuck Berry and Bo Diddley records. Later influenced by James Burton, Scotty Moore and Ritchie Valens. Switched to a Fender Stratocaster in 1961. Attended the Berklee College of Music in 1967 and also studied law. Joined punk band Richard Hell and the Voidoids in 1976. Their Sire EP *Blank Generation* (1976) featured some savage and exciting guitar. Later played with Lou Reed on *The Blue Mask* (1981) and *Legendary Hearts* (1983). Also worked with Tom Waits on *Rain Dogs* (1985), Scritti Politti on *Cupid & Psyche '85* (1985) and Bill Frisell.

Recorded critically-acclaimed album *Basic* (1984) on EG with drummer Fred Maher. An exciting player with a highly individual sound.

Snoozer **QUINN**

Jazz guitarist. Born Edwin McIntosh Quinn in McComb, Mississippi on October 18, 1906. Started playing mandolin and violin at age 7 before switching to guitar at age 10. Toured with the Paul English Travelling Shows by the time he was 17. Later worked with Paul Whiteman and a number of others. Earned a reputation as an outstanding jazz guitarist, but left the Whiteman band because of poor health during 1929. Suffered for many years before his death in New Orleans in 1952. Recordings include *The Legendary Snoozer Quinn With Johnny Wiggs* (Fat Cat).

R

Trevor **RABIN**

Rock player. Born in Johannesburg, South Africa on January 21, 1955. Started learning piano at age 6 and guitar by the time he was 12. Influenced by rock, R&B and classical music. Worked extensively as a session player in South Africa during the '70s. Formed the group Rabbitt, recording albums *Boys Will Be Boys* and *A Croak & A Grunt In The Night* on Capricorn. Joined rock supergroup Yes in the early '80s. Their Atco album *90125* (1983) boasted the US No.1 hit 'Owner Of A Lonely Heart', featuring a tasty solo from the guitarist (and impressive production by Trevor Horn). They later released *Big Generator* (1987) and *Union* (1991). Rabin solo recordings on Chrysalis and Elektra include *Trevor Rabin* (1978), *Face To Face* (1979) and *Can't Look Away* (1989).

Gerry **RAFFERTY**

Folk-rock singer/songwriter. Born in Paisley, Scotland on April 16, 1947. First group the Humblebums also featured future comedian Billy Connolly. Went solo with classic album *Can I Have My Money Back?* (1968), before forming critically-acclaimed band Stealer's Wheel with singer Joe Egan and others. Hit with catchy 'Stuck In The Middle With You' (1973). The band's life was short and turbulent, and they recorded three albums before splitting: *Stealer's Wheel* (1973), *Ferguslie Park* (1974) and *Right Or Wrong* (1975). Rafferty continued solo with highly successful albums *City To City* (1978), featuring the hit 'Baker Street', and *Night Owl* (1979). Later recordings include *Snakes And Ladders* (1980), *Sleepwalking* (1982), *North And South* (1988) and *On A Wing And A Prayer* (1993).

Konrad **RAGOSSNIG**

Classical virtuoso. Also lutanist. Born in Klagenfurt, Austria on May 6, 1932. Started playing guitar at age 9. Studied at the Academy of Performing Arts in Vienna with Karl Scheit. Later studied with Segovia. Won first prize at the Cheltenham Festival in England (1960) and at the Concours International in Paris, France

(1961). Toured Europe and soon earned a reputation as an outstanding guitarist. Commissioned a number of works from Joaquin Rodrigo, Mario Castelnuovo-Tedesco and many other composers. Recordings include *Guitar Recital* (Supraphon), *Master Of The Guitar* (RCA) and *The Spanish Guitar* (Turnabout).

Bonnie **RAITT**

Singer/songwriter/guitarist. Born in Burbank, California on November 8, 1949. Daughter of Broadway singer John Raitt. Picked up acoustic guitar at age 10. Early influences included Joan Baez, Mississippi John Hurt, Fred McDowell and Muddy Waters. Moved over to the East Coast and played in an acoustic duo with

Mark Weiss/Idols

Bonnie Raitt

fretless bassist Freebo. Joined the Bluesbusters with Paul Barrere (ex-Little Feat) and finally went solo. Her music was blues with a country-rock feel. Had considerable success on the East

Coast, which led to a record deal. Albums on Warner Brothers include *Bonnie Raitt* (1971), *Give It Up* (1972), *Streetlights* (1974), *The Glow* (1979), *Green Light* (1982) and *Nine Lives* (1986). Switched to Capitol for *Nick Of Time* (1989) and *Luck Of The Draw* (1991). Also featured as guest guitarist on John Lee Hooker's *The Healer* (1989). A Grammy Award winner, who is highly respected by other musicians.

Elliott RANDALL

Session legend. Born in New York City on June 15, 1947. Started playing the guitar at age 9. Studied with Bill Suyker, Roy Smeck and Sal Salvador. Early influences included the Ventures and Howard Roberts. Started session work in 1963. Worked with the Ronettes and numerous others before forming his own band Randall's Island. They recorded *Randall's Island* (1970) and *Rock 'N' Roll City* (1972) on Polydor. Featured soloist on four Steely Dan albums (famous solo on 1972 hit 'Reeling In The Years'). Randall's outstanding playing and versatility later brought work with the Doobie Brothers, Joan Baez, Carly Simon, David Sanborn and many others. Also film and TV music. Other recordings include *Elliott Randall's New York* (1976) and *Down On The Road By The Beach* (1983). Guitar consultant for Oliver Stone's movie *The Doors* (1991). Regular columnist with *Guitar For The Practicing Musician* magazine during the '80s and early '90s. Publications include *The Guitar And Electronic Sounds* (Silver Burdett). Instructional video: *On Guitar* (DCI).

Jimmy RANEY

Jazz guitarist. Born in Louisville, Kentucky on August 20, 1927. Studied jazz and classical guitar at school and was playing professionally by the time he was 15. Worked with numerous bands in New York and Chicago, before joining Woody Herman's band in 1948. Later worked with Tal Farlow, Sal Salvador, Artie Shaw, Stan Getz (also ex-Woody Herman) and Red Norvo. By the mid-'50s he was voted Best Jazz Guitarist in several jazz journals. Did session, radio and TV work in the late '50s and started studying cello and composition. Later performed in many jazz clubs around the world and recorded a number of albums including *The Jimmy Raney Quintet* (1953), *The Jimmy Raney Quintet II* (1954), *In Three Attitudes* (1956), *Two Jims And A Zoot* (1964),

Momentum (1974), *Strings Attached* (1975), *Live In Tokyo* (1976), *Jimmy Raney: Solo* (1977), *Here's That Raney Day* (1980), *The Master* (1983), *Wisteria* (1990) and *But Beautiful* (1992).

Chris REA

UK singer/songwriter and rock guitarist. Born in Middlesborough, England, 1951. Became influenced by Joe Walsh and Ry Cooder. Played in Magdalene (with David Coverdale) and The Beautiful Losers, before signing a solo deal in 1977. Gained considerable respect and commercial success with his down-to-earth songwriting and guitar playing. Hit singles include 'Fool If You Think It's Over' (1978) and 'The Road To Hell' (1989). Albums on Magnet, WEA and East-West include *Whatever Happened To Benny Santini?* (1977), *Water Sign* (1983), *Shamrock Diaries* (1985), *Dancing With Strangers* (1987), *The Road to Hell* (1989), *Auberge* (1991) and *Espresso Logic* (1993).

Noel REDDING

Guitar/bass player. Born in Kent, England in December 1945. Started playing violin at age 9, before switching to banjo and guitar at 14. Early influences included the Shadows, the Ventures and Buddy Holly. Played in skiffle bands and left art college to become a professional musician. Joined the Jimi Hendrix Experience in 1966. The band did not have a bass player so he became one, trading his Fender Telecaster in for a Fender Jazz Bass. They recorded blues-rock classics *Are You Experienced* (1967), *Axis: Bold As Love* (1968) and *Electric Ladyland* (1968). After Hendrix, Redding worked in a band called Fat Mattress and with Lord Sutch, before forming the Noel Redding Band.

Lou REED

Singer/songwriter and rock guitarist. Born in New York on March 2, 1944. Grew up in middle-class Long Island. Played in a local rock'n'roll band as a teenager. Forced to have electro-shock therapy by his parents. Studied poetry and journalism at Syracuse University (NY). Formed the Velvet Underground in 1966 with John Cale (bass, keyboards, viola), Sterling Morrison (guitar) and Maureen Tucker (drums). Wrote songs about drugs, paranoia and sado-masochism. First album *The Velvet Underground And Nico* (1967) was a collaboration with model/singer Nico and artist Andy Warhol (famous banana album sleeve). *White Light/White Heat* (1968) was raw and uncompromising. Cale left and was replaced by Doug Yule for *The Velvet Underground* (1969), which was lighter and more mainstream. *Loaded* (1970) featured more optimistic songs and Billy Yule on drums. Reed left that year, signed to RCA and eventually recorded *Lou Reed* (1972) in London. *Transformer* (1972) was produced by David Bowie and included the

Mark Weiss/Idols

Lou Reed

US/UK hit single 'Walk On The Wild Side'. Many later albums: *Berlin* (1973), a concept LP about doomed relationship of two junkies; *Metal Machine Music* (1975), a double album of guitar feedback and machinery noise, considered to be one of the most unlistenable albums ever; *Growing Up In Public* (1980) was autobiographical; *The Blue Mask* (1981) and *Legendary Hearts* (1983) featured ex-Voidoid guitarist Robert Quine; *New York* (1989), hailed as one of his best; *Songs For Drella* (1990) with John Cale was critically acclaimed homage to Warhol; *Magic And Loss* (1992) featured songs about death. Books include *Lou Reed: Growing Up In Public* by Peter Doggett. One of the most original and influential figures in rock.

Hans **REICHEL**

Experimental guitarist and luthier. Born in Hagen, Germany on May 10, 1949. Studied violin and cello before taking up the guitar during the '60s. Became influenced by Derek Bailey and other experimental musicians by the early '70s. Built special guitars with unusual necks and developed a free-form technique that was unheard of and highly personal. Invented the daxophone (an unusual stringless instrument consisting of a clamped wooden 'tongue') which is played by bowing, striking or tapping. Recordings on Free Music Production include *Bonobo* (1975), duets with Achim Knispel on *Erdmännchen* (1977), *The Death Of The Rare Bird Ymir* (1979), *Bonobo Beach* (1981), *The Dawn Of Dachsman* (1987), *Angel Carver* (1989) with Tom Cora, *Coco Bolo Nights* (1989), *Stop Complaining / Sundown* (1991) with Fred Frith / Kazuhisa Uchihashi (1991) and the all-daxophone *Shanghaied On Tor Road* (1992). An astonishing musician.

Vernon **REID**

Progressive rock player. Born in London c.1959. Moved to the United States and grew up in New York. Picked up the guitar at age 15. Played with Kashif (R&B singer) and the Decoding Society during his teens. Later worked with Mick Jagger, Defunkt and Public Enemy. Recorded experimental rock album *Smash & Scatteration* (1986) with Bill Frisell and played on John Zorn's *The Big Gundown* (1986). Formed black heavy rock band Living Colour with Corey Glover (vocals), Muzz Skillings (bass) and William Calhoun (drums). They recorded unique and impressive rock albums on Epic such as *Vivid* (1988), *Time's Up* (1990) and *Stain* (1992). Reid's playing is dangerous and outstanding: blends raw heavy metal with avant-garde and harmolodic jazz concepts. Founder of the Black Rock Coalition (dedicated to combating racial stereotypes in the music industry).

Django **REINHARDT**

Legendary gypsy jazz guitarist. Born Jean Baptiste Reinhardt in Liverchies, Belgium on January 23, 1910. Played banjo-guitar by the time he was 13. Became greatly influenced by American jazz players such as Eddie Lang and Charlie Christian. Lost the use of 3rd and 4th fingers of his left hand in a caravan fire when he was 18, but carried on playing and developed a new technique. Formed famous jazz group, the

Django Reinhardt

'Quintet of the Hot Club of France', with violinist Stephane Grappelli in 1934. Went to America in 1946 and toured with Duke Ellington. Impressed Segovia with his playing. Died of a stroke in Fontainebleau, France on May 16, 1953. An innovator and the first European musician to exert an influence on American jazz. His strong vibrato, octave playing and exciting rhythm techniques inspired players as diverse as Julian Bream, B.B.King, Eric Johnson, Bireli Lagrene, Eddie Duran and John Etheridge. Mainly used French-made Maccaferri guitars, although he played some electric guitar during his later years. Recordings include compilations such as *Djangology* (RCA) and *Django Reinhardt & Stephane Grappelli* (GNP Crescendo). One of the most influential guitar players of all time. Included in *Guitar Player* magazine's 'Gallery Of The Greats' (1984) for his lifetime achievement. Biography: *Django Reinhardt* by Charles Delauney (Ashley Mark).

Emily **REMLER**

Jazz guitar player. Born in New York City on September 18, 1957. Grew up in Englewood Cliffs. Started listening to folk and rock guitar players such as Jimi Hendrix and Jimmy Page. Initially self-taught. Later studied at Berklee College of Music in Boston. Became influenced by Wes Montgomery and Pat Martino. Developed her own unique and beautiful technique. Worked with Tal Farlow, Barney Kessel, Larry Coryell, Charlie Byrd, Astrud Gilberto and Herb Ellis. Also formed her own

quartet. Recorded several albums on Concord Jazz including *The Firefly* (1981), *Take Two* (1982), *Transitions* (1983), *Catwalk* (1985) and *East To West* (1988). Hot Licks instructional videos include *Bebop And Swing* and *Advanced Jazz And Latin Improvisation*. Highly respected as a player and teacher. Died suddenly of a heart attack on May 4, 1990. Concord later released *Retrospective* (1991).

John **RENBOURN**

UK folk guitarist, sitar player and singer. Played in the London folk club circuit before recording critically acclaimed albums such as *John Renbourn* (1965) and *Bert And John* (1966), the latter with Bert Jansch. They formed unique folk group Pentangle in 1967 with Jacqui McShee (vocals), Danny Thompson (bass) and Terry Cox (drums). They played an innovative blend of folk, blues and jazz. Recordings include *The Pentangle* (1968), *Sweet Child* (1968), *Basket Of Light* (1969), *Cruel Sister* (1970), *Reflections* (1971) and *Solomon's Seal* (1972). Renbourn had also recorded solo albums such as *Another Monday* (1967), *Sir John Alot Of Merre Englandes Musik Thynge And Ye Grene Knyghte* (1968) and *Faro Annie* (1972). The Pentangle split up in 1973 and Renbourn continued with *The Hermit* (1977), *Maid In Bedlam* (1977), *Black Balloon* (1979), *Enchanted Garden* (1980), *Nine Maidens* (1988), *Ship Of Fools* (1988) and *The Essential John Renbourn* (1992). Also columnist with *Guitar Player* magazine. Renbourn and Jansch influenced many other folk-orientated singer-songwriters including John Martyn, Ralph McTell and Roy Harper.

Randy **RHOADS**

Heavy rock guitarist. Born in Santa Monica, California on December 6, 1956. Started learning guitar at age 6. Influences included Jeff Beck, Ritchie Blackmore, Gary Moore, Eddie Van Halen and classical music. Taught guitar extensively as a teenager. Joined heavy metal band Quiet Riot with Kevin DuBrow (vocals), Rudy Sarzo (bass) and Frankie Banali (drums) in 1975. The band became very popular in the LA music circuit and released the albums *Quiet Riot I* (1977) and *Quiet Riot II* (1978) on CBS. Left to join Ozzy Osbourne's band in 1979. They recorded *Blizzard Of Oz* (1981) and *Diary Of A Madman* (1981) for Jet Records, before Rhoads' untimely death in a plane crash on March 20, 1982. He was highly respected as

R

93

a melodic lead guitarist and teacher. Osbourne later released the 1987 double-album *Tribute* (recordings of 1981 concerts featuring Rhoads) in memory of the guitarist.

Marc **RIBOT**

Experimental rock guitarist. Born in 1955. Grew up in South Orange, New Jersey. Influences included jazz giants such as Ornette Coleman, Eric Dolphy and Thelonius Monk. Worked with Tom Waits on Island albums *Rain Dogs* (1985), *Frank's Wild Years* (1987) and *Big Time* (1988). With the Lounge Lizards on *The Lounge Lizards* (1986), *Live In Tokyo: Big Heart* (1987), *No Pain For Cakes* (1987) and *Big Time* (1989). Also with Elvis Costello on *Spike* (1989) and Marianne Faithful on *Blazing Away* (1990). Formed his own experimental group the Rootless Cosmopolitans. They recorded uncompromising and highly unpredictable albums on Island and Crepuscule: *Rootless Cosmopolitans* (1990) and *Requiem For What's His Name* (1993). Both recordings heavily feature Ribot's unique and jagged playing. His style incorporates angular chromatic runs, graunchy bends and "out" comping.

Keith **RICHARDS**

Legendary rock guitarist. Born in Dartford, Kent on December 18, 1943. Received his first guitar in 1956. Went to the same school as vocalist Mick Jagger. They shared musical interests (Chuck Berry, Muddy Waters and Elvis Presley) and became close friends. Met multi-instrumentalist Brian Jones, at Alexis Korner's blues club in London and decided to form a band. Brian named it the Rolling Stones, after the title of a Muddy Waters song. By 1963 they were joined by bass player Bill Wyman and drummer Charlie Watts, completing the now famous line-up. Initially supported Blues Incorporated (see Alexis KORNER) at the Marquee club in London. Signed to Decca and released a relatively unsuccessful version of Chuck Berry's 'Come On' (1963). After several other cover versions, Jagger and Richards worked on original songs and covered new ground. Developed a fresh and raunchy two-guitar sound. Their single 'Satisfaction' went to No.1 on both sides of the Atlantic in 1965 and helped popularise the fuzztone. They went on to have several other famous hit singles and best-selling albums. Jagger, Richards and Jones were arrested on drug offences in 1967, although

Keith Richards

Denis O'Regan/Idols

prison terms were eventually quashed. Soon Jones' drug problem was so serious he was eased out of the band. He drowned in his swimming pool on July 3, 1969 and was replaced by Mick Taylor (ex- John Mayall), who was in turn replaced by Ron Wood in 1974. The Rolling Stones continued to be a successful live and recording act. Albums on Decca/London include *Rolling Stones* (1964), *Rolling Stones 2* (1965), *Out Of Our Heads* (1965), *Aftermath* (1966) and *Beggar's Banquet* (1968). On Rolling Stones Records: *Sticky Fingers* (1971), *Exile On Main Street* (1972), *It's Only Rock And Roll* (1974), *Black & Blue* (1976), *Emotional Rescue* (1980) and *Steel Wheels* (1989). Richards also released solo albums on Virgin: *Talk Is Cheap* (1988) and *Main Offender* (1992). One of the most influential guitar players of all time.

Carlos **RIOS**

Jazz and rock guitarist. Born in San Antonio, Texas in 1954. Family moved to Torrance, California. While he was at high school het met Larry Carlton, who became a big influence and mentor. Got into session work and soon became one of the most sought-after players on the West Coast. Worked with Yellowjackets (on

1985 album *Samurai Samba*), Herbie Hancock, Stanley Clarke, Chet Atkins, Robben Ford, Chaka Khan, Chick Corea's Elektric Band (on 1987 album *Chick Corea Elektric Band*), David Sanborn, Gino Vanelli, Kenny Rogers and Lionel Richie (lyrical guitar solo on Richie's famous 1984 hit 'Hello'). A versatile all-rounder.

Lee **RITENOUR**

Jazz and classical player. Born in Hollywood, California on January 1, 1952. Started playing guitar at age 5. Played in local bands from age 12. Inspired by Jim Hall, Joe Pass and Wes Montgomery. Studied with Joe Pass, Howard Roberts and Christopher Parkening. Later taught classical guitar at the University of Southern California. Worked with Steely Dan, Stanley Clarke, Pink Floyd, Stevie Wonder, Carly Simon and many others. His own albums on Coral, Epic, Elektra and JVC are a light fusion of latin, jazz, rock and soul. They include *Guitar Player* (1976), *Captain Fingers* (1977), *Rit* (1981), *Rio* (1982). On GRP: *Earth Run* (1986) featuring SynthAxe, *Portrait* (1987), *Stolen Moments* (1990), *Collection* (1991) and *Wes Bound* (1993). The Columbia book *The Lee Ritenour Collection* (1985) features arrangements and transcriptions of 12 of his tunes.

Howard **ROBERTS**

Jazz player. Born in Phoenix, Arizona on October 2, 1929. Started playing the guitar from an early age. Studied with Horace Hutchett at age 12 and played in local bands during WWII. Moved to Los Angeles in 1950 and became a studio guitarist, recording on many television and film soundtracks. Also worked with the Beach Boys, Frank Sinatra, Ella Fitzgerald, Duane Eddy, the Monkees and many others. Later gave seminars regularly throughout the United States and became a regular columnist with *Guitar Player* magazine. Author of several instruction books including *The Howard Roberts Guitar Book* and *The Guitar Compendium Vols 1,2 & 3* (both Playback Publishing). Founder of the Guitar Institute of Technology (G.I.T.) in Hollywood. Highly respected player and teacher. Died of prostate cancer in Seattle on June 28, 1992. Recordings on Verve, Capitol and Concord include *Mr. Roberts Plays Guitar* (1957), *Good Picking* (1957), *H.R. Is A Dirty Guitar Player* (1963) and *The Real Howard Roberts* (1977).

Robbie **ROBERTSON**

Singer/songwriter, rock guitarist and producer. Born in Toronto, Canada on July 5, 1943. Formed The Band with Richard Manuel (piano, vocals), Garth Hudson (organ, sax), Rick Danko (bass) and Levon Helm (drums) in the early '60s. They backed up Ronnie Hawkins, before working as Bob Dylan's band for his 1966 World Tour (played at notorious Albert Hall concert). The Band's first two Capitol albums, *Music From The Big Pink* (1968) and *The Band* (1969), caused a sensation. Later recorded *Rock Of Ages* (1972) and *Northern Lights, Southern Cross* (1975). Backed Dylan on *Planet Waves* (1974) and *Basement Tapes* (1975). The Band split in 1976. Robertson spent more time in production and films. Later recorded critically acclaimed solo albums on Geffen: *Robbie Robertson* (1987) and *Storyville* (1991). His songs have also been covered by Joan Baez, Emmylou Harris and many others.

Duke **ROBILLARD**

Blues player. Born in Burrillville, Rhode Island in 1950. Started playing guitar at age 12. Early influences included James Burton, Chuck Berry, Hubert Sumlin, Muddy Waters and B.B.King. Formed the nine-piece blues band Roomful of Blues in 1967 with pianist Al Copley and others. Gigged extensively before recording Island and Antilles albums *Roomful Of Blues* (1977) and *Let's Have A Party* (1979). Robillard left to form the Pleasure Kings. Recordings on Rounder include *Duke Robillard & The Pleasure Kings* (1983) and *Swing* (1987). Instructional video: *Uptown Blues, Jazz Rock and Swing Guitar* (Hot Licks 1992).

Steve **RODBY**

Bass player. Born in Joliet, Illinois in 1954. Wanted to play bass at age 3 but had to wait until he was 7 (big enough to tackle the upright bass). Started playing classical music and improvising at age 10. Studied bass performance with Warren Benfield of the Chicago Symphony Orchestra. Self-taught on electric bass. After graduating from college in 1977, he played in Chicago for a while and toured with Monty Alexander and Michael Franks. Also worked with Ross Traut on his eponymous solo album and with Simon & Bard on various Flying Fish recordings. Joined the Pat Metheny Group in 1981 and played on ECM albums *Off Ramp* (1982), live *Travels* (1983) and *First Circle* (1984). On Geffen: *Still*

Life Talking (1987), *Letter From Home* (1989) and *Secret Story* (1992).

Nile **RODGERS**

Jazz-funk guitarist and producer. Born in New York City on September 19, 1952. Grew up with his grandparents in California, where he played flute, clarinet and saxophone at school. Moved back to the Bronx and started playing the guitar at age 16. Taught himself from books. Played in garage bands and then at clubs and sessions. Formed Chic (disco band) in 1977 with bassist Bernard Edwards and others. The combination of Rodgers' infectious rhythm guitar playing, Edwards' up-front funk bass, and very catchy tunes made the band extremely popular during the late '70s: singles 'Le Freak' (1978) and 'Good Times' (1979) both reached No.1 in the US charts (both top ten in UK). Albums on Atlantic include *C'est Chic* (1978), *Risqué* (1979), *Real People* (1980) and *Tongue In Chic* (1982). The band were the most commercially successful act on the Atlantic label. Split up in 1983 and Rodgers recorded solo album *Adventures In The Land Of The Good Groove* (1983) on Mirage. Also worked with David Bowie, Mick Jagger, Sister Sledge, Diana Ross, Debbie Harry and many others.

Angel & Pepe **ROMERO**

Classical/flamenco guitar players. Sons of famous flamenco player Celedonio Romero. Both born in Malaga, Spain (Pepe in 1944 and Angel in 1946). Both picked up the guitar at a very young age and played in the family guitar quartet the Romeros. Moved to California in 1958. Formed a duo and premiered Rodrigo's 'Concerto Madrigal' for two guitars and orchestra in 1970. Both later gave many outstanding solo performances. Angel's recordings include *Rodrigo Concerto And Fantasia* and *Spanish Virtuoso* (both EMI Angel), while Pepe recorded *Famous Guitar Music*, *Rodrigo For Solo Guitar*, *Boccherini Quartets* and *Flamenco* (all on Philips).

Mick **RONSON**

British rock guitarist. Born in Hull, England on May 26, 1945. Started learning violin at age 11 and switched to guitar at 17. Played in various bands and worked as a gardener. Met David Bowie in London and joined his band. They recorded classic pop albums such as *Hunky Dory* (1971), *The Rise And Fall Of Ziggy*

Stardust And The Spiders From Mars (1972) and *Aladdin Sane* (1973) on RCA. Ronson's power chords gave extra solidity to Bowie's music. Also worked with Lou Reed (on 1972 classic *Transformer*), Ian Hunter, Mott the

Denis O'Regan/Idols

Mick Ronson

Hoople, David Johansen and Bob Dylan. Played on Roger McGuinn's highly praised CBS album *Cardiff Rose* (1976). Solo albums on RCA include *Slaughter On Tenth Avenue* (1974) and *Play, Don't Worry* (1975). Later worked with Ellen Foley, Morrissey (on his *Your Arsenal* album in 1992) and many others. Appeared with Bowie at the Freddie Mercury Aids Benefit Concert in 1992. Died of liver cancer on April 30, 1993.

Francis **ROSSI**

UK rock guitarist and singer. Born in Peckham, London on April 29, 1949. Formed Status Quo (originally the Spectres) in 1967 with Rick Parfitt (guitar), Alan Lancaster (bass), Roy Lynes (keyboards) and John Coughlan (drums). Started off playing psychedelic pop and changed into an infectious 12-bar boogie band by the time Lynes left in the early-'70s. Despite being unfashionable with critics, Quo became one of the most popular British bands of the '70s and '80s. Hits include 'Caroline' (1973), 'Down Down' (1974) and 'Whatever You Want' (1979). There were a number of personnel changes over the years but Rossi and Parfitt were always the nucleus of the band. Albums include *Picturesque Matchstickable Messages* (1968), *Ma Kelly's Greasy Spoon* (1970), *Piledriver* (1973), *Hello* (1973), *Quo* (1974), *Whatever You Want* (1979), *Back To Back To Back* (1983), *In The Army Now* (1986), *Ain't*

Francis Rossi

Complaining (1988) and *Rock Till You Drop* (1991). Included in the *Guinness Book Of Records* after playing charity concerts in four UK cities within 12 hours. Books include *Status Quo: The Authorised Biography* by John Shearlaw.

Arlen **ROTH**

Rock guitarist and teacher. Grew up in the Bronx, New York. Started learning guitar at age 11. Studied art and photography at New York's High School of Music and Art. Became influenced by blues players Mike Bloomfield and B.B.King. Moved upstate at age 19 and began doing session work at A&R Studios in New York. Worked with Phoebe Snow, Duane Eddy and Ry Cooder (on the film *Crossroads*). Author of several guitar instruction books including *Arlen Roth's Complete Electric Guitar* (Doubleday), *Arlen Roth's Complete Acoustic Guitar* (Schirmer) and *Slide Guitar* (Oak). Founder of the 'Hot Licks' instruction tapes (which now have special editions hosted by Tal Farlow, Steve Morse, Joe Pass, Emily Remler, John Entwistle, Vivian Campbell and others). Recorded a number of solo albums on Rounder and Breaking Records including *Hot Pickups* (1980) and *Paint Job* (1983).

Uli Jon **ROTH**

Heavy-rock guitarist. Born in Dusseldorf, Germany in December 1954. Started learning trumpet before switching to guitar and bass at 14. Influences included Jimi Hendrix, Jan Akkerman, Eric Clapton and Django Reinhardt. Played in a number of local bands. Joined the Scorpions (replacing Michael Schenker) in 1974, while still in his teens. Soon built up a considerable reputation for his dramatic and melodic soloing. Featured on Scorpions albums *Fly To The Rainbow* (1974), *In Trance* (1975), *Virgin Killer* (1976) and *Best Of The Scorpions* (1979). Left the Scorpions in 1979 to form classically-orientated rock band Electric Sun. They recorded *Earthquake* (1979), *Firewind* (1981) and *Beyond The Astral Skies* (1985).

Todd **RUNDGREN**

Singer/songwriter. Also multi-instrumentalist and producer. Born in Philadelphia, Pennsylvania on June 22, 1948. Began playing electric guitar at age 17. Early influences included Eric Clapton, Jeff Beck and Harvey

Todd Rundgren

Mandel. Formed the Nazz in the late '60s, releasing three albums on Screen Gems/Columbia: *Nazz* (1968), *Nazz Nazz* (1969) and *Nazz 3* (1969). Worked on a number of solo projects before forming Utopia in the mid '70s with Roger Powell (keyboards, vocals), Kasim Sulton (bass, vocals) and Willie Wilcox (drums, vocals). They recorded a number of progressive albums on Bearsville, including *Todd Rundgren's Utopia* (1974), *RA* (1977) and *Adventures In Utopia* (1980). Switched to Passport for *Oblivion* (1983) and *POV* (1985). Rundgren solo albums on Bearsville, Warner Brothers and Forward include *Runt* (1970), *Something/Anything* (1972), *A Wizard/A True Star* (1973), *Todd* (1974), *Initiation* (1975), *Hermit Of Mink Hollow* (1978), *The Ever Popular Tortured Artist Effect* (1983), *Nearly Human* (1989) and *No World Order* (1993). Also produced albums by New York Dolls, Fanny, Meat Loaf, Steve Hillage, the Tubes, Patti Smith, Cheap Trick, XTC and many others. A highly influential all-rounder with a distinctive and expressive guitar style.

Otis RUSH

Blues guitarist and singer/songwriter. Self-taught. Born in Philadelphia, Pennsylvania on April 29, 1934. Grew up on a farm. Started playing guitar at age 10. Left-handed player. Moved to Chicago when he was 14. Early influences included Muddy Waters, Howlin' Wolf, Jimmy Rogers and John Lee Hooker. Formed a group and performed as Little Otis. Became popular in the Chicago blues scene. Had a hit with 'I Can't Quit You Baby' (1956). Recordings on Delmark, Bullfrog and other labels include *Mourning In The Morning* (1969), *Cold Place In Hell* (1975), *Right Place, Wrong Time* (1976), *So Many Roads* (1978), *Troubles, Troubles* (1979), *Screamin' And Cryin'* (1979) and *Tops* (1985). Influenced many other players including Jimmy Page and Mick Taylor.

David RUSSELL

Classical virtuoso. Born in Glasgow, Scotland on June 1, 1953. Grew up in Scotland and Menorca. Studied classical guitar at the Royal Academy of Music in London and won the Julian Bream Prize two years in succession. Later studied with Jose Tomas in Spain. Took the first prize in the Benicasim contest, the International Tarrega Competition and the Andrés Segovia Competition in 1977. Later gave many recitals and master classes around the world and appeared at a number of international guitar festivals. Made recordings on Guitar Masters including *David Russell Plays Antonio Lauro* and critically-acclaimed *Recital* (featuring transcriptions of works by Bach, Handel and Scarlatti). On Overture: *Something Unique*.

Ray RUSSELL

UK guitarist/composer. Born in London on April 4, 1947. Started playing the guitar at age 10. Formed a jazz trio as a teenager. Influences included John Coltrane, Herbie Hancock and Wes Montgomery. Worked with Georgie Fame before assembling his own quartet for CBS albums *Turn Circle* (1968), *Dragon Hill* (1969) and *Rites & Rituals* (1970). Later made a number of recordings on various labels with numerous musicians: *Live At The ICA* (1971), *Secret Asylum* (1973), *Ready Or Not* (1977), atmospheric *Childscape* (1989), *Live At Montreux Vols I&II* (1989) and *A Table Near The Band* (1990). With Tina Turner on *Private Dancer* (1984) and jazz composer Gil Evans on *Take Me To The Sun* (released 1990). Formed fusion trio Protocol with bassist Anthony Jackson and drummer Simon Phillips for *Force Majeure* (1993). Also worked with Alex Harvey, Phil Collins, Brian Ferry and many others. TV/film scores include *Bergerac*, *BBC Screen On One*, *Down Among The Big Boys* and *The Alleyn Mysteries*. A talented and versatile musician.

Corrado RUSTICI

Italian rock/fusion player. Born in 1955. Grew up in Naples. Started playing folk mandolin at age 5 and switched to guitar by the time he was 8. Heavily influenced by John McLaughlin. Played in bands Cervello and Uno before forming the fusion group Nova in the mid-'70s. Rustici's tasteful songwriting and intricate soloing can be heard on Nova albums on Arista: *Vimana* (1976), *Wings Of Love* (1977) and *Sun City* (1978). The band line-up changed several times before they finally split up in 1978. Rustici later worked for Narada Michael Walden, Angela Bofill, Herbie Hancock and Sister Sledge.

Mike RUTHERFORD

UK rock bassist and guitarist. Born in England on October 2, 1950. Formed art-rock band Genesis in 1967 with schoolmates Peter Gabriel (vocals), Tony Banks (keyboards) and others. Gave a demo tape to Jonathan King, who organised recording of debut album on Decca: *From Genesis To Revelation* (1969). Signed to Charisma and recorded *Trespass* (1970). Steve Hackett (guitar) and Phil Collins (drums) were added for *Nursery Cryme* (1971). By then the band had a distinctive sound and unique stage show, fronted by Gabriel in a number of spectacular costumes. Recorded *Foxtrot* (1972),

Mike Rutherford (left) of Genesis

Genesis Live (1973), *Selling England By The Pound* (1973) and the epic conceptual *The Lamb Lies Down On Broadway* (1974), before Gabriel left in 1975. Collins eventually took over on vocals. *A Trick Of The Tail* (1976) was a huge success, with Collins sounding uncannily like Gabriel. Also released *Wind And Wuthering* (1977) and live *Seconds Out* (1977), before Hackett left to go solo (see Steve HACKETT). Commercial success continued with more mainstream albums: *And Then There*

Were Three (1978), *Duke* (1980), *Abacab* (1981), *Genesis* (1983), *Invisible Touch* (1986), *We Can't Dance* (1991) and live *The Way We Walk - Vol 1/2* (1992/3). One of the most original and popular bands of the '70s and '80s. Collins also became successful solo artist and Rutherford formed Mike And The Mechanics for *Mike And The Mechanics* (1986) and *The Living Years* (1988).

Terje **RYPDAL**

Jazz guitar player. Born in Oslo, Norway on August 23, 1947. Started learning the piano at age 5 and picked up the guitar at age 13. Played in local rock groups before joining saxophonist Jan Garbarek's band in 1968. Influenced by Charlie Christian, Wes Montgomery and Kenny Burrell. Studied classical music with composer Finn Mortenson. Also formed a fusion group called Odyssey during the mid-'70s. Recordings on ECM include *Odyssey* (1975), *Waves* (1978), *To Be Continued* (1981), *Eos* (1984), *Chaser* (1985), *Blue* (1987), *Works* (1989), *Afric Pepperbird* (1990) and *Undisonus* (1990).

Sal **SALVADOR**

Jazz guitarist. Born in Monson, Massachusetts on November 21, 1925. Started playing guitar at an early age. Early influences included hillbilly music and the jazz styles of Charlie Christian, Carl Kress and George Van Eps. Took correspondence courses with Oscar Moore and Hy White. Joined the staff at the Radio City Music Hall in New York in 1949. Worked with the Columbia Recording Company, supporting famous artists such as Tony Bennett, Rosemary Clooney, Frankie Laine and Marlene Dietrich. Also played in the Stan Kenton Orchestra and a quartet of his own during the early '50s. Later became a respected teacher and author of instruction books including *Sal Salvador's Single String Studies* (Henry Adler Music), as well as performing regularly on the East Coast. Recordings on Stash include *The World's Greatest Jazz Standards* (1984) and *Sal Salvador & Crystal Image* (1990).

Richie Sambora (second from right)

Richie **SAMBORA**

US rock guitarist. Born on July 11, 1959. Joined Bon Jovi in the early-'80s, with John Bongiovi (vocals), David Bryan (keyboards), Alec Such (bass) and Tico Torres (drums). Signed to Phonogram and released *Bon Jovi* (1984) and

7,800 Degrees Farenheit (1985) with limited success. However, the third recording *Slippery When Wet* (1986) contained much stronger material and constant touring paid off: the album went to the top of the US charts, stayed there for two months and was the biggest selling rock album of the year. Follow up *New Jersey* (1988) went to No.1 in both US and UK charts. Also first American rock album to be issued in the CIS (formerly USSR) on the state-owned Melodiya label. Headlined the Moscow Peace Festival in 1989. Later recording: *Keep The Faith* (1992).

Carlos SANTANA

Rock guitarist and songwriter. Born in Autlan de Navarro, Mexico on July 20, 1947. Started playing the guitar at an early age. Performed in Tijuana night clubs as a teenager. Moved to San Francisco in 1962. Developed a melodic blues-influenced lead guitar style. Appeared as a guest on *Live Adventures Of Mike Bloomfield & Al*

Steve Gillett/Redferns

Carlos Santana

Kooper in 1969. Formed the band Santana (originally Santana Blues Band), playing at the Woodstock festival the same year. Signed to CBS and recorded debut album *Santana* (1969), a unique blend of blues-rock and Afro-Cuban

rhythms. Made US Top 5. *Abraxas* (1970) was even more successful and boasted classic tracks 'Black Magic Woman' and 'Samba Pa Ti'. The next two albums, *Santana III* and *Caravanserai* (both 1972), had a more jazz-rock feel. Became influenced by guru Sri Chimnoy and recorded *Love, Devotion, Surrender* (1973) with John McLaughlin (another Chimnoy convert). Later Santana albums include *Amigos* (1976), *Moonflower* (1977), *Zebop!* (1981), *Havana Moon* (1985), *Freedom* (1987), *Blues For Salvador* (1987), *Persuasion* (1989), *Spirits Dancing In The Flesh* (1990) and *Milagro* (1991). Santana's bands have included many notable players over the years, such as Neal Schon, Jan Hammer, Stanley Clarke, Herbie Hancock and Billy Cobham.

Blues SARACENO

Heavy rock guitarist. Born c.1972. Started playing the guitar at around age 9. Self-taught. Early influences included Chuck Berry, the Beatles, Deep Purple, Johnny Winter and Eddie Van Halen. Worked with Jack Bruce and Kingdom Come. Albums on Guitar Recordings include *Never Look Back* (1989) and *Plaid* (1992). The latter features a mean version of Cream's track 'Cat's Squirrel'. Also featured on Guitar Recordings compilation *Guitar's Practicing Musicians* (1993). Joined heavy metal band Poison in 1993 (replacing Richie Kotzen). Columnist with *Screamer* magazine during the '90s. An impressive player with a maturity that belies his years.

Rudy SARZO

Rock bass player. Born in Havana, Cuba in 1952. Family relocated to Miami, Florida. Started playing trombone and guitar and took up bass by the time he was 15. Played in rock and roll clubs and topless bars in Miami. Moved to New York, Chicago and eventually Los Angeles. Joined heavy metal band Quiet Riot in 1975. They had considerable success as a live act and recorded a number of best-selling albums on CBS and Epic: *Quiet Riot* (1977), *Quiet Riot II* (1978), *Metal Health* (1983), *Critical Condition* (1984) and *Quiet Riot III* (1986). Joined Project Driver with Tony MacAlpine (guitar), Rob Rock (vocals) and Tommy Aldridge (drums). Also played bass on Ozzy Osbourne's album *Tribute* (1977) and Whitesnake's *Slip Of The Tongue* (1989). Instructional video: *Sarzo Master Class* (Hot Licks).

Joe **SATRIANI**

Rock virtuoso. Born in Long Island, New York in 1952. Started playing drums and switched to

Joe Satriani

guitar on the day Jimi Hendrix died (Sept 18, 1970). Early influences included his sister Marion, as well as Hendrix, Wes Montgomery and John McLaughlin. Played in local bands before moving over to California. Formed a rock trio Squares and released a solo EP *Joe Satriani* (1984) on Rubina. Became well-known as a teacher (famous pupils include Steve Vai and Kirk Hammett of Metallica). Also worked with Greg Kihn, Mick Jagger, Tony Williams and drummer Danny Gottlieb. Other Satriani recordings on Relativity and Epic include *Not Of This Earth* (1986), *Surfing With The Alien* (1987), *Flying In A Blue Dream* (1990) featuring brilliant title track, and *The Extremist* (1992). Combines formidable scalar soloing with strong use of tremolo arm, two-handed techniques, unusual harmonics and other effects. One of the most outstanding and influential rock players of the '80s and '90s. Best-selling video on Relativity: *The Satch Tapes* (1992).

Boz **SCAGGS**

Rock singer/guitarist. Born William Royce Scaggs in Ohio on June 8, 1944. Grew up in Dallas, Texas. Joined the Marksmen with Steve Miller at high-school. Played with R&B band

the Wigs before touring Europe as a solo performer. Recorded debut album *Boz* (1965) in Sweden. Returned to the US to join the Steve Miller Band for albums *Children Of The Future* (1968) and *Sailor* (1968). Left Miller in 1969 to resume solo career. Hits with 'Lowdown' (1976), 'What Can I Say' (1977), 'Lido Shuffle' (1977), 'Breakdown Dead Ahead' (1980) and 'Miss Sun' (1981). Albums include *Boz Scaggs* (1969), *Moments* (1971), *Boz Scaggs And Band* (1971), *My Time* (1972), *Slow Dancer* (1974), *Silk Degrees* (1976), *Two Down Then Left* (1977), *Middle Man* (1980) and *Other Roads* (1988). His songs are bluesy and soulful.

Michael **SCHENKER**

Heavy metal player. Born in Sarstedt, Germany on January 10, 1955. Picked up a guitar at age 9 and began teaching himself. Worked with a number of bands as a teenager. Early influences included Jeff Beck, Jimmy Page, Eric Clapton

Ulf Magusson/Idols

Michael Schenker

and Leslie West. Played with the Scorpions on the album *Lonesome Crow* (1972). Left to join UFO in 1973 and gained a considerable reputation for his melodic lead playing. Albums on Chrysalis include *Phenomenon* (1974), *Force It* (1975), *No Heavy Petting* (1976), *Lights Out* (1977) and *Obsession* (1978). Left the band in 1979 to form the Michael Schenker Group. Albums on Chrysalis include *Michael Schenker*

Group (1980), *Assault Attack* (1982) and *Built To Destroy* (1983). On EMI: *Perfect Timing* (1987), *Save Yourself* (1989) and *Never Ending Nightmare* (1992). An outstanding rock player who influenced Carlos Cavazo, Warren De Martini and many others.

Tom SCHOLTZ

Rock player and guitar effects inventor. Born in Toledo, Ohio on March 10, 1947. Started playing piano at age 8 and did not pick up guitar until he was 20. Early influences included the Beatles, the Hollies, the Yardbirds and Led Zeppelin. Graduated from Massachusetts Institute of Technology and went into research work for Polaroid. Spent his spare time making unique guitar effects, which he used later in his AOR band Boston. Signed to Epic: debut album *Boston* (1976) sold more than 7 million copies and is considered a classic. Other albums on Epic and MCA include *Don't Look Back* (1978) and *Third Stage* (1986). All three recordings reached the US Top 5, with total sales of more than 20 million. Inventor of the revolutionary and extremely successful Rockman (portable guitar amplifier with built in distortion, chorus and delay effects), marketed by his own company Scholtz Research & Development.

Neal SCHON

Rock guitarist. Born in Oklahoma on February 27, 1954. Picked up the guitar at a very young age. Joined Santana at age 15 and played on *Santana III* (1971) and *Caravanserai* (1972). Left to form AOR band Journey in 1973 with George Tickner (guitar), Ross Valory (bass) and Prairie Prince (drums). They were later joined by keyboardist Greg Rolie. Journey had considerable success with albums such as *Journey* (1975), *Infinity* (1978), *Departure* (1980), *Escape* (1981), *Frontiers* (1983), *Raised On Radio* (1986) and *Greatest Hits* (1988). Schon also recorded *Untold Passion* (1982) and *Here To Stay* (1983) with keyboardist Jan Hammer. Joined John Waite's Bad English in 1988. A tasteful and melodic rock player.

John SCOFIELD

Jazz/fusion guitarist and composer. Born in Wilton, Connecticut on December 26, 1951. Started playing guitar at high school. Later studied at Berklee College of Music in Boston. Became heavily influenced by Jim Hall, Mick

Goodrick and John McLaughlin. Developed his own angular bebop style, incorporating elements of blues, funk and rock. Worked with Charles Mingus, Tony Williams, Ron Carter, Lee Konitz, Larry Coryell, Gerry Mulligan, Billy Cobham, Gary Burton and Miles Davis. Later went solo. Recorded a number of critically acclaimed albums. On Enja: *Shinola* (1982). On Gramavision: *Electric Outlet* (1984), *Still Warm* (1986), *Blue Matter* (1987) and *Loud*

John Scofield

Jazz (1988) all featured exciting and sophisticated funk grooves; emphasis switched more to bebop for *Flat Out* (1989). Changed to Blue Note for *Time On My Hands* (1990), *Meant To Be* (1991), *Grace Under Pressure* (1992) and *What We Do* (1993). Instructional videos include *John Scofield On Improvisation* (DCI) and *Jazz-Funk Guitar* (REH). His unique, blues-influenced style often combines across-the-beat phrasing with advanced modal passages. One of the most adventurous, expressive and respected jazz guitar/composers of the '80s and '90s. Voted Best Jazz Guitarist in *Guitar Player* (1992).

Andrés SEGOVIA

Legendary classical virtuoso. Born in Granada, Spain on February 21, 1893. Started playing guitar at age 10. His parents were worried because the guitar was not seen as a 'respectable' instrument in those days. Segovia changed that during his lifetime. He adapted music composed for other instruments to the guitar and created the classical guitar technique. Initially found enormous opposition to the instrument from other musicians and the press. However, his reputation as an outstanding musician grew and he was invited to play for Queen Victoria of Spain in 1920. By 1928 he had astounded audiences around the world with his performances. His arrangements of pieces by Bach, Handel and Tarrega became standards for the classical guitar. Also commissioned works by composers such as Villa-Lobos, Falla, Castelnuovo-Tedesco, Ponse and Tansman, thus broadening the repertoire of the instrument. Taught many outstanding classical players including Julian Bream, Christopher Parkening, John Williams and Alexandre Lagoya. Died in 1987. Recordings include *Maestro* (MCA), *Granada* (MCA), *Guitar Recital* (Decca/Ermitage), *Concerto* (MCA), *An Evening With Andrés Segovia* (Decca), *The Genius Of Andrés Segovia: A Bach Recital* (Everest), and *The Intimate Guitar* (RCA Red Seal). Included in *Guitar Player* magazine's 'Gallery Of The Greats' after being voted Best Classical Guitarist (1970-1974).

Paul SENEGAL

Zydeco (Cajun) guitarist. Born in Lafayette, Louisiana in 1944. Started playing guitar at age 12 and eventually worked with most of the major Zydeco bands, including Stanley Dural and his Ils Sont Partis Band, Rockin' Dopsie, Sampy and the Bad Habits, Fernest Arceneaux and the Thunders and Clifton Chenier and his Red Hot Louisiana Band. Recordings made during the '70s with Chenier include *The King Of Zydeco, Bogalusa Boogie* and *Clifton Chenier And His Red Hot Louisiana Band* (all Arhoolie). With Rockin' Dopsie: *Crowned Prince Of Zydeco* (1987) on Sonet.

Eldon SHAMBLIN

Bluegrass/swing rhythm guitar player. Born in Weatherford, Oklahoma on April 24, 1916. Began teaching himself guitar as a teenager. Early influences included jazz players such as Eddie Lang, Django Reinhardt, Frank Victor and Harry Volpe. Played in Oklahoma bars at age 17. Developed an outstanding western swing style, incorporating chord melodies with complex bass lines and arpeggios. Member of Dave Edward's Alabama Boys and later in Bob Wills' Texas Playboys. Given a gold-finished Stratocaster by Leo Fender in 1954. Texas Playboys recordings on Columbia and Delta include *Bob Wills Anthology* (1973), *Bob Wills & His Texas Playboys In Concert* (1976), *The San Antonio Rose Story* (1982) and *Heaven, Hell or Houston* (1983).

Elliott SHARP

Experimental guitarist, composer. Born in Cleveland in 1951. Grew up in White Plains, New York. Started playing guitar in 1968 after seeing Jimi Hendrix. Later became influenced by Sonny Sharrock, Ornette Coleman, Iannis Xenakis, Conlon Nancarrow and Cecil Taylor. Studied at Cornell University and Bard College. Plays guitars (often with overdrive), prepared guitars, bass, mandolin, clarinet, soprano sax and trombone. Also various home-made instruments, including a 'tubinet' (bass clarinet with a tuba mouthpiece). Developed an unusual two-handed tapping technique (producing overtones by hitting very lightly). Albums on Glass, Zoar, Dossier, SST and Enemy include *Nots* (1982), *Carbon* (1984), *Marco Polo's Argali* (1985), *In The Land Of The Yahoos* (1987), *Monster Curve* (1989) and *Tocsin* (1992).

Sonny SHARROCK

Free-improvisational jazz guitarist. Born in Ossining, New York on August 27, 1940. Started singing baritone in an amateur vocal group. Took up the guitar at age 20. Early influences included Miles Davis and John Coltrane. Studied at Berklee College of Music in Boston during 1961/62 and also had lessons with Sun Ra. Later worked with Don Cherry, Wayne Shorter, Miles Davis and Last Exit. One of the most remarkable and unconventional guitar players in modern jazz. Recordings on Vortex and Atco include *Black Woman* (1970) and *Paradise* (1974). On Enemy: *Guitar* (1986), *Seize The Rainbow* (1987), *Live In New York* (1990), *Ask The Ages* (1991) and *High Life* (1991).

Aaron SHEARER

Classical guitarist, author and teacher. Born in Anatone, Washington on December 6, 1919. Started playing guitar at age 9. Gave many classical guitar recitals, before working with Benny Goodman and a number of others. Later concentrated on teaching and wrote a variety of successful instruction books including *Classical Guitar Technique, Scale Pattern Studies, Guitar Note Speller* (all Bellwin Mills) and *Learning The Classic Guitar Parts I & 2* (Mel Bay). Respected teacher (pupils include David Tanenbaum and many others) and author.

Billy **SHEEHAN**

Rock bass virtuoso. Born c.1953. Started playing the guitar, before switching over to bass guitar at age 15. Influences included Jimi Hendrix, Frank Zappa and Tim Bogert. Developed a unique and impressive two-handed hammering technique. Formed Talas with Phil Naro (vocals), Mitch Perry (guitar) and Mark Miller (drums). Recordings on Zorro, Relativity and Evenfall include *Talas* (1980), *Sink Your Teeth Into That* (1982) and *Live Speed On Ice* (1983). Left to join David Lee Roth's band, playing bass on Warner Brothers albums *Eat 'Em And Smile* (1986) and *Skyscraper* (1988). Formed Mr Big in 1988, with Paul Gilbert (guitar), Eric Martin (vocals) and Pat Torpey (drums). They released sophisticated hard-rock albums *Mr Big* (1989), *Lean Into It* (1991) and *Bump Ahead* (1993) on Atlantic. Included in *Guitar Player* magazine's 'Gallery Of The Greats' after being voted Best Rock Bassist (1986-89, 1992).

Gene **SIMMONS**

Heavy rock bassist/singer. Born Gene Klein in New York on August 25, 1949. Formed Kiss with Paul Stanley (guitar, vocals), Ace Frehley

Gene Simmons

(lead guitar, vocals) and Peter Criss (drums, vocals) during the early '70s. Manic/theatrical performances with outrageous costumes and make-up earned them a reputation as a flamboyant and exciting stage act. Image brought them considerable popularity during the late '70s: *Marvel* produced comics of the band and Kiss merchandise included board games, pinball machines and make-up kits. Each of the four members released a solo album in 1978. Criss and Frehley left in 1979 and 1982 respectively. The guitarist was replaced by a number of others including Vinnie Vincent, Mark St. John and Bruce Kulick. Albums include *Kiss* (1974), *Hotter Than Hell* (1974), *Dressed To Kill* (1975), *Kiss Alive* (1975), *Destroyer* (1976), *Rock And Roll Over* (1976), *Love Gun* (1977), *Alive II* (1977), *Dynasty* (1979), *Unmasked* (1980), *Music From The Elder* (1981), *Creatures Of The Night* (1982), *Lick It Up* (1983), *Animalize* (1984), *Asylum* (1985), *Crazy Nights* (1987), *Hot In The Shade* (1989) and *Revenge* (1992). Simmons also worked as an actor and released solo albums including *Cajun Country* (1988) and *Haunted House* (1989).

Paul **SIMON**

Singer/songwriter and guitarist. Born in Newark, New Jersey on November 5, 1941. Met singer Art Garfunkel at school. They had a minor hit with 'Hey Schoolgirl' in 1957. Studied at Queens College in New York, before collaborating with Garfunkel again in 1964. Signed to Columbia/CBS. First album *Wednesday Morning 3am* (1964) was a flop. Went to Europe and recorded *The Paul Simon Songbook* (1965) with some success. Meanwhile a new folk-rock backing was grafted on to 'The Sound Of Silence' (track from the first album) and it became a US No.1 hit. Simon hurriedly returned from Europe to record a number of similarly-treated tunes with Garfunkel. The result was the album *Sounds Of Silence* (1966), which featured two more hits: 'I Am A Rock' and 'Homeward Bound'. Success continued with a number of albums including *Parsley, Sage, Rosemary & Thyme* (1966), soundtrack *The Graduate* (1968), featuring 'Mrs. Robinson', and *Bridge Over Troubled Water* (1970). Split up and Simon pursued a successful solo career. *Paul Simon* (1972) featured 'Mother And Child Reunion'. *Still Crazy After All These Years* (1975) dealt with the break up of his marriage. Switched to Warner Brothers for *Hearts & Bones* (1983), multi-cultural *Graceland* (1986) and *Rhythm Of The Saints* (1990). A highly original and influential songwriter.

Ricky **SKAGGS**

Country singer and multi-instrumentalist. Born near Cordell, Kentucky on July 18, 1954.

Ricky Skaggs

Started playing mandolin at age 5 and later learned guitar, banjo and fiddle. Recorded debut album *That's It* (1975). Also worked with Ralph Stanley, the Country Gentlemen and his own band Boone Creek during the mid-'70s. Joined Emmylou Harris' Hot Band in 1977, featuring heavily on her Reprise albums *Blue Kentucky Girl* (1979) and *Roses In The Snow* (1980), before going solo. Albums on Sugar Hill and Epic include *Sweet Temptation* (1980), *Favorite Country Songs* (1981), *Highways And Heartaches* (1982), mean picking on *Country Boy* (1984), *Live In London* (1985), *Love's Gonna Get Ya!* (1986), *Home To Stay* (1988), *Kentucky Thunder* (1989) and *My Father's Son* (1991). Produced Dolly Parton's *White Limozeen* (1989). Grammy winner and Entertainer of the Year in 1985. One of country music's most successful and influential contemporary performers.

SLASH

Heavy metal player. Born Saul Hudson in Stoke, England on July 23, 1965. Joined pop-metal band Guns N' Roses in 1985, with Axl Rose (vocals), Izzy Stradlin (rhythm guitar), Michael 'Duff' McKagen (bass) and Steven Adler (drums). They enjoyed considerable success with commercial heavy metal singles including 'Sweet Child O'Mine' (1988), 'Patience' (1989) and a version of Dylan's 'Knockin' On Heaven's Door' (1990). Achieved notoriety after a number of incidents involving drugs, drunkenness and public disturbances (two fans died during their performance at the Donington Monsters Of Rock Festival in 1988). Albums on Geffen include *Appetite For Destruction* (1987), *GN'R Lies* (1988) and *Use Your Illusion Vols I & II* (1991). First band to have two albums simultaneously in US and UK Top 5 during the '80s.

Slash

Gene Kirkland/Idols

Earl **SLICK**

US blues-rock guitarist. Born on October 1, 1951. Grew up in New York. Early influences included British 60's supergroups such as The Yardbirds, Cream and Led Zeppelin. Picked up the guitar in his early teens. Taught himself to play from Rolling Stones and Ventures records. Started playing professionnally at age 15. Joined David Bowie's band in 1974 and played on RCA recordings *David Live* (1974), *Young Americans* (1975) and *Station To Station* (1976). Featured heavily on the latter. Left Bowie during '76 (rejoined later) and toured with Ian Hunter in '77. Formed his own band the Earl Slick Band. Their two Capitol albums *The Earl Slick Band* and *Razor Sharp* are now out of print. Sessioned extensively during and after the late '70s. Played on John Lennon and Yoko Ono albums *Double Fantasy* (1980) on Geffen and *Milk And Honey* (1984) on Polydor. Formed Phantom, Rocker & Slick with ex-Stray Cats members Lee Rocker (bass/vocals) and Slim Jim Phantom (drums). They released an eponymous album in 1985.

Johnny **SMITH**

Jazz legend. Born John Henry Smith in Birmingham, Alabama on June 25, 1922. Started playing the guitar at age 5. Self-taught. Moved to Portland, Maine at age 12. Played in local bands as a teenager. Joined the Air Force as a student pilot in 1942 but had to stop flying due to defect in his left eye. Moved to New York in 1946 to work as an arranger for NBC. Became staff guitarist, composer and arranger for the NBC orchestra. Formed his own band the Johnny Smith Trio. Became well-known for his full guitar sound and fast arpeggios. His many recordings on Royal Roost include *Moonlight In Vermont*, *The Man With The Blue Guitar*, *The Guitar World Of Johnny Smith*, *Reminiscing*, *Flowerdrum Song*, *The Sound Of The Johnny Smith Guitar* and *Johnny Smith With Strings*. Author of *The Complete Johnny Smith Approach To Guitar* (Mel Bay) and original composer of the Ventures' hit 'Walk Don't Run'.

SNAKEFINGER

UK avant-garde/rock guitarist. Born Philip Lithman in Streatham, London on June 17, 1949. Started playing the guitar at age 11. Influences included blues players such as Blind Blake and Sonny Boy Williamson. Formed cult-rock band Chilli Willi & The Red Hot Peppers in 1972 with guitarist Martin Stone and others. They recorded the albums *Kings Of Robot Rhythm* (1972) and *Bongos Over Balham* (1974). The band split up in 1975 and Lithman relocated to the United States. Re-emerged as Snakefinger on the Ralph label (owned by the mysterious avant-garde band the Residents). Highly original style: laced eccentric songs with bizarre and twisting guitar lines, combined with unique/extreme effects. Recordings were manic, inventive and highly-entertaining: *Chewing Hides The Sound* (1979), *Greener Postures* (1980) and *Manual Of Errors* (1982). Formed Snakefinger And The Vestal Virgins for *Night Of Desirable Objects* (1984). Died after a heart attack on July 1, 1987.

Fernando **SOR**

Early classical guitarist and composer. Born in Barcelona, Spain on February 14, 1778. Grew up in a monastery in Montserrat and studied guitar, organ and violin. Returned to Barcelona at age 16 and spent four years at the military academy there, during which time he was already composing prolifically. His first opera was performed in Barcelona by the time he was 19. Moved to London in 1815 and enjoyed considerable success as a composer and guitar recitalist. Moved to Russia in 1823 and played for the Imperial Royal family. By 1827, Sor was living in Paris and concentrated specifically on the guitar. Composed more than 400 guitar pieces overall and wrote a famous method book (published in 1827 by Robert Cocks & Co.). Died in Paris on July 8, 1839. Recordings of his work include *Segovia Plays Sor And Tarrega* (MCA) and *Alice Artzt Plays Sor* (Meridian). Some transcriptions of his works (edited by Brian Jeffrey) were published as *Fernando Sor: Easy Studies For Guitar* (TECLA 1981).

Chris **SPEDDING**

UK rock guitarist. Born in Sheffield, Yorkshire on June 17, 1944. Formed The Battered Ornaments with Pete Brown, before working with Gilbert O'Sullivan, John Cale, Donovan, Lulu, Dusty Springfield, Jack Bruce, David Essex, Roy Harper, Bryan Ferry, Ian Carr's Nucleus, Paul McCartney and many others. Became one of the Wombles for Mike Batt, donning a furry costume on Top Of The Pops. Teamed up with producer Mickie Most for unlikely punkish hit 'Motorbiking' in 1975. Albums on Harvest, RAK, Island, Passport and

See For Miles include *Backward Progression* (1971), *Jab It In Your Eye* (1974), *Chris Spedding* (1976), *Friday The 13th* (1981), *Enemy Within* (1986), compilation *Motorbikin': The Best Of Chris Spedding* (1991) and *Mean And Moody* (1993).

Peter SPRAGUE

Jazz guitar player. Born on October 11, 1955. Started learning blues and jazz guitar at age 12 and was concentrating on mainly bebop by the time he was 15. Studied with Pat Metheny in Boston and with Albin Czak at the New England Conservatory of Music. Later became interested in Indian and Latin American music, as well as guitar synthesis. Worked with Chick Corea, Al Jarreau, Hubert Laws and others. Solo recordings on Concord and Xanadu include *Bird Raga* (1984), *Musica Del Mar* (1984) and *Napali Coast* (1985). His fluid style combines bebop with classical ideas. Respected teacher of the instrument (pupils include Jennifer Batten, who wrote *The Transcribed Guitar Solos Of Peter Sprague*). Author of *The Sprague Technique* (1989).

Bruce SPRINGSTEEN

Rock singer, songwriter and guitarist. Born in Freehold, New Jersey on September 23, 1949. Started learning the guitar at age 13. Played in various local bands. Introduced to John Hammond, who signed him to CBS/Columbia in 1972. First album *Greetings From Asbury Park* (1973) was raw and vibrant. *The Wild, The Innocent & The E Street Shuffle* (1974) introduced his backing group, the E Street Band. The big break came with heavily produced *Born To Run* (1975), a key album of the decade, charting on both sides of the Atlantic. Appeared on the covers of *Time* and *Newsweek* simultaneously. Gained a fanatical following through epic and dynamic live shows. Became the most bootlegged artist of the '70s. Fell out with manager, who took out an injunction against recording for three years. *Darkness On The Edge Of Town* (1978) was more sombre, but still went platinum. *The River* (1980) was first US No.1 album, promoted by marathon world tour. Solo acoustic *Nebraska* (1982) was recorded on a four-track recorder, but still reached the US and UK Top 3. *Born In The USA* (1984) topped the US and UK charts, boasting 7 US hit singles. Later recordings include multi-disc *Live 1975-1985* (1986), *Tunnel Of Love* (1987), *Human*

Bruce Springsteen (left) with Nils Lofgren

Touch (1992), *Lucky Town* (1992) and *Bruce Springsteen In Concert* (1993). A charismatic performer with a down-to-earth rock style. Some consider him to be the last true rock and roll star.

Chris SQUIRE

UK rock bassist. Born in London on March 4, 1948. Formed Yes with Jon Anderson (vocals), Peter Banks (guitar), Tony Kaye (keyboards) and Bill Bruford (drums). Signed to Atlantic, recording *Yes* (1969) and *A Time And A Word* (1970), before Banks was replaced by Steve Howe on guitar. Breakthrough came with *The Yes Album* (1971), which made the UK Top 10 and US Top 40. Kaye was replaced by Rick Wakeman on keyboards for *Fragile* (1971), which reached the US Top 5 and featured the hit single 'Roundabout'. By then the band's unique brand of 'classical rock' was fully developed. There were a number of personnel changes over the years, later members including keyboardist Patrick Moraz and guitarist Trevor Rabin. Recordings include *Close To The Edge* (1972), triple-album *Yessongs* (1973), *Tales From Topographic Oceans* (1973), *Relayer* (1974), Squire solo album *Fish Out Of Water* (1975), *Going For The One* (1977), *Tormato* (1978), *Drama* (1980), *90125* (1983), *Big Generator* (1987) and *Union* (1991). Yes were one of the most original and influential rock bands of the '70s and remained popular throughout the '80s. Squire's solid bass playing inspired many other rock musicians.

Mike **STERN**

Fusion/bebop guitarist. Born in Boston, Massachusetts in 1953. Grew up in Washington DC. Picked up the guitar at age 12 and played in numerous high school bands as a teenager. Early influences included Buddy Guy, Jimi Hendrix, Eric Clapton, Wes Montgomery and Jim Hall. Studied at Berklee College, where he met Pat Metheny, who got him gigs with Blood Sweat & Tears. Developed an impressive rock-influenced bebop lead style (high-energy overdriven solos over syncopated jazz-influenced grooves, although he also uses a cleaner sound reminiscent of Metheny). Worked

Ola Bergman/Idols

Mike Stern

with Billy Cobham, Jaco Pastorius, Steps Ahead, Michael Brecker and many others. With Miles Davis on Columbia: *The Man With The Horn* (1981) and *We Want Miles* (1982). Solo albums on Atlantic include *Upside Downside* (1986), *Time In Place* (1988), *Jigsaw* (1989), *Odds Or Evens* (1991) and more traditional *Standards* (1992). A number of his solos have been transcribed by Daniel Kynaston for the book *Mike Stern: Jazz Guitar Solos* (Corybant 1991). One of the guitar giants of the '90s.

William Hames/Idols

Steve Stevens

Steve **STEVENS**

Rock player. Born in Brooklyn, New York c.1959. Started learning acoustic guitar at age 7. Played electric by the time he was 14. Studied guitar at school and later at the Usdan Center on Long Island. Early influences included Pete Townshend and Steve Howe. Joined Billy Idol's band in the early '80s. They recorded the Chrysalis albums *Billy Idol* (1982), *Rebel Yell* (1984) and *Whiplash Smile* (1986), which highlight his fiery soloing and creative use of effects. Also worked with Michael Jackson, Steve Lukather and the Thompson Twins. Formed his own band Steve Steven's Atomic Playboys in 1988 with Perry McCarty (vocals), Phil Ashley (keyboards) and Tommy Price (drums). Later with Michael Monroe and Vince Neil (ex-Mötley Crüe). Featured on Guitar Recordings compilation CD *Guitar's Practicing Musicians* (1993).

Dave **STEWART**

Rock singer/songwriter, multi-instrumentalist and producer. Born in Sunderland, England on September 9, 1952. Played in folk groups, Amazing Blondel and Longdancer during the '60s and '70s. Formed the Tourists in 1977, with talented vocalist Annie Lennox and others. Had hits with Dusty Springfield cover 'I Only

Want To Be With You' and 'So Good To Be Back Home', before splitting up in 1980. Stewart and Lennox carried on together as the Eurythmics. Went on to be one of the most successful UK pop groups of the '80s, with Top 20 hits including 'Sweet Dreams (Are Made Of This)' and 'There Must Be An Angel (Playing With My Heart)'. Albums on RCA include *In The Garden* (1981), *Sweet Dreams (Are Made Of This)* (1983), *Touch* (1984), *Be Yourself Tonight* (1985), *Revenge* (1986), *Savage* (1987), *We Two Are One* (1989) and compilation *Eurythmics Box Set* (1990). Stewart also recorded *Spiritual Cowboys* (1991) and produced for Bob Dylan, Tom Petty, Mick Jagger, Darryl Hall and many others.

Stephen STILLS

Singer/songwriter/guitarist. Born in Dallas, Texas on January 3, 1945. Picked up guitar as a teenager and taught himself. Became influenced by Jimi Hendrix. Formed Buffalo Springfield in 1966 with Neil Young (guitar), Richie Furay (vocals), Bruce Palmer (bass) and Dewey Martin (drums). The band split up during the late '60s and Stills also worked with Judy Collins, Jimi Hendrix and Joni Mitchell. Formed supergroup Crosby, Stills, Nash & Young (initially Crosby, Stills & Nash) with David Crosby (guitar, vocals), Graham Nash (vocals) and Neil Young (guitar, piano, vocals). They signed to Atlantic and recorded *Déjà Vu* (1970) and *Four Way Street* (1971), before Stills left for solo career. Albums include *Stephen Stills* (1970), *Stephen Stills 2* (1971) and *Throughfare Gap* (1978). Reunited with Crosby and Nash for *CSN* (1977) and *Daylight Again* (1982). CSN & Y reunited for the 'Live Aid' concert in 1985 and *The American Dream* (1988). Later solo album: *Stills Alone* (1991).

STING

UK singer/songwriter/bassist. Born Gordon Sumner in Wallsend, Northumberland on October 2, 1951. Initially worked as a schoolteacher and played in local jazz-rock band Last Exit. Joined the Police in 1976 with Stewart Copeland (drums, son of CIA man) and Henri Padovani (guitar). They released a punk single that sold 2000 copies, before guitarist Andy Summers was added to make the band a quartet. Padovani soon left to join Wayne County. The remaining trio developed a unique 'white reggae' style and signed to A&M. First album *Outlandos d'Amour* (1978) featured UK

Top 20 hits 'Roxanne' and 'Can't Stand Losing You'. Died their hair blond for a Wrigleys gum advert and inadvertently gave themselves a stronger image. Hit the big time with *Regatta De Blanc* (1979), which topped the UK album charts and featured No.1 hits 'Message In A Bottle' and 'Walking On The Moon'. Later albums enjoyed similar success on a global scale: *Zenyatta Mondatta* (1980) boasted 'Don't Stand So Close To Me'; *Ghost In The Machine* (1981) featured 'Every Little Thing She Does Is Magic'; *Synchronicity* (1983) spawned 'Every Breath You Take'. Sting later went solo, enlisting the services of top session players such as Omar Hakim (drums) and

Sting

Branford Marsalis (saxophone). Albums on A&M include *Dream Of The Blue Turtles* (1985), *Nothing Like The Sun* (1987) and *The Soul Cages* (1991). Also appeared in a number of films, including *Brimsone And Treacle* (1982) and *Dune* (1985).

Joe STRUMMER

UK rock guitarist. Born John Mellors in Ankara, Turkey on August 21, 1952. Formed punk band the Clash in 1976 with Mick Jones (guitar), Keith Levine (guitar), Paul Simonon (bass) and Terry Chimes (drums). The line-up changed a number of times, although Strummer and Simonon remained at the nucleus. Took a political stance, refused to appear on BBC TV's

Top Of The Pops and wrote songs about unemployment and racism. One of the most original and influential punk bands, with outstanding songs such as 'Tommy Gun' (1977) and 'London Calling' (1979). Later diversified and included elements of country, latin, reggae and rap. Albums include *Give 'Em Enough Rope* (1978), *London Calling* (1979), *Combat Rock* (1982) and *Cut The Crap* (1985). The band split in 1986 and Strummer composed soundtracks for Alex Cox films *Sid & Nancy* and *Walker*. Later worked with Irish band The Pogues. Clash compilations: *The Story Of The Clash* (1988) and *The Singles Collection* (1991).

Jorge **STRUNZ**

Acoustic/electric flatpicking virtuoso. Born in Costa Rica on May 15, 1944. Started playing guitar at age 12. Early influences included Paco de Lucía, Sabicas, John McLaughlin and Jimi Hendrix. Settled in Los Angeles in 1973. Formed fusion band Caldera with keyboardist Eduardo del Barrio and others during the mid-'70s. They released several impressive albums on Capitol including *Time And Chance* (1978) and *Dreamer* (1979). These highlighted Strunz's advanced and inventive compositional skills, as well as his impressive playing on acoustic and electric guitar. Later formed an acoustic duo with Persian guitarist Ardeshir Farah. They developed a unique and exotic blend of latin, jazz and Eastern music. Albums on Ganesh, Milestone and Mesa including *Mosaico* (1982), *Frontera* (1984), *Guitarras* (1985), *Primal Magic* (1990) and *Americas* (1992). Strunz is a highly talented musician and one of the world's premier guitar players.

Hubert **SUMLIN**

Blues player. Born in Greenwood, Mississippi on November 16, 1931. Grew up in Hughes, Arkansas. Worked as a plantation hand. Started playing guitar at age 11. Early influences included Robert Johnson and Charley Patton. Studied at the Chicago Conservatory of Music. Played in James Cotton's band at age 18 and later worked as Howlin' Wolf's guitarist. Became well-known for his sparse, raw playing and mastery of different textures. Howlin' Wolf albums on Chess featuring Sumlin include *Howlin' Wolf* (1962), *The Real Folk Blues* (1963), *Big City Blues* (1966) and *The Howlin' Wolf Album* (1969). Their collaborations lasted until Wolf's death in 1976. Later concentrated

on various solo projects. Albums on Black Top and other labels include *Hubert Sumlin: Blues Party* (1987) and *Blues Guitar Boss* (1991). Also worked with Muddy Waters, Eddie Taylor and others.

Andy **SUMMERS**

Rock guitarist. Born in Blackpool, Lancashire on December 31, 1942. Started playing piano before taking up the guitar at age 14. Early influences included jazz players such as Django Reinhardt, Barney Kessel, Kenny Burrell and Wes Montgomery. Worked with Zoot Money's Big Roll Band, Dantalion's Chariot, Soft Machine and the Animals during the '60s. Later with Kevin Coyne and Kevin Ayers in the early '70s. Joined the Police in 1976 with Gordon 'Sting' Sumner (bass, vocals), Henri Padovani (guitar) and Stewart Copeland (drums). Padovani left the band and the remaining trio went on to become one of the most successful and influential bands of the early '80s (see STING for further information on the Police). Also recorded duo albums with Robert Fripp: *I Advance Masked* (1982) and *Bewitched* (1984) on A&M. Worked on film soundtracks including *2010* and *Down And Out In Beverly Hills* (both made in 1985). Later recordings on Private: *Mysterious Barricades* (1988), *Charming Snakes* (1990) and *World Gone Strange* (1991). Summers' unique style often combines sparse textural leadwork with subtle rhythm playing.

Ichiro **SUZUKI**

Classical guitarist. Born in Kobe, Japan on May 9, 1948. Started playing guitar at age 7 and gave his first public recital in Japan at age 16. Won second prize in both the 1968 and 1969 Tokyo International Guitar Competitions. Later studied with Segovia, Tomas, Ghiglia and Brouwer. Worked with Victoria de Los Angeles, Leo Brouwer, the Tokyo Philharmonic and the Stuttgart Orchestra. Recordings on Camerata include *Ichiro Suzuki Plays Villa Lobos* and *Ichiro Suzuki Plays Sonatina Meridonial*. With Leo Brouwer: *Penny Lane*. One of Japan's leading composers Toru Takemitsu dedicated his work *To The Edge Of Dream* (published by Editions Salabert) to Suzuki.

Steve **SWALLOW**

Jazz bass player. Born in Fair Lawn, New Jersey on October 4, 1940. Initially started learning piano and trumpet, before picking up string bass at age 18. Studied at Yale but left to become full-time musician. Played with Paul Bley, Jimmy Giuffre, Art Farmer, George Russell and Stan Getz during the '60s. Won a *Downbeat* critic's poll in 1964. Switched to electric bass in 1968 and pioneered the use of the instrument in contemporary jazz (one of the first jazz bass players to extensively use a pick). Later worked with Gary Burton, John Scofield, Carla Bley, Andy Sheppard, Jim Hall and many others. Recordings on ECM include *Home* (1980) and *Carla* (1987). With Burton: *Hotel Hello* (1974), *Passengers* (1976), *Easy As Pie* (1980), *Picture This* (1983), *Real Life Hits* (1984) and *Whizz Kids* (1987). With Scofield: *Bar Talk* (1980) and *Shinola* (1982).

Gabor **SZABO**

Guitarist/composer. Born in Budapest, Hungary on March 8, 1936. Started playing guitar at age 14. Self-taught. Played in local groups as a teenager. Wrote music for Hungarian radio and films by 1956. Became a freedom fighter in the revolution and entered the United States as a refugee. Studied at the Berklee School of Jazz (1957-59). Worked with Chico Hamilton and the Charles Lloyd Quartet in the '60s. *Downbeat* voted him the 'Best New Jazz Guitarist' in 1964. Released a highly acclaimed early fusion album *The Sorcerer* (1967) on Impulse!. Later formed the eclectic band Perfect Circle and recorded albums for MCA and Mercury: *Greatest Hits* (1975) and *Nightflight* (1976).

T

David **TANENBAUM**

Classical player. Born in New York City on September 10, 1956. Grew up in New Rochelle. Started learning piano and cello from age 5 and later switched to guitar. Studied classical guitar at high school, later at the Peabody Conservatory in Maryland (with Aaron Shearer) and at the San Francisco Conservatory of Music. Gained first prize at the Carmel Classic Guitar Competition (1977) and second in the International Guitar Competition in Toronto (1978). Taught at San Francisco Conservatory from 1981. Attended Segovia's masterclass in New York in 1982. Recordings on Innova, Audiophon, New Albion and GSP include *Lute Masterworks* (1987), *Royal Winter Music* (1989), *Acoustic Counterpoint* (1990) and *Estudios* (1990). Sheet music available includes transcriptions of pieces by Bach and Scarlatti: *The David Tanenbaum Concert Series* (Guitar Solo 1986).

Francisco **TÁRREGA**

Early classical player and composer. Born in Castellon, Spain on November 29, 1854. Started playing from an early age. Studied at the Madrid Conservatory of Music in 1874 and was awarded first prize for harmony and

composition a year later. Toured successfully in Europe. Later became Professor of the Guitar at the Madrid and Barcelona conservatories. He improved the then existing playing techniques and also transcribed works by composers such as Bach, Beethoven and Chopin. Paved the way for Segovia. Died of apoplexy on December 5, 1909. Recordings of his works include *Segovia Plays Tárrega* (MCA) and *Recuerdos de la Alhambra* (Narciso Yepes/Deutsche Grammophon).

James **TAYLOR**

Singer/songwriter. Born in Boston, Massachusetts on March 12, 1948. Played in various teenage bands including the Fabulous Corsairs. Formed the Flying Machine in 1967 with another guitarist Danny Kortchmar. Suffered from chronic depression and heroin addiction before recording first album *James Taylor* (1968) with Paul McCartney and George Harrison for the Beatles' Apple label. Developed a unique style that was deep and introspective. His intricate acoustic guitar accompaniments were influenced by folk and jazz. Warner Brothers album *Sweet Baby James* (1970) won him critical acclaim. Coincided with success of other singer/songwriters such as

Carole King and Joni Mitchell. Married Carly Simon in 1972. They divorced ten years later. Worked with Simon & Garfunkel, Bruce Springsteen, Jackson Browne and many others. Other recordings on Warners and Columbia include *One Man Dog* (1972), *In My Pocket* (1976), *JT* (1977), *Flag* (1979), *Dad Loves His Work* (1981), *That's Why I'm Here* (1986), *Never Die Young* (1988) and *New Moon Shine* (1991).

Martin **TAYLOR**

UK jazz guitarist. Born in Harlow on October 20, 1956. Started playing the guitar from an early age. Joined his father's band at age 12. Left school at 15 because he had too many gigs. Early influences included Eddie Lang, Django Reinhardt, Carl Kress, Pat Martino and Ike Isaacs. Later worked with Isaacs, Stephane Grappelli, John Dankworth, John Patitucci, Peter King, David Grisman, Barney Kessel, Charlie Byrd, Gordon Giltrap and Joe Pass. Recordings with Grappelli on Concord include *At The Winery* (1980), *Vintage 1981* (1981) and *Together At Last* (1987). With Gordon Giltrap on Prestige: *A Matter Of Time* (1991). Solo albums on Wave, Concord, Gaia, HEP and Linn include *Taylor Made* (1978), *Skye Boat* (1981), *A Tribute To Art Tatum* (1984), *Sarabanda* (1988), *Don't Fret* (1991) and *Artistry* (1993). Author of instructional video *Jazz Guitarist* (Starnite). A number of his pieces have been transcribed in the book *Martin Taylor - Jazz Guitar Artistry* (IMP). A master of self-accompanied jazz guitar (simultaneous melodies, chords and walking bass lines). One of the world's premier jazz players.

Mick **TAYLOR**

UK rock guitarist. Born in Welwyn Garden City, Hertfordshire on January 17, 1948. Started learning the guitar at age 15. Played in local group Gods before joining John Mayall's Bluesbreakers in 1967. Featured on Decca recordings *Crusade* (1967) and *Diary Of A Band* (1968). Left the group to join the Rolling Stones, replacing Brian Jones in 1969. He played on classic Stones albums such as *Let It Bleed* (1969), *Sticky Fingers* (1971), *Exile On Main Street* (1972) and *It's Only Rock And Roll* (1974), before leaving the band in 1974. Later worked with Gong on fusion album *Expresso II* (1978) on Virgin. Also with Mike Oldfield, Bob Dylan, Carla Bley and many others. Solo albums on CBS and Maze include

Mick Taylor (1979) and *Stranger In This Town* (1990). Instructional video: *Mick Taylor - Rock, Blues & Slide Guitar* (Hot Licks).

Tommy **TEDESCO**

Session ace. Born c.1931. Grew up in Niagara Falls, New York. Started playing the guitar at age 6, but didn't become seriously interested in the instrument until his mid-teens. Influences included Charlie Christian, Django Reinhardt, Barney Kessel and Tal Farlow. Moved to LA at age 24 to work with Ralph Marterie. Earned a reputation for being an excellent sight-reader and later worked with the Beach Boys, Jan and Dean, Phil Spector, Frank Zappa (on 1968 album *Lumpy Gravy*), the Monkees, Elvis Presley, Frank Sinatra and many more. Film and TV work included Bonanza, the Godfather, Cocoon and Bonnie & Clyde. One of the most respected columnists with *Guitar Player* magazine during the '80s. Also plays mandolin, bouzouki and banjo. Recordings on UA, Dot and Discovery include *The Guitars Of Tom Tedesco*, *Twangy 12 Great Hits*, *12-String Guitar*, *Calypso Beat*, *When Do We Start?*, *Autumn*, *Alone At Last* and *My Disiree*.

Toots **THIELEMANS**

Jazz harmonica and guitar player. Born Jean Baptiste Thielemans in Brussels, Belgium on April 29, 1922. Started playing the accordion as a child. Later switched to harmonica and guitar. Influenced by Django Reinhardt. Self-taught. Toured with Benny Goodman in 1950 and settled in the United States a year later. Worked with George Shearing, Quincy Jones, Oscar Peterson, Zoot Sims, Joe Pass and many others. A gifted guitarist who often whistles in unison with his guitar solos. Also an exceptional harmonica player. Recordings on Riverside, Polydor, Pablo, Verve, Concord and Emarcy include *Man Bites Harmonica* (1957), *Live* (1975), *Live In The Netherlands* (1980), *Sun Games* (1982), *Aquerela do Brazil* (1987), *Only Trust Your Heart* (1988) and *For My Lady* (1991).

Richard **THOMPSON**

Folk-rock guitarist and songwriter. Born in London on April 3, 1949. Started playing guitar at age 10. Later learned some classical guitar. Formed the pioneering folk-rock band Fairport Convention in 1967 at age 18, with Simon Nicol (guitar), Judy Dyble (vocals), Ashley

Hutchings (bass) and Martin Lamble (drums). Dyble soon left and was replaced by Sandy Denny, who gave the band a more traditional feel. Fairport albums on Polydor, Island and A&M include *Fairport Convention* (1968), *What We Did On Our Holidays* (1969) and *Liege And Lief* (1969). First band to fuse English folk with rock. Thompson left the band

Richard Thompson

in 1971 and recorded a number of duo albums on Hannibal with wife Linda including *Hokey Pokey* (1974), *Pour Down Like Silver* (1975) and *Sunnyvista* (1979). They separated in 1982 and later solo albums on Hannibal, Polydor and Capitol include *Hand Of Kindness* (1983), *Across A Crowded Room* (1985), *Dangerous Adventures* (1986), *Amnesia* (1988), *Sweet Talker* (1991) and compilation *The History Of Richard Thompson* (1993). Also critically acclaimed experimental projects with John French, Fred Frith and Henry Kaiser on Rhino and Demon labels: *Live, Love, Larf And Loaf* (1987) and *Invisible Means* (1990). Instructional cassette: *The Guitar Of Richard Thompson* (Homespun). Much respected songwriter and guitar player.

George **THOROGOOD**

R&B singer/guitarist. Born in Wilmington, Delaware on December 31, 1952. Early influences included Chuck Berry, Elmore James and John Lee Hooker. Initially a street busker. Formed The Destroyers in 1973 with Ron Smith (guitar, later replaced by saxophonist Hank Carter), Billy Blough (bass) and Jeff Simon (drums). Soon earned a reputation as an outstanding live act in the US. Debut album on Rounder *George Thorogood & The Destroyers* (1976) featured a version of John Lee Hooker's 'One Bourbon, One Scotch, One Beer'. Major success came later with the graunchy 1982 song 'Bad To The Bone' (later featured in the Schwarzenegger film 'Terminator II'). Appeared at *Live Aid* with blues legend Albert Collins in 1985. Albums on Rounder and EMI include *Move It On Over* (1978), *Bad To The Bone* (1982), *Maverick* (1985), *Born To Be Bad* (1988), *The Baddest Of George Thorogood & The Destroyers* (1992) and *Haircut* (1993).

Glen **TIPTON**

British heavy rock player. Born on October 25, 1948. Noted for his playing (melodic blues-based style) in conjunction with other guitarist K.K.Downing in heavy metal band Judas Priest. The group was formed during the early '70s in Birmingham and the line-up for the first album *Rocka Rolla* (1974) was Tipton (guitar), K.K.Downing (guitar), Rob Halford (vocals), Ian Hill (bass) and John Hinch (drums). They later became one of the most popular heavy metal outfits in the world with CBS albums such as *Stained Glass* (1978), *British Steel* (1980) and *Screaming For Vengeance* (1982). (See K.K.DOWNING for more information on Judas Priest, including full discography).

David **TORN**

Experimental guitarist, composer. Born in Amityville, New York on May 26, 1953. Started playing at 12. Early influences included Jimi Hendrix, Cream, Led Zeppelin, the Mahavishnu Orchestra and minimalist Terry Riley. Studied at Berklee College of Music in Boston and later with Pat Martino. Since worked with Don Cherry and Jan Garbarek. Developed a highly unusual avant-garde fusion style. Albums on ECM include *Best Laid Plans* (1985) and *Cloud About Mercury* (1986). The latter featured contributions from drummer/percussionist Bill Bruford and multi-instrumentalist Mark Isham. Changed to the Windham Hill label for *Door X* (1990). Torn is a unique player who uses a complex guitar effects set-up.

Ralph TOWNER

Multi-instrumentalist and composer. Born in Chehalis, Washington on March 1, 1940. Started playing the piano at age 3 and later studied trumpet at the University of Oregon. Became attracted to the guitar during his last year there. Later travelled to Europe to study with Austrian classical guitarist Karl Scheit in 1963. After further studying in Oregon and Austria, Towner eventually settled in New York and worked with Astrud Gilberto, Dave Holland, Miles Davis and Keith Jarrett. Formed his own instrumental band Oregon in 1971. They created a unique mellow sound; a combination of earthy folk blended with elements of classical music and bebop. Oregon recordings on ECM and Vera Bra include *Distant Hills* (1973), *Crossing* (1984), *Ecotopia* (1987), *45th Parallel* (1990) and *Always, Never & Forever* (1992). Towner albums on ECM include *Diary* (1973), *Solstice* (1975), *Sargasso Sea* (1976 with John Abercrombie), *Sounds & Shadows* (1977), *Blue Sun* (1983) and *City Of Eyes* (1989). Author of *Improvisation And Performance Techniques For Classical And Acoustic Guitar* (21st Century). Sheet music includes highly-acclaimed *Suite For Guitar* (Distant Hills).

Pete Townshend

Pete TOWNSHEND

Legendary rock guitarist and songwriter. Born in Chiswick, London on May 19, 1945. Started playing guitar at age 12. Met John Entwistle while playing banjo in a traditional jazz band. They formed the Detours with singer Roger Daltrey. The band eventually became the Who, with Keith Moon added later on drums. Townshend's powerful rhythm style became an essential component of the Who's sound and live act. Considered to be the inventor of the 'power-chord', which has since been used extensively by rock guitar players. The Who had a number of major hits in the sixties, including 'My Generation' (1965) and 'Substitute' (1966). Went on to become one of the most original and popular UK rock bands. Became notorious for smashing up their instruments on stage. Albums on Track, Polydor and MCA include *Tommy* (1969), *Live at Leeds* (1970), *Who's Next* (1971), the epic concept *Quadrophenia* (1973), *The Who By Numbers* (1975), *Who Are You* (1978), *Face Dances* (1981), *It's Hard* (1982) and live *Who's Last* (1984). Townshend solo albums on Track, WEA, Atco, Virgin and Atlantic include *Who Came First* (1972), *Empty Glass* (1980), *All The Best Cowboys Have Chinese Eyes* (1982), *White City* (1986), *Iron Man* (1989) and *Psychoderelict* (1993). His songs have also been recorded by Elton John, David Bowie, Billy Fury, Tina Turner and many others. Also released book of prose *Horse's Neck* (Faber 1985). Highly influential guitarist and songwriter.

Pat TRAVERS

Canadian rock guitarist. Early influences included the Jimi Hendrix Experience, Led Zeppelin and other rock bands. Moved to London and formed the Pat Travers Band in 1976 with Peter 'Mars' Cowling (bass) and Roy Dyke (drums). The line-up changed a number of times and notable members included guitarist Pat Thrall and drummer Tommy Aldridge. Recordings on Polydor, Episode and Shrapnel include *Pat Travers* (1976), *Makin' Magic* (1977), *Puttin' It Straight* (1977), impressively raunchy *Heat In The Street* (1978), *Go For What You Know* (1979), *Crash And Burn* (1980), *Radioactive* (1981), *Black Pearl* (1982), *Hot Shot* (1984), *School Of Hard Knocks* (1990), *An Anthology* (1990), *The Best Of Pat Travers* (1991) and *Blues Tracks* (1992). A big influence on major rock players such as Paul Gilbert (Mr Big) and Kirk Hammett (Metallica).

George Bodnar/Idols

Merle **TRAVIS**

Country guitar legend. Singer/songwriter. Born in Rosewood, Kentucky on November 29, 1917. Son of a tobacco farmer. Played guitar from an early age. Worked with the Tennessee Tomcats and Clayton McMichen's Georgia Wildcats during the '30s, before recording and appearing in minor film roles. Had hits in the '40s with 'Divorce Me C.O.D.' and 'Nine-Pound Hammer'. Later worked with Tex Williams and the Nitty Gritty Dirt Band. Albums on Capitol, Country Musical Heritage and other labels include *The Merle Travis Guitar* (1957), *Walking The Strings* (1960), *Travis!* (1962), *Strictly Guitar* (1969), *The Merle Travis Story* (1979) and *Travis Pickin'* (1981). Elected to the Country Music Hall Of Fame in 1977. Suffered from chronic alcoholism and died in Tahlequah, Oklahoma on October 20, 1983. Popularised the thumb and index finger style of playing ('Travis Picking'). Inspired guitar players as diverse as Chet Atkins, Doc Watson, Scotty Moore and Duane Eddy. Compilation on Rhino: *The Best Of Merle Travis* (1990). Included in *Guitar Player* magazine's 'Gallery Of The Greats' (1983) for his lifetime achievement.

Robin **TROWER**

Blues-rock guitarist. Born in Catford, South London on March 9, 1945. Influenced by Jimi Hendrix, Albert King, B.B.King, Otis Rush and Hubert Sumlin. Made his professional debut in 1962 with the Paramounts. Joined Procol Harum in 1967, playing guitar on numerous albums on Deram and A&M: *Procol Harum* (1967), *Shine On Brightly* (1968), *Salty Dog* (1969) and *Broken Barricades* (1971). Left the band in 1971 to go solo. Developed a blues-rock style reminiscent of Hendrix. Albums on Chrysalis, Passport and Atlantic include *Twice Removed From Yesterday* (1973), rock classic *Bridge Of Sighs* (1974), *Robin Trower Live* (1976), *Back It Up* (1983), *Beyond The Mist* (1985), *Take What You Need* (1988) and *In The Line Of Fire* (1990). Also joined forces with Jack Bruce (bass) and Bill Lordan (drums) for the US Top 40 album *B.L.T* (1981) on Chrysalis.Instruction video: *Classic Blues/Rock Guitar* (Hot Licks 1990).

U

James Blood **ULMER**

Blues/jazz guitarist and vocalist. Born in St. Matthews, South Carolina on February 2, 1942. Started playing guitar at age 7. Influenced by gospel, blues and jazz. Played in various musical groups and bands in his teens. Studied in Detroit during the '60s. Moved to New York in 1971. Worked with John Patton, Art Blakey and Joe Henderson. Studied with Ornette Coleman in 1974 (a devotee of Coleman's *harmolodics* concept). Recorded several solo albums highlighting his passionate funky/jazzy/free sound, on Artists House, Rough Trade, Columbia, Blue Note and DIW: *Tales Of Captain Black* (1978), *Are You Glad To Be In America?* (1980), *Odyssey* (1984), *America, Do You Remember The Love?* (1987) and *Blues Preacher* (1993).

Phil **UPCHURCH**

Blues and jazz player. Born in Chicago, Illinois on July 19, 1941. Started learning ukulele at age 11 and switched to guitar a couple of years later. Played in local groups such as the Kool Gents and the Dells while still at high school. Recorded the hit instrumental single 'You Can't Sit Down' in 1961. Later joined Chess Records in Chicago to play guitar with Howlin' Wolf and Muddy Waters. Also worked with Cannonball Adderley, Dizzy Gillespie, Ramsey Lewis, Quincy Jones, Michael Jackson and George Benson. Recorded several solo albums including *Feeling Blue* (Milestone) *Darkness Darkness* (Blue Thumb), *Phil Upchurch* (Marlin), *Revelation* (JAM), *Name Of The Game* (JAM) and 1992 recording *Whatever Happened To the Blues?* (GoJazz). A soulful player who fuses blues, jazz and funk.

V

Steve **VAI**

Rock virtuoso. Born in Carleplace, Long Island on June 6, 1960. Picked up the accordion at age 11 but soon switched to guitar. Had lessons with Joe Satriani. Later studied jazz and classical music at the Berklee College of Music in Boston. Transcribed a complex piece by Frank Zappa, who was so impressed he hired Vai initially as a transcriber. Played guitar in Zappa's band at age 18, and appeared on Barking Pumpkin/Zappa albums including *Shut Up And Play Yer Guitar* (1981), *You Are What*

William Hames/Idols

Steve Vai

You Is (1981), *Ship Arriving Too Late To Save A Drowning Witch* (1982), *The Man From Utopia* (1983) and *Them Or Us* (1984). Joined Alcatrazz for *Disturbing The Peace* (1985) and played with Public Image on *Album* (1986). Later with David Lee Roth for *Eat 'Em And Smile* (1986) and *Skyscraper* (1988) on Warner Brothers. Also played on the Whitesnake album *Slip Of The Tongue* (1989). Transcribed solos

by Allan Holdsworth, Steve Morse, Eric Clapton and Eddie Van Halen for *Guitar Player* magazine. Columnist with *Guitarist* during the '90s. An outstanding and formidable player who has delighted audiences with his exquisite harmonics, flashy scalar runs and extraordinary (often humorous) tremolo effects. Extended the boundaries of rock guitar technique. Solo albums on Relativity/Food For Thought include *Flexable* (1984), *Leftovers* (1984) and *Passion And Warfare* (1990). Formed his own band Vai with Terry Bozzio (drums), T.M. Stevens (bass) and Devin Townshend (vocals) for Epic recording *Sex And Religion* (1993). One of the most popular rock guitarists, and deservedly so.

George **VAN EPS**

Legendary 7-string guitar pioneer. Born in Plainfield, New Jersey on August 7, 1913. Son of Fred Van Eps, a noted banjoist. George took up the instrument at age 10 and switched to guitar by the time he was 13. Started gigging with his older brothers in the late '20s. Later worked with Freddy Martin, Benny Goodman and Ray Noble. Started playing a 7-string Epiphone guitar from 1938. The new guitar had a seventh string tuned to a low A (one octave below the fifth string). Developed a unique style, being able to play melodies, chords and bass lines all at the same time. Worked extensively in the studio and for radio. Influenced many jazz players including Joe Pass, Barney Kessel, Howard Roberts and Earl Klugh. Recordings on Columbia, Capitol and Concord include *Mellow Guitar* (1956), *Soliloquy* (1968) and *Hand-Crafted Swing* (1992) with Howard Alden. Included in *Guitar Player* magazine's 'Gallery Of The Greats' (1989) for his lifetime achievement.

Eddie **VAN HALEN**

Legendary heavy metal guitarist. Born in Nijmegen, Holland on January 26, 1957. Early influences included Eric Clapton and Jimi Hendrix. Formed heavy metal band Van Halen (originally called Mammoth) in 1973 with brother Alex Van Halen (drums), Michael

Anthony (bass) and David Lee Roth (vocals). Played the LA club circuit during the mid '70s.

Eddie Van Halen

Their exciting and flamboyant stage act soon earned them a large following. Gene Simmons (of Kiss) was amazed by the guitarist's revolutionary playing and the singer's over-the-top theatrics; convinced Warner Brothers to sign them up. First album *Van Halen* (1978) made the US Top 20 and sold two million units in the first year. Went on to have even more commercial success with *Van Halen II* (1979), *Women And Children First* (1980), *Fair Warning* (1981), *Diver Down* (1982) and *1984* (1984). Roth left the band in 1985 and was replaced by Sammy Hagar on vocals. They continued with further albums on Warner Brothers: *5150* (1986), *OU812* (1988), *For Unlawful Carnal Knowledge* (1991) and *Van Halen Live: Right Here, Right Now* (1993). Eddie also played solo on Michael Jackson's 'Beat It' in 1984. He was the first rock guitarist to use sophisticated two-handed techniques extensively and also showed an impressive control of harmonics. A pioneer, who influenced a whole new generation of players, including

Steve Vai, Joe Satriani and Warren De Martini (even Bill & Ted). Eddie Van Halen is clearly one of the most important names in the history of rock guitar. Included in *Guitar Player* magazine's 'Gallery Of The Greats' after being voted Best New Talent (1978) and Best Rock Guitarist (1979-1983).

Jimmy **VAUGHAN**

R&B guitarist. Born in Dallas, Texas on March 20, 1951. Older brother of Stevie Ray. Started playing from an early age. His first guitar was a cheap acoustic with three strings on it, but he soon progressed to a Gibson hollowbody. Early influences included the Kinks, the Yardbirds and Little Richard, although bluesmen Muddy Waters, B.B.King and Buddy Guy made a bigger impact on him later. Played in a rock and roll band the Chessmen at age 15. Moved to Austin in 1970 and later formed the Fabulous Thunderbirds. By then Jimmy had earned a reputation of being one of the best blues players around. Fabulous Thunderbirds albums on Takoma, Chrysalis and CBS include *The Fabulous Thunderbirds* (1979), *What's The Word* (1980), *Tuff Enuff* (1985) and *Hot Number* (1987). Also recorded with brother Stevie Ray, Carlos Santana and George Harrison. His blues leadwork is highly spontaneous, emotive and subtle.

Stevie Ray **VAUGHAN**

R&B guitarist. Born in Dallas, Texas on October 3, 1954. Started playing guitar at 8, although he originally wanted to play drums. His older brother Jimmy was an early influence, as were Lonnie Mack, Albert King, Albert Collins and Django Reinhardt. Played in the Cobras and Triple Threat Revue during the '70s. Formed the band Double Trouble (named after an Otis Rush song) with Tommy Shannon (bass) and Chris 'Whipper' Layton (drums) in 1981. They became a popular live act and received rave reviews at the Montreux Jazz Festival in 1982. Albums on Epic include *Texas Flood* (1983), *Couldn't Stand The Weather* (1984), *Soul To Soul* (1986), *Live Alive* (1986) and *In Step* (1989). Also played on the David Bowie album *Let's Dance* (1983) on EMI. His career was blighted by drug problems, but exciting and gutsy lead and rhythm playing made him one of the outstanding R&B players of the '80s. Died in a helicopter crash in Wisconsin on August 27, 1990. A Grammy winner, who was also Included in *Guitar Player* magazine's 'Gallery

George Bodnar/Idols

Stevie Ray Vaughan

Of The Greats' after being voted Best Electric Blues Player (1983-1986, 1989).

Suzanne **VEGA**

US singer/songwriter and guitarist. Born in New York City, New York on August 12, 1959. Studied dance and songwriting at the High School of Performing Arts in 1975. Early influences included artists such as Joni Mitchell, Woody Guthrie, Laura Nyro, Leo Kottke and Lou Reed. Developed a minimalistic folk-rock guitar style (she describes as "circular"), often using open strings on the instrument. Started playing the folk club circuit in 1977. Had hits during the '80s with singles such as 'Marlene On the Wall' and 'Luka'. One song, the acapella 'Tom's Diner', became a surprise hit with a remixed version by dance team DNA in 1990. Albums on A&M include *Suzanne Vega* (1985), *Solitude Standing* (1987), *Days Of Open Hand* (1990) and *99.9°F* (1992).

Benjamin **VERDERY**

Classical virtuoso. Born c.1956. Started listening to rock'n'roll and jazz before becoming exposed to classical composers. Early influences included B.B.King and Bill Connors. Studied at the music conservatory of New York State University. Later with Philip de Fremery and Frederic Hand. Attended master classes held by Leo Brouwer and Alirio Diaz during 1976 in France. Went on to teach at New York University, the Manhattan School of Music and the Wisconsin Conservatory. Recordings on Musical Heritage Society and Newport Classic include *Bach Two Generations: Concerti For Guitar And Chamber Orchestra* (1987), *American Guitar Music* (1990) and *Some Towns And Cities* (1992). Instructional video: *The Essentials Of Classical Guitar, Vol.1* (Workshop Arts 1990).

Tom **VERLAINE**

New wave guitarist/singer. Born Thomas Miller in New Jersey on December 13, 1949. Worked with bassist Richard Hell in punk band the Neon Boys, before they formed Television in 1974 with Richard Lloyd (guitar) and Billy Ficca (drums). They released raw independent single 'Little Johnny Jewell' in 1975. Hell left that year after various disagreements (replaced by Fred 'Sonic' Smith on bass). Signed to Elektra. Debut album *Marquee Moon* (1977) featured the guitarist's sneering vocals and jagged guitar work. It boasted classic tracks 'Venus' and 'Torn Curtain' and received critical acclaim in the UK. The band split after disappointing *Adventure* (1978), with Verlaine going solo. Later albums on Elektra, Warners, Virgin, Fontana and Rough Trade include *Tom Verlaine* (1979), *Dreamtime* (1981), *Words From The Front* (1982), *Cover* (1984), *Flash Light* (1987), *The Wonder* (1990) and *Warm & Cool* (1992). A big influence on many punk and post-new wave guitarists.

Heitor **VILLA-LOBOS**

Early classical player and composer. Born in Rio de Janeiro, Brazil on March 5, 1887. Started playing the viola at age six and soon became a multi-instrumentalist. Played in local groups before studying at the National Institute of Music. Later incorporated aspects of Brazilian folk music into his own unique style. Travelled to France in 1923 and soon excited the European music world with his performances and compositions. Met Segovia and composed many superb pieces for him. Returned to Brazil in 1929. There he was appointed Director of Musical Education in 1932 and devised new methods of musical instruction. Also became President of the

Brazilian Academy. Died in 1959. Recordings of his compositions include *Julian Bream Plays Villa-Lobos* (RCA), *Lagoya Plays Villa-Lobos/Sor* (Philips) and *John Williams Plays Villa-Lobos* (Capitol).

T-Bone WALKER

Legendary blues guitarist and singer/songwriter. Born Aaron Walker in Linden, Texas on May 28, 1910. Raised in Dallas. Influenced by swing and big bands, as well as blues performers such as Blind Lemon Jefferson. Initially worked as a solo act (singing, playing and dancing) in Dallas before touring with Ida Cox. Won Cab Calloway contest in 1930. Later worked with Jack McVea, Memphis Slim and Jimmy Witherspoon. Developed a smooth and sophisticated jazz-blues style which became a big influence on B.B.King, Freddie King, Chuck Berry, Clarence Gatemouth Brown and many others. Classics include 'T-Bone Shuffle' and 'Stormy Monday'. One of the first electric guitar players. Died in Los Angeles on March 16, 1975. Albums on Atlantic, Polydor and Charly include *T-Bone Blues* (1956), *Good Feelin'* (1968), *Stormy Monday Blues* (1978), *T-Bone Jumps Again* (1981), *Plain Ole Blues* (1982) and *The Natural Blues* (1983). Included in *Guitar Player* magazine's 'Gallery Of The Greats' (1985) for his lifetime achievement. Biography: *Stormy Monday* by Helen Oakley Dance (1987 Louisiana State University Press).

T-Bone Walker

Joe WALSH

Rock guitarist. Singer/songwriter. Born in Wichita, Kansas on November 20, 1947. Started playing oboe and clarinet at high school. Took up electric guitar at university (Kent State, Ohio). Influences included the Ventures, Jimmy Page, Jimi Hendrix, Leo Kottke, Cream and Albert King. Joined the James Gang, recording albums on ABC such as *James Gang Rides Again* (1970) and *Thirds* (1971). Later joined the Eagles during the mid-'70s. They had considerable success with *Hotel California* (1976) on Asylum, which featured two US No.1 hits 'New Kid In Town' (1976) and 'Hotel California' (1977). Next album *The Long Run* (1979) was also a success, spawning US No.1 hit 'Heartache Tonight' (1979). Solo albums on ABC, Asylum, Warner Brothers, Full Moon and Epic include *Barnstorm* (1972), *But Seriously Folks* (1978), *The Best Of Joe Walsh* (1978), *The Confessor* (1985), *Got Any Gum?* (1987) and *Ordinary Average Guy* (1991). Also worked with B.B.King, Dan Fogelberg, Rick Derringer, Rod Stewart and many others. Well-

Joe Walsh

known for his melodic soloing (and sense of humour).

Kazumi **WATANABE**

Fusion and jazz player. Born in Tokyo, Japan on October 14, 1953. Started playing guitar at age 13. Early influences included Jimi Hendrix, Eric Clapton, Larry Coryell, John McLaughlin and Wes Montgomery. Played with Sadao Watanabe and Isao Suzuki by the time he was 17. Later moved to New York and has since worked with Gary Burton, David Sanborn, Lee Ritenour, Larry Coryell, Jeff Berlin and Michael Brecker. Developed a unique and striking lead guitar technique (frequently and effortlessly leaves the key centre and returns during solos). Albums include *To Chi Ka* (1981), *Mobo I* (1984), *Mobo II* (1984), the extremely inventive *Mobo Club* (1985), *Mobo Splash* (1986), *The Spice Of Life I* (1987), *The Spice Of Life II* (1988), *Kilowatt* (1990) and *Pandora* (1992).

Doc **WATSON**

Country guitarist. Born Arthel Watson in Deep Gap, North Carolina on March 2, 1923. Blind since birth. Played harmonica and guitar from childhood. Later became influenced by the Delmore Brothers and Bill Monroe. Played at local functions and performed on the radio by the time he was 18. Developed impressive flatpicking and fingerpicking techniques. Recordings on Vanguard, Popp, Flying Fish and Sugar Hill include *Doc Watson & Family* (1963), *Doc Watson* (1964), *Doc Watson & Son* (1965), *Southbound* (1966), *Doc Watson On Stage* (1968), *The Elementary Doc Watson* (1972), *Then And Now* (1973), *Two Days In November* (1974), *Doc & Merle Watson's Guitar Album* (1983), *Ridin' The Midnight Train* (1986), *Portrait* (1987) and *Praying Ground* (1990). The recordings from 1973 and 1974 won Grammy awards. Instruction video: *Fingerpicking & Flatpicking* (Homespun Tapes). His son Merle Watson is also a noted guitarist.

Jeff **WATSON**

US heavy rock player. Born c.1957. Grew up in Sacramento, California. Picked up guitar at age 7. Early influences included Johnny Winter, Ritchie Blackmore and Eddie Van Halen. Formed the Jeff Watson Band and later joined heavy rock band Night Ranger with co-lead guitarist Brad Gillis and others. Night Ranger albums on MCA include *Dawn Patrol* (1982), *Midnight Madness* (1983), *Big Life* (1977) and *Greatest Hits* (1989). The band split up in the early '90s and Watson later released an instrumental solo album *Lone Ranger* (1992) on Shrapnel, featuring guest guitar players Steve Morse and Allan Holdsworth. His impressive soloing incorporates rapid scalar runs and an advanced eight-fingered technique.

Johnny 'Guitar' **WATSON**

Blues-funk guitarist and singer. Born in Houston, Texas on February 3, 1935. Took up blues guitar at age 11. Early influences included T-Bone Walker and Clarence 'Gatemouth' Brown. Moved to Los Angeles at age 15. Won various talent contests before working with Big Jay McNeely, Joe Houston and Amos Milburn. His biting high-treble tone on songs such as 'Three Hours Past Midnight' influenced many other guitarists including Jimi Hendrix and Frank Zappa. Also well known for his sense of humour and extrovert personality. Albums on

Okeh, Fantasy, DJM and A&M include *Johnny Guitar Watson* (1963), *Bad* (1966), *Gangster Of Love* (1973), *Ain't That A Bitch* (1976), *A Real Mutha For Ya* (1977), *Funk Beyond The Call Of Duty* (1977), *That's What Time It Is* (1982) and *Strike On Computers* (1984). Compilations: *Three Hours Past Midnight*

Johnny 'Guitar' Watson

(1991) and *Listen/I Don't Want To Be Alone, Stranger* (1992).

Bert **WEEDON**

UK guitarist, author and teacher. Born in East Ham, London on May 10, 1920. Started playing the guitar at age 13. Also studied classical music. Played in local bands before working with Django Reinhardt, Stephane Grappelli, Ted Heath, Cliff Richard, Dickie Valentine, Frank Sinatra, Nat 'King' Cole, Judy Garland and many others. Had a UK Top 10 hit with 'Guitar Boogie Shuffle' in 1959. The Shadows dedicated their track 'Mr. Guitar' to him in 1961. Best known as an author of best-selling instruction books *Play In A Day* (over 2 million copies sold worldwide) and *Play Every Day*. The books influenced guitarists such as

Eric Clapton and Brian May during their early development. Albums include Top Rank and K-Tel recordings: *King Size Guitar* (1960) and compilation 22 *Golden Guitar Greats* (1976).

Bob **WEIR**

Rock guitarist. Born in San Francisco on October 16, 1947. Picked up guitar at age 14. Met other guitarist Jerry Garcia two years later. They formed a band which eventually became the Grateful Dead. His jazzy rhythm and slide playing became an essential part of the band's sound (see Jerry GARCIA for more information on the Grateful Dead). Also formed Bobby & The Midnites with Alphonso Johnson (bass), Billy Cobham (drums) and Brent Mydland (keyboards). Solo albums on Grateful Dead Records and Arista including *Ace* (1971), *Kingfish* (1976) and *Heaven Help The Fool* (1978). With Bobby & The Midnites: *Bobby & The Midnites* (1981) and *Where The Beat Meets The Street* (1984).

Paul **WELLER**

UK singer/songwriter and rock guitarist. Born in Woking, Surrey on May 25, 1958. Formed and fronted new wave band The Jam in 1974 with Bruce Foxton (bass) and Rick Butler (drums). Initially started out as a brash Mod band. Signed to Polydor and released albums *In The City* (1977) and *This Is The Modern World* (1977). Weller's songwriting skills matured considerably for *All Mod Cons* (1978), which included hit singles 'Down In The Tube Station At Midnight' and Kinks cover 'David Watts'. In 1980 their single 'Going Underground' was the first of three to go straight to No. 1 in the UK charts. Three more successful albums followed: *Sound Affects* (1980), *The Gift* (1982) and the live *Dig The New Breed* (1982). The Jam disbanded in 1982. One of the most influential bands of their time. Weller formed a soul/jazz influenced band The Style Council and released a number of hit singles including 'My Ever Changing Moods' (1984). Albums on Polydor include *Cafe Bleu* (1984), *Our Favourite Shop* (1985) and *The Cost Of Living* (1987). Solo: *Wild Wood* (1993) on Go! Discs.

Leslie **WEST**

Rock guitarist and singer. Born Leslie Weinstein in Queens, New York on October 22, 1945. Played in the Vagrants during the late '60s. Impressed bassist/producer Felix Pappalardi, who helped record solo debut *Leslie West-Mountain* (1969), named after the guitarist's physique. They formed Mountain with Steve Knight (keyboards) and Corky Laing (drums), making heavy music with extended guitar and keyboard solos. Albums on Bell, Island and CBS include *Mountain Climbing* (1970), *Nantucket Sleighride* (1971), *Flowers Of Evil* (1971), *Mountain Live* (1972) and *Avalanche* (1974). West also formed a trio with Laing and Jack Bruce, releasing three albums. Mountain split in 1975 and two more solo albums followed: *The Great Fatsby* (1975) and *The Leslie West Band* (1976) on RCA. West faced financial and drug problems during the late '70s and Pappalardi was shot and killed by his wife in 1983. West and Laing reformed Mountain in 1985, with Mark Clarke (ex-Rainbow) on bass. They toured with Deep Purple in Europe and recorded *Go For Your Life* (1985) on Bellaphon. West's chunky, blues-influenced sound influenced many other players.

John **WETTON**

Bass player and singer. Born in Derby, England on July 12, 1949. Joined Family in 1971 and played on the albums *Fearless* (1971) and *Bandstand* (1972). Left a year later to play bass with progressive rock band King Crimson for Island recordings: *Larks Tongues In Aspic* (1973), *Starless And Bible Black* (1974) and *Red* (1974). Became well-known for his sharp, aggressive bass style. Later joined fusion/rock band UK in 1977. They split up in 1979 and Wetton did some session work while releasing a solo album *Caught In The Crossfire* (1980) on EG. Formed AOR 'supergroup' Asia in 1981 with Steve Howe (guitar), Carl Palmer (drums) and Geoff Downes (keyboards). Debut Geffen album *Asia* (1982) topped the US charts for 9 weeks and featured hits 'Heat Of The Moment' and 'Only Time Will Tell'. Later recordings include *Alpha* (1983) and *Astra* (1985).

Tina **WEYMOUTH**

Rock bassist. Born Martina Weymouth in Coronado, California on November 22, 1950. Joined Talking Heads in 1974 with design-school colleagues David Byrne (guitar, vocals) and Chris Frantz (drums). Her imaginative bass playing became an essential part of the band's sound. One of the most original and successful groups of the '80s, with albums on Sire and EMI such as *Talking Heads '77* (1977), *Fear Of Music* (1979), *Remain In Light* (1980),

Speaking In Tongues (1983) and *Naked* (1988). Formed a spin-off band Tom Tom Club with her sisters and husband Frantz on drums. Recordings on Island and Fontana include *Tom Tom Club* (1981) and *Boom Boom Chi Boom Boom* (1988).

Clarence **WHITE**

Bluegrass and country-rock guitarist. Born in Lewiston, Maine on June 7, 1944. The whole family was musical and used to play as a band. Clarence became interested in the guitar at age 4. Later influenced by Django Reinhardt. Worked with Nashville West, Linda Ronstadt and the Byrds. Formed the Kentucky Colonels with his brothers Roland and Eric during the early '60s. They were considered to be one of the finest ever bluegrass bands. Recordings on Briar and Rounder include *Appalachian Spring* (1964), *Kentucky Colonels* (1974), *Living In The Past* (1975) and *On Stage* (re-issued 1984). Recordings with the Byrds include *Dr Byrds & Mr Hyde* (Columbia) and *Untitled* (Columbia). Clarence's ground-breaking flatpicking and electric playing influenced guitarists as diverse as Vince Gill, Marty Stewart, Jimmy Page and Pete Townshend. Killed by a drunk driver while unloading instruments in Palmdale, California on July 14, 1973.

Snowy **WHITE**

UK blues-rock player. Born in Barnstaple, North Devon on March 3, 1948. Grew up on the Isle of Wight. Took up the acoustic guitar at age 11 and switched to electric by the time he was 16. Influences included Otis Rush, B.B.King and Peter Green. Played in local bands before working with Cockney Rebel, Cliff Richard and Pink Floyd during the late '70s. Featured on the Peter Green album *In The Skies* (1979). Joined Thin Lizzy in 1980; played on *Chinatown* (1980), featuring controversial hit single 'Killer On The Loose', and *Renegade* (1981). Left to go solo: *White Flame* (1984) on Towerbell featured catchy hit ballad 'Bird Of Paradise'. Followed up with *Snowy White* (1985) and *That Certain Thing* (1986). Formed the Blues Agency for *Change My Life* (1988) and *Open For Business* (1989). Appeared at *The Wall* concert (in aid of the Disaster Relief Fund) with Roger Waters at the site of the dismantled Berlin Wall in 1990. Later album *Highway To The Sun* (1994) also features contributions from Gary Moore, Chris Rea and Dave Gilmour.

Verdine WHITE

Bass player. Born on July 25, 1951. Brought up in Chicago. Listened to a lot of soul, pop and jazz as a youngster. Studied classical string bass from age 15 and played in clubs while still a teenager. Formed the latin-influenced soul band Earth, Wind & Fire in 1969 with his older brother Maurice White (vocals, drums) and several other musicians. They were extremely successful during the '70s and early '80s with albums on Columbia including *The Last Days And Time* (1972), *That's The Way Of The World* (1975), *Spirit* (1976), *All 'N' All* (1977) and *Powerlight* (1983). All featured White's solid and fluid bass lines (tended to avoid typical funk techniques such as slapping and popping). He also worked with the Emotions, Level 42, Ramsey Lewis, Deniece Williams and many others.

Big Joe WILLIAMS

Blues guitarist and singer. Born in Crawford, Mississippi on October 16, 1903. One of 16 children. Built a one-string instrument as a child and later played a nine-string guitar. Developed a gruff folk-blues style. Worked in railroad gangs and at lumber camps. Recorded a number of songs for Bluebird Records in the late '30s. Some of these can be heard on the compilation *Baby Please Don't Go* (Charly). Other recordings on Delmark, Sonet and Arhoolie include *Nine String Guitar Blues* (1961), *Legacy Of The Blues Vol 6* (1974) and *Thinking Of What They Did* (1981). Died in Macon, Mississippi on December 17, 1982.

John WILLIAMS

Classical virtuoso. Born in Melbourne, Australia on April 24, 1941. Started playing guitar at age 7. Family moved to London in 1952. Took lessons from Segovia at age 11. Later studied guitar at the Academia Musicale Chigiana in Siena and piano at the Royal College of Music in London. Following highly successful debuts in Europe, he toured Russia and the United States during 1962-63. Made several appearances at Ronnie Scott's Jazz Club in London. Became an artistic director of the Wavendon Theatre in 1970. Premiered André Previn's Guitar Concerto in 1971. Recorded several successful classical albums on CBS and Cube: *John Williams Plays Spanish Music* (1970), *Concerto de Aranjuez* (1976) and *Cavatina* (1979). Formed classical-rock fusion group Sky in the late '70s with Kevin Peek (guitar), Francis Monkman (keyboards), Herbie Flowers (bass) and Tristan Fry (drums and percussion). Arista recordings *Sky* (1979), *Sky 2* (1980) and *Sky 3* (1981) sold well on both sides of the Atlantic and helped to introduce larger

John Williams

audiences to classical music. Left the band in 1984 and went on to perform and record other projects for CBS/Sony: *Let The Music Take You* (1983) with Cleo Laine, Paul Hart's *Concerto For Guitar And Jazz Orchestra* (1987), *Takemitsu: To The Edge Of Dream* (1991), *Vivaldi Concertos* (1991) and *The Seville Concert* (1993, also released on video). Also award-winning collaborations with Julian Bream (see Julian BREAM). An outstanding musician.

Carl WILSON

Rock singer/guitarist. Born in Los Angeles, California on December 21, 1946. Formed the Beach Boys with brothers Brian (bass, vocals, main songwriter), Dennis (drums) and others. Developed advanced and unique vocal techniques, inspired by the Four Freshmen.

Songs were mainly about surfing, cars and girls. Signed to Capitol. First three albums were *Surfin' Safari* (1962), *Surfin' USA* (1963) and *Surfer Girl* (1963). The big break came later with *All Summer Long* (1964), which featured the US No.1 hit 'I Get Around'. Later recorded critically acclaimed *Pet Sounds* (1966) and launched US and UK No.1 hit 'Good Vibrations' the same year. There were several personnel changes over the years. Dennis drowned in 1983. Other albums on Stateside, Warner Brothers and Caribou include *Surf's Up* (1971), *15 Big Ones* (1976), *L.A.* (1979) and *The Beach Boys* (1985). One of the most influential pop bands of all time. Carl Wilson solo projects include *Carl Wilson* (1981) and *Young Blood* (1983) on Caribou.

Don **WILSON**

Rock/pop guitarist. Born in the USA on February 10, 1937. Formed instrumental pop band the Ventures (originally the Versatones) with Bob Bogle (guitar), Nokie Edwards (bass) and Howie Johnson (drums). Had a big hit in the US and UK with 'Walk Don't Run' in 1960. Albums on EMI include *Walk Don't Run* and *Best Of The Ventures*. Also released a series of instructional *Play With The Ventures* records during the '60s. Particularly popular in the Far East (first foreign group elected to be in the Top Ten Hall of Fame by the Conservatory of Music of Japan). Their clean, tremolo-drenched sound influenced guitar players as diverse as Hank Marvin, Joe Walsh, Eric Johnson, Jerry Donahue, John Etheridge and Noel Redding. Later compilation: *The EP Collection* (1990) on See For Miles.

Nancy **WILSON**

Rock singer/songwriter and guitarist. Born in San Francisco, California on March 16, 1954. Worked as a solo folksinger before joining Heart (formerly White Heart) with sister Ann Wilson (vocals), Roger Fisher (guitar), Steve Fossen (bass), Howard Leese (keyboards, guitar) and Michael Derosier (drums). Music was a mixture of heavy rock and ballads. Considerable success with albums *Dreamboat Annie* (1976) on Mushroom and *Little Queen* (1977) on CBS. Fisher left in 1980, following relationship problems. Fossen and Derosier were later replaced by bassist Mark Andes and drummer Denny Carmasi in 1982. Commercial success continued and improved with Capitol albums *Heart* (1985), *Bad Animals* (1987) and *Brigade* (1990).

Johnny **WINTER**

Blues guitarist and singer. Born in Leland, Mississippi on February 22, 1944. Started

Johnny Winter

Mick Hutson/Redferns

playing the guitar at age 11. Influences included Howlin' Wolf and Muddy Waters. Built a considerable reputation while playing in various local groups during the '60s. An excellent review in *Rolling Stone* magazine led an entrepreneur to become Winter's manager and sign him to a major label in 1969. Early albums on CBS include *Johnny Winter* (1969), *Second Winter* (1970), *Johnny Winter And...* (1970) and *Johnny Winter And... Live* (1971). Drug addiction forced him into semi-retirement until 1973. Re-emerged with *Still Alive And Well* (1973). Worked with Muddy Waters on *Hard Again* (1977). Later recordings on Blue Sky and Alligator include *Raisin' Cain* (1980), *Guitar Slinger* (1984), Grammy-winner *Third Degree* (1986), *Winter Of '88* (1988), *Let Me In* (1991) and *Hey, Where's Your Brother?* (1992). A gifted blues guitarist with a raw and fiery style.

Ron **WOOD**

UK rock guitarist. Born on June 1, 1947. Started playing guitar at age 8. Biggest early influence was Chuck Berry. Played with the Birds and supported Jeff Beck during the late-'60s. Joined the Jeff Beck group and played on the Columbia albums *Truth* (1968) and *Beck-Ola* (1969). Left in 1969 to form the Faces (originally the Small Faces) with singer Rod Stewart (also ex-Beck). They released several hit singles including 'Maggie May' (1971) and 'You Wear It Well' (1972), before Stewart left the band in 1975. Faces albums on Vertigo and Mercury include *An Old Raincoat Won't Ever Let You Down* (1969), *Gasoline Alley* (1970) and *Never A Dull Moment* (1972). Joined the Rolling Stones as Mick Taylor's replacement in 1976 and recorded on albums such as *Black & Blue* (1976) and *Some Girls* (1978). Solo albums on Warner Brothers, Columbia and Continuum include *Now Look* (1975), *Gimme Some Neck* (1979), *1234* (1981) and *Slide On This* (1992).

Link **WRAY**

Electric guitar pioneer. Born in Fort Bragg, North Carolina in 1930, of Shawnee Indian descent. Started playing the guitar at age 8. Became inspired by a local negro bluesman

Link Wray

called Hambone. Formed a country music band at school. Joined the army in 1950 and contracted tuberculosis while serving in Korea. Practiced the guitar extensively while in hospital. Formed Lucky Wray & the Ranch

Hands with his brothers Ray and Doug. Later formed instrumental band Link Wray and The Ray Men. Developed an aggressive fuzz tone sound which had an impact on later rock players. Instrumental hits include 'Rumble' (1958) and 'Rawhide' (1959). Became popular around the bar circuit. Released albums on Charisma, Ace, Epic and Creation: *Beans & Fatback* (1973), *Bullshot* (1979), *Live At The Paradiso* (1980), *Live In '85* (1985), compilation *Walkin' With Link* (1992) and *Indian Child* (1993). Lived in Denmark since 1983. Highly influential player who inspired guitarists as diverse as Pete Townshend, Jeff Beck, Bob Dylan and Robert Quine.

Zakk **WYLDE**

Heavy metal guitarist. Born in New Jersey on January 14, 1967. Started playing the guitar at age 13. Influences included Eddie Van Halen, Al Di Meola, John McLaughlin, Yngwie Malmsteen and various rock and heavy metal bands of the '70s and '80s. Developed a flashy technique and impressed Ozzy Osbourne, who asked Zakk to join his band (replacing guitarist Jake E.Lee). They recorded *No Rest For The Wicked* (1988) and *No More Tears* (1991). Later put together a southern-rock band inspired by the Allman Brothers and Lynyrd Skynyrd.

Bill **WYMAN**

Rock bass player and singer. Born William Perks in Penge, South London on October 23, 1936. Joined the Rolling Stones in 1962, replacing Dick Taylor on bass. The band were seen as London's rebellious answer to the more squeaky-clean Beatles. Wyman's unassuming manner was in sharp contrast to Jagger's arrogance and Richards' moodiness (see Keith RICHARDS for more information on the Rolling Stones). Had a surprise hit with '(Si, Si) Je Suis Un Rock Star' in the early '80s. Albums include *Monkey Grip* (1974), *Stone Alone* (1976), *Bill Wyman* (1981) and soundtrack *Green Ice* (1982). Formed Willie And The Poor Boys in 1985 for an album in aid of multiple sclerosis. Controversial and troubled marriage with teenager Mandy Smith. His autobiography was published in 1990 by Viking. Formally left the Stones in January 1993.

XYZ

Narciso **YEPES**

Classical virtuoso and 10-string pioneer. Born in Lorca, Spain on November 14, 1927. Started playing guitar at age 6. Studied at the Conservatory of Music in Valencia and later with Vincente Asencio. Joined the Spanish National Orchestra in 1946 and performed as the soloist for Rodrigo's 'Concerto de Aranjuez' in 1947. Played in Europe during the early '50s, giving many highly acclaimed performances. Also toured Japan and America in the early '60s. Played a 10 string guitar since 1963 (commissioned Ramirez to make a special guitar with four extra bass strings tuned to C, B flat, A flat and G flat). His many recordings include *Narciso Yepes*, *Musica Catalana* and *Telemann Guitar Duos* (all on Deutsche Grammophon).

Angus **YOUNG**

Rock guitarist. Born in Glasgow, Scotland on March 31, 1959. Family emigrated to Australia when he was 5. Soon picked up guitar and was playing in local teen bands. Influenced by his older brother George, who played in a band called the Easybeats. Other early influences included the Yardbirds, the Who, Eric Clapton and Paul Butterfield. Formed a band with older brother Malcolm Young (guitar), Bon Scott (vocals), Mark Evans (bass) and Phil Rudd (drums). They named it AC/DC after an inscription on the family vacuum cleaner. The band started playing seedy bars in Sydney; their raunchy brand of rock and roll and outrageous stage antics soon brought them a regular following. Angus dressed as a schoolboy in short trousers onstage. It became one of the band's trademarks, along with his aggressive riffs and solos. They recorded several albums on Atco and Atlantic including *Let There Be Rock* (1977), *Powerage* (1978) and *Highway To Hell* (1979). Scott choked to death after a heavy drinking session on February 20, 1980. He was replaced by Brian Johnson (ex-Geordie) for their appropriately titled *Back In Black* (1980). Later recordings include *For Those About To Rock* (1981), *Fly On The Wall* (1985), *Who Made Who?* (1986), *Blow Up Your Video* (1988), *Razor's Edge* (1990) and *AC/DC Live* (1992).

Angus Young

Erica Echenberg/Redfrens

Neil **YOUNG**

Singer/songwriter and guitarist. Born in Toronto, Canada on November 12, 1945. Suffered from diabetes, polio and epilepsy during childhood. Played local folk gigs before moving to Los Angeles (travelled in a hearse) and joining folk-rock band Buffalo Springfield with Steve Stills. First solo album was the melancholy *Neil Young* (1969). Critically acclaimed *Everybody Knows This Is Nowhere* (1969) featured debut of backing band Crazy Horse and some of his most popular songs, including 'Down By The River' and 'Cinnamon Girl'. Joined Crosby, Stills and Nash while working on highly-successful *After The Gold Rush* (1970). CSN&Y recorded *Déjà Vu* (1970) and live *Four Way Street* (1971), before splitting up in 1971. *Harvest* (1972) was Young's most commercial work, topping both the US and UK album charts and featuring the hit 'Heart Of Gold'. Later albums include

Mimi Steinwehe/Idols

Neil Young

harrowing *Tonight's The Night* (1975), more optimistic *Zuma* (1976), acoustic *Comes A Time* (1978), unexpected tribute to Johnny Rotten on *Rust Never Sleeps* (1979), country-influenced *Hawks & Doves* (1980), hard rock/R&B on *Re-ac-tor* (1981), synthesizers and vocoders on *Trans* (1983), country again on *Old Ways* (1985), blues on *This Note's For You* (1988), mainstream but critically acclaimed *Ragged Glory* (1990), abrasive *Arc* (1991), and acoustic *Harvest Moon* (1992). Also a number of reunions with Crosby, Stills and Nash. One of the most original, experimental and influential singer/songwriters.

Rusty **YOUNG**

Steel guitarist. Born in Long Beach, California on February 23, 1946. Well-known for his fiery steel playing with country-rock band Poco. The band was formed in 1968 and the initial line-up included ex-Buffalo Springfield musicians Richie Furay (guitar, vocals) and Jim Messina (guitar, vocals), augmented with Rusty Young (steel guitar), Randy Meisner (bass) and George Grantham (drums). Went through several personnel changes before eventually splitting up in 1984. Recordings on Epic, CBS, MCA and ABC include *Pickin' Up The Pieces* (1969), *Poco* (1970), *Deliverin' The Goods* (1971), *A*

Good Feelin' To Know (1973), *Crazy Eyes* (1973), *Seven* (1974), *Live* (1976), *Legend* (1978), *Ghost Town* (1982), *Inamorata* (1984), *Legacy* (1989) and compilation *The Forgotten Trail* (1991). Young is an expressive player who turned many rock fans on to the steel guitar.

Frank **ZAPPA**

Composer/guitarist. Born Frank Vincent Zappa Jr. in Baltimore, Maryland on December 21, 1940. Grew up in Lancaster and San Diego in California. Started playing drums at age 12 and switched to guitar at 18. Early influences included Johnny Guitar Watson, Guitar Slim, Matt Murphy and Clarence Brown, as well as 20th-Century composers such as Stravinsky and Varèse. Started playing in cocktail lounges and writing music for B-movies. Incarcerated for 10 days after recording a sex tape that found its way into the hands of the San Bernadino Vice Squad. Formed his own band the Mothers (later renamed the Mothers of Invention by MGM) during mid-'60s with Ray Collins (vocals),

Frank Zappa

Elliot Ingber (guitar), Roy Estrada (bass) and Jimmy Carl Black (drums). Since then his bands have included many talented musicians including George Duke, Jean-Luc Ponty, Aynsley Dunbar, Eddie Jobson, Vinnie Colaiuta, Steve Vai and Adrian Belew. Also worked with Captain Beefheart (an old school-friend). Composed a lot of highly original (and often very complex) rock songs and instrumentals, which have included elements of all kinds of music. Also many orchestral pieces. Probably best known for the satirical humour prevalent in many of his works. Most of the band albums feature extended electric guitar solos, which Zappa describes as "poly-scale oriented harmonically and speech-influenced rhythmically". Employs a heavy right-hand technique. His son Dweezil is also a noted guitarist. Band and solo albums on Zappa/Barking Pumpkin Records include *Freak Out* (1966), *Absolutely Free* (1967), *We're Only In It For The Money* (1967), *Lumpy Gravy* (1968), *Uncle Meat* (1968), *Hot Rats* (1970), *Burnt Weeny Sandwich* (1970), *Chunga's Revenge* (1970), *Fillmore East* (1971), *Overnite Sensation* (1973), *Roxy & Elsewhere* (1974), *Apostrophe* (1974), *Zoot Allures* (1976), *Studio Tan* (1979), *Sleep Dirt* (1979), *Sheik Yerbouti* (1979), *Joe's Garage: Acts I, II & III* (1979), *You Are What You Is* (1981), *Shut Up And Play Yer Guitar* (1981), *The Man From Utopia* (1983), *Them Or Us* (1984), *Jazz From Hell* (1986), *Broadway The Hard Way* (1988) and *Make A Jazz Noise Here* (1991). Orchestral albums include *LSO/Zappa Vol I* (1983) and *Boulez Conducts Zappa: The Perfect Stranger* (1984). With the Ensemble Modern: *The Yellow Shark* (1993). Released *The Frank Zappa Guitar Book* (Music Sales 1982), which contained many Zappa solos transcribed by Steve Vai. Also co-wrote *The Real Frank Zappa Book* (Poseidon 1989) with Peter Occhiogrosso. Included in *Guitar Player* magazine's 'Gallery Of The Greats' (1991) for his lifetime achievement. Died of prostate cancer in Los Angeles on December 4, 1993. One of the most important figures in modern music.

Attila **ZOLLER**

Jazz guitarist. Born in Visegard, Hungary on June 13, 1927. Started playing the violin at age 4 and the trumpet at 9, before taking up the guitar at 18. Played professionally in Budapest by the time he was 20. Moved to Austria in 1948 and formed an award winning quartet with accordionist Vera Auer. Moved to Germany before finally settling in the United States in 1959. Studied at the Lennox School of Jazz in Massachusetts. Worked with Chico Hamilton, Red Norvo and Herbie Mann. Formed his own quartet in 1965. Patented a bi-directional pickup for the guitar in 1971 and later invented a vibraphone pickup. Worked with Jimmy Raney during the early '80s. Recordings include *Zo-Ko-Ma* (1968), *Gypsy Cry* (1971), *Conjunction* (1982) and *Memories Of Pannonia* (1987).

APPENDIX I

A selection of jazz guitar recordings

Laurindo Almeida	Chamber Jazz	Concord (LP/CD)
George Barnes	Swing Guitars (1972)	Famous Door (LP)
George Benson	Benson Burner (1966)	CBS (LP/CD)
	Beyond The Blue Horizon (1971)	CTI (LP)
Ed Bickert	Ed Bickert	PM (LP)
	Border Crossing (1983)	Concord (LP/CD)
Lenny Breau	Guitar Sounds From Lenny Breau	RCA (LP)
	The Velvet Touch Of Lenny Breau	RCA (LP)
	Five O'Clock Bells	Adelphi (LP)
Kenny Burrell	All Day Long & All Night Long	Prestige (LP)
	At The Five Spot Cafe (1959)	Blue Note (LP/CD)
Charlie Byrd	Jazz/Samba (1962)	Verve (LP)
Charlie Christian	Solo Flight (1939-41)	Columbia (LP/CD)
	Charlie Christian (1939-41)	Everest (LP/CD
Herb Ellis	The Midnight Roll (1962)	Epic (LP)
	Rhythm Willie (1975)	Concord (LP/CD)
Tal Farlow	The Tal Farlow Album (1954)	Verve (LP)
	Tal (1956)	Verve (LP)
	The Legendary Tal Farlow (1984)	Concord (LP/CD)
Bruce Forman	Full Circle (1985)	Concord (LP/CD)
	There Are Times (1988)	Concord (LP/CD
	Pardon Me (1989)	Concord (LP/CD)
Goodrick / Diorio	Rare Birds (1993)	RAM (CD)
Jim Hall	Intermodulation (1966)	Verve (LP/CD)
	The Bridge	RCA (LP)
	Jim Hall's Three (1986)	Concord (LP/CD)
Barney Kessel	To Swing Or Not To Swing (1955)	JVC (LP/CD)
	I Remember Django (1969) †	Mob Fidel(LP)
Eddie Lang	A Handful Of Riffs (1988)	Living Era (LP/CD)
	Troubles, Troubles (1988)	Rounder (LP/CD)
Pat Martino	El Hombre (1966)	Prestige (LP)
	The Visit (1972)	Cobblestone (LP)
Pat Metheny	Question & Answer ◆	Geffen (LP/CD)
Wes Montgomery	While We're Young	Milestone (LP)
	So Much Guitar! (1961)	Milestone (LP/CD)
	Movin' Wes (1964)	Milestone (LP/CD)
	Full House (1962)	Riverside (LP/CD)
	Tequila (1966)	Verve (LP/CD)
Joe Pass	Virtuoso (1973)	Pablo (LP/CD)
	Virtuoso 2 (1976)	Pablo (LP/CD)
	Catch Me	Fontana (LP)
	For Django	Fontana (LP)
Django Reinhardt	Djangology	RCA (LP/CD)
	Django Reinhardt & Stephane Grappelli	GNP (LP/CD)
Emily Remler	Firefly (1981)	Concord (LP/CD)
	Together (1986) +	Concord (LP/CD)
Howard Roberts	Mr. Roberts Plays Guitar (1957)	Verve (LP)
	H.R. Is A Dirty Player (1963)	Capitol (LP)
John Scofield	Shinola (1982)	Enja (LP/CD)
Sonny Sharrock	Guitar (1986)	Enemy (LP/CD)
George Van Eps	Mellow Guitar (1956)	Corinthian (LP)

KEY:
  † with Stephane Grappelli; Mob Fidel - Mobile Fidelity
  ◆ with Dave Holland & Roy Haynes; Concord - Concord Jazz.
  + with Larry Coryell

A selection of fusion guitar recordings

Shaun Baxter	Jazz Metal (1993)	Jazz Metal (CD)
Jeff Beck	Blow By Blow (1975)	Epic (LP/CD)
	Wired (1976)	Epic (LP/CD)
Jeff Berlin	Feels Good To Me (1978) †	Polydor (LP/CD)
Larry Carlton	Larry Carlton (1978)	WB (LP/CD)
Stanley Clarke	Journey To Love (1975)	Epic (LP/CD)
Larry Coryell	Spaces (1971)	Vanguard (LP/CD)
Bill Connors	Step It (1984)	Pathfinder (LP/CD)
Al Di Meola	Elegant Gypsy (1977)	CBS (LP/CD)
	Casino (1978)	CBS (LP/CD)
John Etheridge	Softs (1976) ♦	SFM (LP/CD)
Bill Frisell	Rambler (1984)	ECM (LP/CD)
	Where In The World (1991)	Elektra (LP/CD)
Frank Gambale	Eye Of The Beholder (1988) ††	GRP (LP/CD)
John Goodsall	Unorthadox Behaviour (1975)	Virgin (LP/CD)
(& Percy Jones)	Masques (1978) ☆	Virgin (LP/CD)
	XCommunication (1992) ☆	Ozone (LP/CD)
Scott Henderson	Spears (1986)	Relativity (LP/CD)
(with Tribal Tech)	Dr. Hee (1987)	Relativity (LP/CD)
	Illicit (1992)	Blue Moon (LP/CD)
Allan Holdsworth	I.O.U. (1982)	Intima (LP/CD)
	Road Games (1983)	WB (LP/CD)
	Metal Fatigue (1985)	Intima (LP/CD)
	Secrets (1989)	Intima (LP/CD)
	UK (1978) ■	EG (LP/CD)
Steve Khan	Blades (1982)	Passport (LP/CD)
John McLaughlin	Inner Mounting Flame (1972)	CBS (LP/CD)
(& Mahavishnu)	Visions Of The Emeralds Beyond (1975)	CBS (LP/CD)
	Natural Elements (1977) +	CBS (LP/CD)
	Adventures In Radioland (1987)	Relativity (LP/CD)
Pat Metheny	Pat Metheny Group (1978)	ECM (LP/CD)
	New Chautauqua (1979)	ECM (LP/CD)
	Travels (1983)	ECM (LP/CD)
	First Circle (1984)	ECM (LP/CD)
	Still Life Talking (1987)	Geffen (LP/CD)
Gary Moore	Electric Savage (1977)	MCA (LP)
Jaco Pastorius	Jaco Pastorius (1975)	Epic (LP/CD)
	Heavy Weather (1977) ♦♦	CBS (LP/CD)
	Night Passage (1980) ♦♦	CBS (LP/CD)
John Scofield	Electric Outlet (1984)	Grama (LP/CD)
	Still Warm (1986)	Grama (LP/CD)
	Blue Matter (1987)	Grama (LP/CD)
Mike Stern	Upside Downside (1987)	Atlantic (LP/CD)
	Jigsaw (1989)	Atlantic (LP/CD)
Jorge Strunz	Dreamer (1979) ▮	Capitol (LP)
	Frontera (1984) ▼	Milestone (LP/CD)
	Primal Magic (1990) ▼	Mesa (LP/CD)
Ralph Towner	Sargasso Sea (1976) ●	ECM (LP/CD)
Kazumi Watanabe	Mobo Club (1985)	Grama (LP/CD)
	Mobo Splash (1986)	Grama (LP/CD)

KEY:

† with Bruford;   ■ with UK;   ▮ with Caldera;   WB - Warner Brothers,
♦ with Soft Machine;   + with Shakti;   ▼ with Strunz & Farah;   SFM - See For Miles
☆ with Brand X;   ● with John Abercrombie;   †† with Chick Corea Elektric Band.   Grama - Gramavision.
♦♦ with Weather Report;

A selection of blues guitar recordings

Blind Blake	Ragtime Guitar's Foremost Fingerpicker	Yazoo (LP)
Eric Clapton	Bluesbreakers (1965) ▽	Decca (LP/CD)
	Just One Night (1980)	RSO (LP/CD)
Robert Cray	False Accusations (1985)	High Tone (LP/CD)
Rev. Gary Davis	Reverend Gary Davis	Heritage (CD)
Robben Ford	Talk To Your Daughter	Chrysalis (LP/CD)
Rory Gallagher	Live In Europe/Stagestruck	Castle (LP/CD)
Peter Green	A Hard Road (1966) ▽	London (LP/CD)
Buddy Guy	Hold That Plane	Start (LP/CD)
	Stone Crazy	Alligator (LP/CD)
Jeff Healey	See The Light (1988)	Arista (LP/CD)
John Lee Hooker	Boogie Chillun	Charly (LP/CD)
	Boom Boom (1992)	Point Blank (LP/CD)
Son House	Father Of The Folk Blues	Columbia (LP)
	Library Of Congress Sessions	Trav Man (LP/CD)
Mississippi John Hurt	Best Of Mississippi John Hurt	Start (LP/CD)
Leadbelly	Alabama Road	Bluebird (LP/CD
Lightnin' Hopkins	Bad Boogie	Diving Duck (LP)
	Lightnin' Strikes Back	Charly (LP/CD)
Elmore James	Collection: Elmore James	Deja Vu (LP/CD)
Blind Lemon Jefferson	King Of The Country Blues	Yazoo (LP)
	Blind Lemon Jefferson (1925-26)	Document (CD)
Robert Johnson	The Complete Recordings	CBS (LP/CD)
	King Of The Delta Blues Singers	Columbia (LP)
Albert King	Live Wire/Blues Power	Stax (LP/CD)
	Best Of Albert King	Stax (LP/CD)
	Born Under A Bad Sign (1967)	Stax (LP)
B.B.King	Live At The Regal (1965)	ABC/MCA (LP/CD)
	Blues Is King (1967)	SFM (LP/CD)
	Live In Cook County Jail (1971)	MCA (LP/CD)
Earl King	Glazed (1986)	Black Top (LP/CD)
Freddie King	Takin' Care Of Business	Charly (LP/CD)
	Hideaway	King (LP)
	Texas Sensation	Charly (CD)
Gary Moore	Still Got The Blues (1990)	Virgin (LP/CD)
Charley Patton	Founder Of The Delta Blues (1929-34)	Yazoo (LP)
	Remaining Titles (1929-34)	Wolf (LP)
Bonnie Raitt	Bonnie Raitt (1971)	WB (LP)
Otis Rush	Classic Recordings	Charly (LP/CD)
T-Bone Walker	Low Down Blues	Charly (CD)
	T-Bone Blues (1956)	Atlantic (LP)
Muddy Waters	Best Of Muddy waters	MCA (LP/CD)
	Mud In Your Ear (1967)	Muse (LP/CD)
	Hard Again (1977)	Columbia (LP/CD)
Johnny Winter	Second Winter (1970)	Edsel (LP/CD
	Johnny Winter And...(1970)	CBS (LP)
Howlin' Wolf	Howlin' Wolf	Charly (LP/CD)
	The London Howlin' Wolf Sessions (1971)	Chess (LP/CD)
	Howlin' For My Baby	Charly (LP/CD)

KEY:
▽ with John Mayall's Bluesbreakers.   W B – Warner Bros.,
Trav Man – Travelling Man,
SFM – See For Miles.

A selection of country and folk guitar recordings

Chet Atkins	Early Years Of Chet Atkins & His Guitar	RCA (LP)
	Best Of Chet Atkins	RCA (LP/CD)
Jimmy Bryant	Country Cabin Jazz	Capitol (LP)
James Burton	Corn Pickin' & Slick Slidin' (1968)	Capitol (LP)
Jim Croce	Photographs & Memories (1974)	ABC (LP/CD)
Bob Dylan	The Freewheelin' Bob Dylan (1963)	CBS (LP/CD)
	Greatest Hits	CBS (LP/CD)
John Fahey	I Remember Blind Joe Death	Rounder (LP/CD)
	Rainforests, Oceans & Other Themes (1985)	Rounder (LP/CD)
Emmylou Harris	Pieces Of The Sky (1975)	Reprise (LP)
	Elite Hotel (1976)	Reprise (LP/CD)
	Bluebird (1989)	Reprise (LP/CD)
Leo Kottke	Greenhouse (1972)	Capitol (LP/CD)
Adrian Legg	Mrs. Crowe's Blue Waltz (1993)	Relativity (CD)
Joni Mitchell	Blue (1971)	Reprise (LP/CD)
	For The Roses (1972)	WEA (LP/CD)
Albert Lee	Hiding (1979)	A&M (LP)
	Speechless (1986)	MCA (LP/CD)
Ricky Skaggs	Country Boy (1984)	Epic (LP/CD)
Merle Travis	Walkin' The Strings (1960)	Capitol (LP)
Doc Watson	Essential Doc Watson Vol 1	Vanguard (LP/CD)
	Doc Watson On Stage (1968)	Vanguard (LP)
Clarence White	Nashville West (1967)	Briar (LP)
Neil Young	Old Ways (1985)	Geffen (LP)

A selection of experimental guitar recordings

Derek Bailey	Solo Vol I (1971)	Incus (LP/CD)
	Solo Vol II (1991)	Incus (LP/CD)
Eugene Chadbourne	Corpses Of Foreign Wars (1986)	Fund (LP/CD)
	Blotter (1992)	Delta (LP/CD)
Hans Reichel	Bonobo (1975)	FMP (LP)
	Death Of The Rare Bird Ymir (1979)	FMP (LP)
	Coco Bolo Nights (1989)	FMP (LPCD)
Fred Frith	Unrest (1974) ○	Virgin (LP/CD)
	Guitar Solos (1974)	Caroline (LP)
	Guitar Solos II (1976)	Caroline (LP)
	Guitar Solos III (1981)	Rift (LP)
	Live, Love, Larf, Loaf (1987) ✱	Demon (LP/CD)
Henry Kaiser	Protocol (1979)	Metalanguage (LP)
	Those Who Know History...(1988)	SST (LP/CD)
	Hearts Desire (1990)	Reckless (LP/CD)
Marc Ribot	Rootless Cosmopolitans (1990)	Island (LP/CD)
Elliott Sharp	In The Land Of The Yahoos (1987)	SST (LP/CD)

KEY:
○ with Henry Cow;
✱ with French, Kaiser & Thompson.

Fund – Fundamental records.
FMP – Free Music Production.

A selection of classical guitar recordings

Alice Artzt	Variations, Passacaglias & Chaconnes (1990)	Hyperion (CD)
Manuel Barrueco	Works For Guitar By Albiniz & Granados	Turnabout (LP)
	Albiniz/Turina: Works For Guitar	EMI (CD)
	Guitar Works (1989)	EMI (CD)
Liona Boyd	Liona Live In Tokyo (1984)	CBS (LP)
	Persona (1986)	CBS (LP)
Julian Bream	20th Century Guitar (1966)	RCA (LP)
	Music Of Spain	RCA (CD)
	Plays Granados & Albiniz	RCA (CD)
Eduardo Fernàndez	Avant-garde guitar (1993)	Decca (CD)
Eliot Fisk	Works By Baroque Composers (1985)	MM (LP)
	Latin American Guitar Music (1988)	EMI (LP/CD)
Nicola Hall	Virtuoso Guitar Transcriptions (1991)	Decca (CD)
Sharon Isbin	Dances For Guitar (1984)	Pro Arte (LP)
	J.S.Bach: Complete Lute Suites (1989)	Virgin (CD)
	Guitar Works (1990)	Virgin (CD)
Alexandre Lagoya	Transcriptions For Guitar	Erato (CD)
Vladimir Mikulka	Compositions By J.S.Bach (1982)	Supraphon (LP)
	Iberoamerican Guitar Music (1987)	BIS (CD)
	Vladimir Mikulka Plays Stephan Rak	GHA (CD)
	Masterpieces For Guitar †††	Denon (CD)
Christopher Parkening	A Tribute To Segovia	EMI (CD)
	Virtuoso Duets (1990) ◆	EMI (LP/CD)
Konrad Ragossnig	Flute & Guitar Works	Claves (LP/CD)
	Lieder With Guitar Accompaniment (1989)	Novalis (LP/CD)
Angel Romero	Music Of Celedonio Romero	Angel (LP)
	Guitar Recital (1990)	Telarc (CD)
	Barcelona '92 (1992)	EMI (CD)
Pepe Romero	Boccherini Guitar Quintets	Philips (LP)
	Famous Guitar Music	Philips (LP)
David Russell	Guitar Recital	GHA (CD)
	Plays Antonio Lauro	GM (LP)
Andrés Segovia	HMV Recordings (1927-39)	EMI (LP/CD)
David Tanembaum	Royal Winter Music (1989)	Audiophon (CD)
	Acoustic Counterpoint (1990)	New Albion (CD)
Benjamin Verdery	American Guitar Music (1990)	Newport (LP)
	Vivaldi Concertos (1991) ✳	Sony (LP/CD)
John Williams	Boccherini: Quintets, etc. (1981)	CBS (LP)
	Virtuoso Arrangements For Guitar	CBS (LP)
	Albiniz: Guitar Works (1984)	CBS (CD)
	Hart: Concerto For Gtr & Jazz Orch. (1987)	CBS (LP/CD)
	Takemitsu: To The Edge Of Dream (1991)	Sony (CD)
	The Seville Concert (1993)	Sony (CD)
Narciso Yepes	Tàrrega: Recuerdos de la Alhambra (1987)	DG (CD)
	Villa-Lobos: Guitar Works (1989)	DG (CD)
	Spanish Guitar Works (1991)	DG (CD)

KEY:

◆ with David Brandon;
✳ with John Williams;
††† with Sharon Isbin.

M – Musicmasters,
Virgin – Virgin Classics,
GM – Guitar Masters,
DG – Deutsche Grammophon.

A selection of rock and pop guitar recordings

Duane Allman	Allman Bros At The Fillmore East (1971)	Polydor (LP/CD)
Jan Akkerman (Focus)	Moving Waves (1971)	Polydor (LP)
	Focus 3 (1972)	Polydor (LP)
Jennifer Batten	Above, Below & Beyond (1992)	Voss (CD)
Chuck Berry	The Great Twenty Eight	Chess (LP/CD)
Ritchie Blackmore	Deep Purple In Rock (1970)	Harvest (LP/CD)
	(Deep Purple) Made In Japan (1972)	Purple (LP/CD)
James Burton	Best Of Ricky Nelson	EMI (LP/CD)
J.J.Cale	Troubadour (1976)	Mercury (LP/CD)
Eric Clapton	Five Live Yardbirds (1964) ×	EMI (LP/CD)
	Bluesbreakers (1965) †	Decca (LP/CD)
	Wheels Of Fire (1968) ◆	RSO (LP/CD)
	Layla (1970) ✳	RSO (LP/CD)
	Just One Night (1980)	RSO (LP/CD)
Kurt Cobain (Nirvana)	Nevermind (1991)	Geffen (LP/CD)
Steve Cropper	Best Of Booker-T & The MG's	London (LP/CD)
Bo Diddley	Road Runner	Charly (LP/CD)
Duane Eddy	Have Twangy Guitar, Will Travel	Outline (LP/CD)
The Edge (U2)	Boy (1980)	Island (LP/CD)
	The Unforgettable Fire (1984)	Island (LP/CD)
Robert Fripp	In The Court Of The Crimson King (1969)	Polydor (LP/CD)
(King Crimson)	Lizard (1971)	Polydor (LP/CD)
	Discipline (1981)	EG (LP/CD)
Danny Gatton	Unfinished Business (1989)	NRG (LP/CD)
	88 Elmira Street (1991)	Elektra (LP/CD)
Billy Gibbons (ZZ Top)	Tres Hombres (1973)	London (LP/CD)
	Eliminator (1983)	WB (LP/CD)
David Gilmour	Meddle (1971)	Harvest (LP/CD)
(Pink Floyd)	Dark Side Of The Moon (1973)	Harvest (LP/CD)
	Wish You Were Here (1975)	Harvest (LP/CD)
Steve Hackett	Spectral Mornings (1979)	Charisma (LP/CD)
Jimi Hendrix	Are You Experienced? (1967)	Polydor (LP/CD)
	Axis: Bold As Love (1968)	Polydor (LP/CD)
	Electric Ladyland (1968)	Polydor (LP/CD)
Steve Hillage	Fish Rising (1975)	Virgin (LP/CD)
Steve Howe (Yes)	Fragile (1971)	Atlantic (LP/CD)
	Close To The Edge (1972)	Atlantic (LP/CD)
Tony Iommi	Paranoid (1970)	Vertigo (LP/CD
(Black Sabbath)	Volume Four (1972)	Vertigo (LP/CD)
	Sabbath, Bloody Sabbath (1974)	NEMS (LP/CD)
Eric Johnson	Tones (1986)	Reprise (LP/CD)
	Ah Via Musicom (1990)	Capitol (LP/CD)
Mark King (Level 42)	Level 42 (1981)	Polydor (LP/CD)
Mark Knopfler	Dire Straits (1978)	Vertigo (LP/CD)
(Dire Straits)	Love Over Gold (1982)	Vertigo (LP/CD)
	Brothers In Arms (1985)	Vertigo (LP/CD)
Shawn Lane	Powers Of Ten (1992)	WB (CD)
Paul Kossoff (Free)	All Right Now (1991)	Island (LP/CD)
Lemmy (Motorhead)	Ace Of Spades (1980)	Bronze (LP/CD
Alex Lifeson (Rush)	Permanent Waves (1980)	Mercury (LP/CD)
Phil Lynott (Thin Lizzy)	Live & Dangerous (1978)	Vertigo (LP/CD)
Yngwie Malmsteen	Eclipse (1990)	Polydor (LP/CD)
Johnny Marr (Smiths)	Meat Is Murder (1985)	RT (LP/CD)

KEY:
× with the Yardbirds;   ◆ with Cream;   WB – Warner Brothers.
† with John Mayall's Bluesbreakers;   ✳ with Derek & The Dominoes.

	The Queen Is Dead (1986)	RT (LP/CD)
Barry Martin (Hamsters)	Electric Hamsterland (1990)	On The Beach (CD)
Hank Marvin	Shadows: 20 Golden Greats (1977)	EMI (LP/CD)
Paul McCartney	A Hard Day's Night (1964) ✿	Parlo (LP/CD)
(& John Lennon)	Rubber Soul (1965) ✿	Parlo (LP/CD)
	Sgt. Pepper's Lonely Hearts Club Band (1967) ✿	Parlo (LP/CD)
Joni Mitchell	Shadows Of Light (1980)	Asylum (LP/CD)
	Wild Things Run Fast (1982)	Geffen (LP/CD
Ronnie Montrose	Montrose (1974)	WB (LP)
Gary Moore	G-Force (1981)	Ten (LP/CD)
	Run For Cover (1985)	Ten (LP/CD)
Scotty Moore	Elvis Presley (1956)	RCA (LP/CD)
Van Morrison	Astral Weeks (1968)	WB (LP/CD)
Steve Morse	What If (1978) ✳	Polydor (LP/CD)
	Unsung Heroes (1981) ✳	Arista (LP/CD)
	The Introduction (1984)	Elektra (LP/CD
Ted Nugent	Free For All (1976)	Epic (LP)
Mike Oldfield	Tubular Bells (1973)	Virgin (LP/CD)
Jimmy Page	Led Zeppelin II (1969)	Atlantic (LP/CD)
	Led Zeppelin III (1970)	Atlantic (LP/CD)
	Led Zeppelin IV (1971)	Atlantic (LP/CD)
Andy Partridge (XTC)	Black Sea (1980)	Virgin (LP/CD)
	English Settlement (1982)	Virgin (LP/CD)
Prince	Purple Rain (1984)	WB (LP/CD)
Trevor Rabin (Yes)	90125 (1983)	Atco (LP/CD)
Lou Reed	Velvet Underground & Nico (1967)	Polydor (LP/CD)
	New York (1989)	WEA (LP/CD)
Vernon Reid	Vivid (1988)	Epic (LP/CD)
(Living Colour)	Time's Up (1990)	Epic (LP/CD)
Todd Rundgren	Todd Rundgren's Utopia (1974)	Bearsville (LP/CD)
(Utopia)	Oblivion (1983)	Passport (LP)
Carlos Santana	Santana (1969)	CBS (LP/CD
	Abraxas (1970)	CBS (LP/CD)
Joe Satriani	Flying In A Blue Dream (1990)	Rela (LP/CD)
	The Extremist (1992)	Rela (LP/CD)
Bruce Springsteen	Born To Run (1975)	CBS (LP/CD)
Sting & Andy Summers	Regatta De Blanc (1979)	A&M (LP/CD)
(The Police)	Zenyatta Mondatta (1980)	A&M (LP/CD)
	Ghost In The Machine (1981)	A&M (LP/CD)
Pete Townshend	Tommy (1969)	Polydor (LP/CD)
(The Who)	Live At Leeds (1970)	MCA (LP/CD)
	Quadraphenia (1973)	Polydor (LP/CD)
Robin Trower	Bridge Of Sighs (1974)	Chrysalis (LP/CD)
Steve Vai	Eat 'Em And Smile (1986) ◆	WB (LP/CD)
	Passion & Warfare (1990)	Rela (LP/CD)
Eddie Van Halen	Van Halen (1978)	WB (LP/CD)
Don Wilson/Ventures	Walk Don't Run	EMI (LP/CD)
Angus Young (AC/DC)	Highway To Hell (1979)	Atlantic (LP/CD)
Neil Young	After The Gold Rush (1970)	Reprise (LP/CD)
	Rust Never Sleeps (1979)	Reprise (LP)
Frank Zappa	Hot Rats (1970)	BP (LP/CD)
	Zoot Allures (1976)	BP (LP/CD)
	Shut Up And Play Yer Guitar (1981)	BP (LP/CD)

Ace Records;

KEY:

✿ with the Beatles;

✳ with the Dregs/Dixie Dregs;

◆ with David Lee Roth.

BP – Barking Pumpkin,
Parlo – Parlophone,
Rela – Relativity/Food For Thought.
RT – Rough Trade,
WB – Warner Bros,

CONTACT ADDRESSES FOR RECORDINGS, BOOKS AND INFORMATION

Ace Records
48-50 Steele Rd., London NW10 7AS, UK
Alfred Publishing;
163 Roscoe Blvd., Van Nuys, CA 91410, USA
Alligator Records;
Box 60234, Chicago, Illinois 60660, USA
American Educational Music Publications, Inc;
1106 E. Burlington, Fairfield, Iowa 52556, USA
Arhoolie;
10341 San Pablo Ave, El Cerrito, CA 94530, USA
Bass Player;
P.O. Box 57324, Boulder, CO 80322-7324, USA
Berklee College Of Music;
1140 Boylston Street, Boston, MA 02215, USA (Tel: 800-421-0084)
BIS;
Qualiton, 3928 Crescent, Long Island City, NY 11101, USA
Black Top; Box 56691, New Orleans, LA 70156, USA
Bold Strummer Ltd, The;
P.O. Box 2037, Dept 10, Westport, CT 06880, USA
Caroline Records; 5 Crosby St., New York, NY 10013, USA
CMP;
Box 1129, 5166 Kreuzau, Germany
Concord;
Box 845, Concord, CA 94522, USA
Criss Cross;
Box 1214, 7500 BE, Enschede, Holland
DCI Music Video;
15800 NW 48th Ave, Miami, FL 33014, USA (Tel: 800-628-1528)
Enigma Records;
1750 East Holly Ave., Box 2428, El Segundo, CA 90245-2428, US
Flying Fish;
1304 W.Schubert, Chicago, IL 60614, USA
Free Music Production (H.Reichel CD's);
Lübecker Strasse 19, D-10559 Berlin, Germany (Tel: 30/394-17-56)
Grove School Of Music;
14539, Sylvan Street, Van Nuys, CA 91411, USA
Guitar For The Practicing Musician;
110 Midland Ave, Port Chester, NY 10573-1490, USA
Guitar Institute;
6 Warple Way, Acton, London W3 0UE, UK (081-740-1031)
Guitar Magazine, The;
Link House, 9 Dingwall Avenue, Croydon, CR9 2JA, UK
Guitar Player;
Miller Freeman Publications, 411 Borel Avenue, Suite 100, San Mateo, CA 94402, US
Guitar World;
1115 Broadway, New York, NY 10010, US
Guitarist/Guitar Techniques;
Alexander House, Forehill, Ely, Cambs CB7 4AF, UK
Hal Leonard;
8112 Bluemound Rd., Milwaukee, WI 53213, USA
Hamsters, The;
P.O. Box 835, Westcliff-on-Sea, Essex, SS0 0SQ, UK
High Tone;

Box 326, Alameda, CA 94501, USA
Homespun Video;
Box 694GP, Woodstock, NY 12498, USA (Tel: 914-679-7832/Fax: 914-246-5282)
Hot Licks Productions Inc;
P.O. Box 337, Pound Ridge, New York 10576, USA (Tel: 800-388-3008)
Inak/Timeless;
Wm. Wigt Productions, Box 201, Wagenigen, Holland
Incus Records;
14 Downs Rd., London E5 8DS, UK
Innova;
947 Walnut St #530, Boulder, CO 80302, USA
International Music Publications;
Southend Road, Woodford Green, Essex IG8 8HN, UK
Jennifer Batten Fan Club (Sprague transcriptions book);
PO BOX 52107, Riverside, CA 92517-3107, USA
London College Of Music;
Northwood House, 67 Northwood Avenue, Purley, Surrey CR8 2ER, UK
Mix Bookshelf (Carol Kaye videos);
6400 Hollis St #12, Emeryville, CA 94608, USA
Modern Blues Recordings;
Box 248, Pearl River, NY 10965, USA
Musical Heritage Society;
1710 Hwy. 35, Ocean, NJ 07712, USA
Musician's Institute (Hollywood);
Box 4011, Hollywood, CA 90028, USA (Tel: 213-462-1384)
Musician's Institute (London);
131 Wapping High Street, London E1 9NQ, UK (Tel: 071-265-0284)
NRG;
Box 100, Alpharetta, GA 30201, USA
REH Video (UK);
Music Mail Ltd, P.O. Box 69, Gravesend, Kent DA12 3AD, UK (Tel: 0474-813813)
REH Video (US);
15800 NW 48th Ave, Miami, FL 33014, USA (Tel: 800-628-1528)
REH Video (US);
Box 31729, Seattle, WA 98103, USA
Rhino;
2225 Colorado Blvd., Santa Monica, CA 90404, USA
Rosewood Press;
85 N. Whitney, Amherst, MA 01002, USA
Rounder;
1 Camp St., Cambridge, MA 02140, USA
Shanachie;
Dalebrook Park, Ho-Ho-Kus, NJ 07423, USA
SST;
Box 1, Lawndale, CA 90260, USA
Stefan Grossman's Guitar Workshop;
P.O. Box 802, Sparta, NJ 07871, USA
Suede Information Service;
P.O. Box 3431, London N1 7LW, UK
Workshop Arts;
Box 55, Lakeside, CT 06758, USA
Zoo/Praxis;
6363 Sunset Boulevard, Hollywood, CA 90028, USA

APPENDIX II

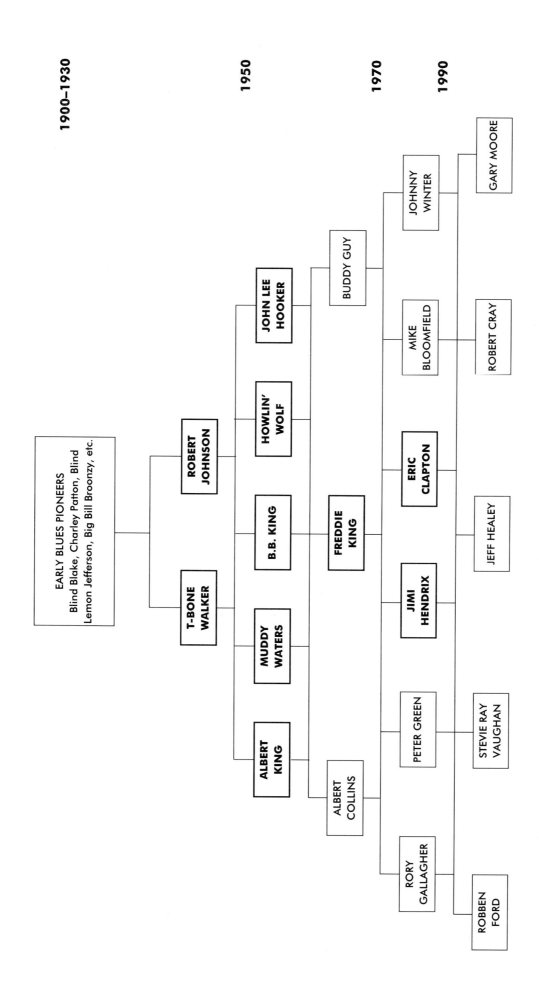

1900–1930

1950

1970

1990

EARLY BLUES PIONEERS
Blind Blake, Charley Patton, Blind
Lemon Jefferson, Big Bill Broonzy, etc.

ROBERT JOHNSON

T-BONE WALKER

JOHN LEE HOOKER

HOWLIN' WOLF

B.B. KING

MUDDY WATERS

ALBERT KING

BUDDY GUY

FREDDIE KING

ALBERT COLLINS

JOHNNY WINTER

MIKE BLOOMFIELD

ERIC CLAPTON

JIMI HENDRIX

PETER GREEN

RORY GALLAGHER

GARY MOORE

ROBERT CRAY

JEFF HEALEY

STEVIE RAY VAUGHAN

ROBBEN FORD

SIMPLIFIED INFLUENCE TREE OF BLUES GUITARISTS

137

SIMPLIFIED INFLUENCE TREE OF JAZZ AND FUSION GUITARISTS

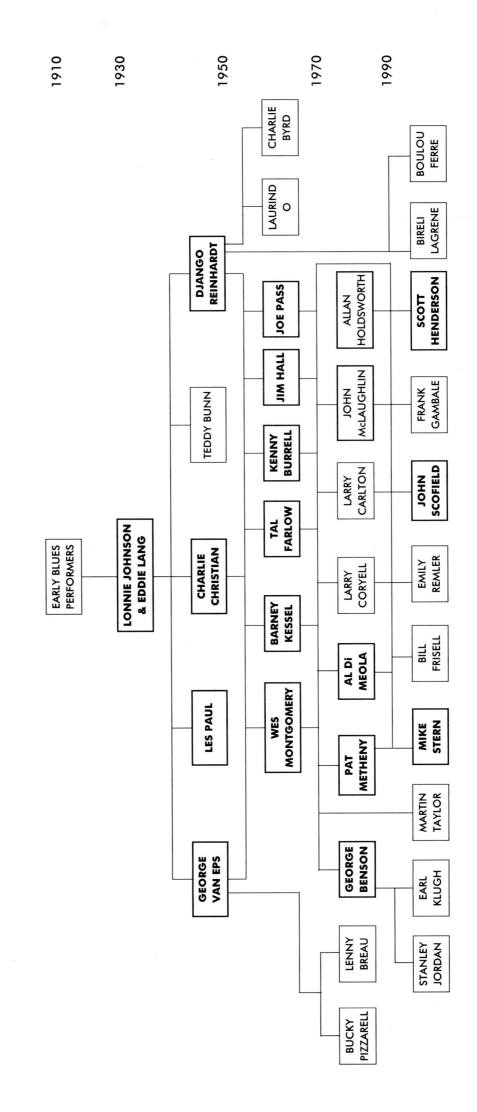

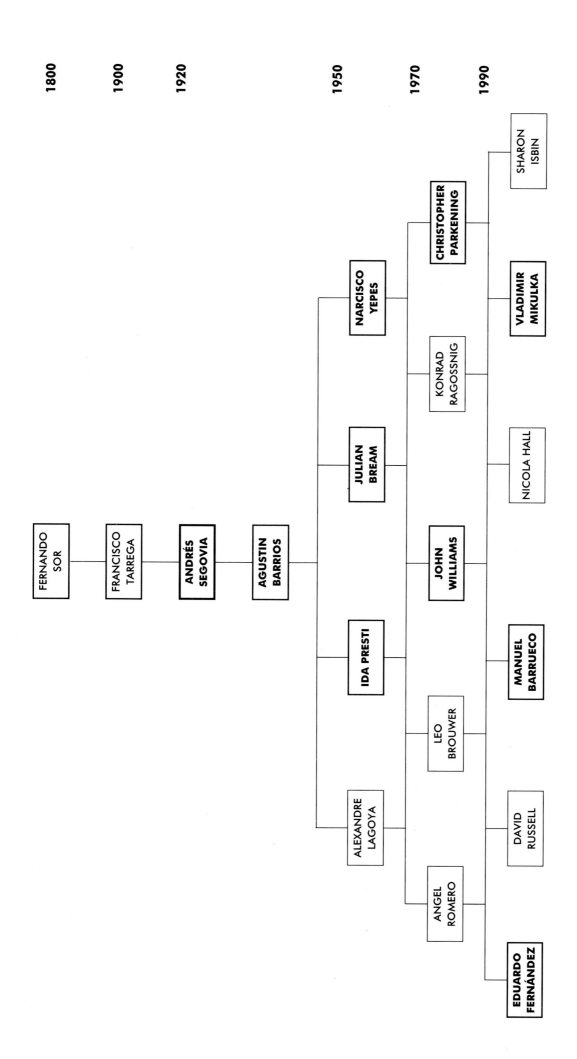

1800

1900

1920

1950

1970

1990

FERNANDO
SOR

FRANCISCO
TARREGA

ANDRÉS
SEGOVIA

AGUSTIN
BARRIOS

ALEXANDRE
LAGOYA

IDA PRESTI

JULIAN
BREAM

NARCISCO
YEPES

ANGEL
ROMERO

LEO
BROUWER

JOHN
WILLIAMS

KONRAD
RAGOSSNIG

CHRISTOPHER
PARKENING

EDUARDO
FERNÁNDEZ

DAVID
RUSSELL

MANUEL
BARRUECO

NICOLA HALL

VLADIMIR
MIKULKA

SHARON
ISBIN

SIMPLIFIED INFLUENCE TREE OF CLASSICAL GUITARISTS

SIMPLIFIED INFLUENCE TREE OF ROCK GUITARISTS

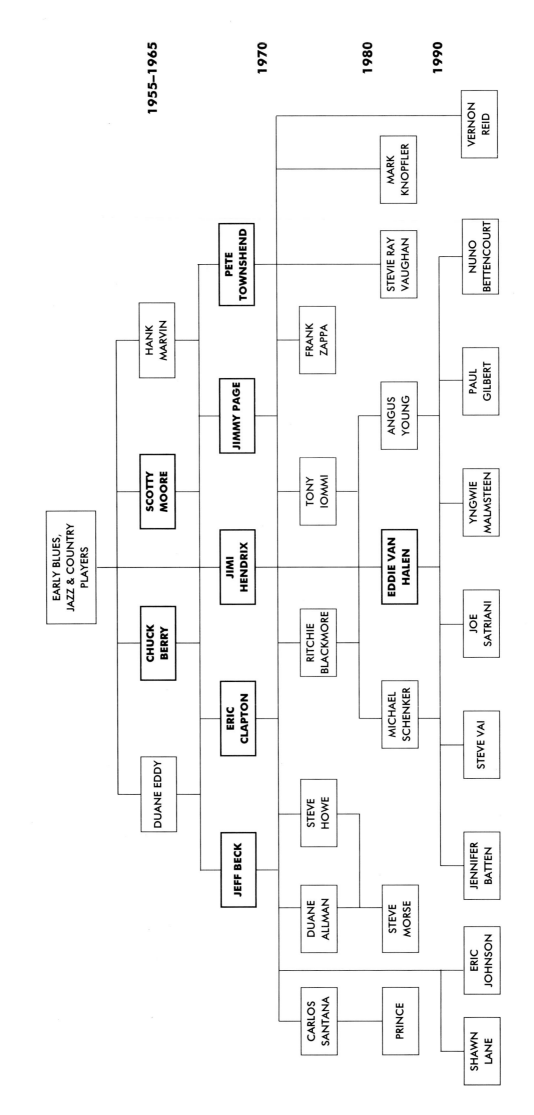

1955–1965

1970

1980

1990

EARLY BLUES, JAZZ & COUNTRY PLAYERS

DUANE EDDY

HANK MARVIN

SCOTTY MOORE

CHUCK BERRY

PETE TOWNSHEND

JIMMY PAGE

JIMI HENDRIX

ERIC CLAPTON

JEFF BECK

MARK KNOPFLER

STEVIE RAY VAUGHAN

FRANK ZAPPA

TONY IOMMI

ANGUS YOUNG

RITCHIE BLACKMORE

EDDIE VAN HALEN

MICHAEL SCHENKER

STEVE HOWE

DUANE ALLMAN

STEVE MORSE

VERNON REID

NUNO BETTENCOURT

PAUL GILBERT

YNGWIE MALMSTEEN

JOE SATRIANI

STEVE VAI

JENNIFER BATTEN

CARLOS SANTANA

PRINCE

ERIC JOHNSON

SHAWN LANE